W. Bert Hill's Daybooks

1897–1908

Book Design & Production:
Columbus Publishing Lab
www.ColumbusPublishingLab.com

Paperback ISBN: 978-1-63337-876-6
Hardcover ISBN: 978-1-63337-877-3

Printed in the United States of America
1 3 5 7 9 10 8 6 4 2

W. Bert Hill's Daybooks

1897-1908

A Life to Be Remembered, a Story to Be Told, a Book to Visit Memories for Generations to Come

Sarah E. Dunn

INTRODUCTION

Mr. Hill (as I always addressed him) said that we met when I was three years old. I don't recall our first meeting, but I can't recall a time when he was not part of my childhood.

He introduced me to a wide variety of flowers and vegetables grown in his gardens. My neighborhood friends and I would pick grapes, quinces, and a variety of apples from his orchard, which he used to make jelly and jams on his woodburning stove.

One of his outbuildings held his "to do" list. He would always show me his latest project. In turn, I would ask many questions which he would patiently answer.

He loved baseball! I spent time in his parlor listening to baseball on the radio. Even at 99, with that glint in his blue eyes, he would recite baseball statistics to me.

His personal stories are my most cherished memories. He conveyed, with such detail, stories about his childhood and the history of our hometown of Waterloo, Indiana.

His home's only source of heat was a potbelly parlor stove with isinglass doors and the woodburning cookstove in the kitchen. Winter months proved to be increasingly hard for him. So in his nineties, he went to live closer to his niece Laura Hill Smith in Michigan for those months. We would say our goodbyes and then exchange letters until spring. He would let me know when to expect his return, and I would welcome him home with a card and sometimes a pie. If his arrival was later than expected, he would write and give me permission to pick his tulips and daffodils so they could be enjoyed. I hold a special place in my heart for all these times we shared.

He lived an interesting life, and he chose to share some of it with me. His curiosity kept him young at heart. He was a man of many interests and stayed engaged in the world around him. He said, "In my lifetime there have been more discoveries than any other period on this earth. And think of it—I have even lived to see men land on the moon!"

When doing research, I discovered this excerpt from a 1901 issue of *Waterloo Press* within the "Neighbor News" section:

"Bert Hill, who is farming over in Illinois, came home last week to visit his father, Elijah Hill, and will remain several weeks. He is a graduate of the Waterloo High School, and a lively student of current events—a very worthy young man."

Obviously, he was always engaged and aware of the world around him.

William Bert Hill was born on August 21, 1876, in a two-story, wood framed house in Waterloo, Indiana, built by his father, Elijah Hartshorn Hill, in 1867. As a young man, he would walk miles a day, and only on a rare occasion would he borrow a horse. He never owned an automobile. He used the hand tools and scythe that his father had bequeathed him in 1902.

In 1893, he graduated from Waterloo High School, one of five boys and one girl. He received a four-year scholarship to DePauw University at New Castle, Indiana, which he chose not to accept.

Two years later in 1895, with $5.61 in his pocket, he hit the road to find work, and along the way found a journey that led him across the Midwest, the South, and the Southwest. His first stop was thirty miles from home, on a farm east of Fort Wayne, Indiana. He worked doing physical labor for 75-cents per day. Then he proceeded to work for a year or so in the St. Mary, Ohio, area. He spoke of the Smith family and the Postmaster from Ohio who remained his lifelong friends. When hearing that farm positions in Illinois were paying about $18 per month, he felt it was time to move on. He wanted to continue to gain experience in the farming business, so on May 11, 1897, he purchased a train ticket to Paxton, Illinois.

And this is where his journal entries begin . . .

Approximately 100 years after Bert's daybooks were written, I was gifted the original journals from his niece, Laura Hill Smith. I read them immediately and began the task of copying them. All were written in pencil, and some entries are faded, smudged, and almost impossible to decipher. Nevertheless, having spent forty-plus years compiling this book, I feel confident that all questionable passages were translated correctly.

This project has been a true labor of love. In 2014, while attending spring training for the Chicago Cubs in Arizona, my husband, Dan; grandson, Andrew; and I retraced much of Mr. Hill's journey in 1899/1900, as he and Noel B.Shaffer searched for precious minerals.

In 2015, I took a road trip to Illinois and visited the lovely towns and countryside where from 1896 to 1907, he worked and lived. Over the course of the next decade, I would continue this research at libraries and historical societies, seeking to fill in the gaps of Mr. Hill's daybook entries and to give future readers historical context to better understand these snippets of his life.

By compiling his journals, my hope is that the reader will come to know and gain a sense of this kind man. His spirit of integrity and fairness can be found between the pages of these daybooks. His mother, Sarah Agnes Hill, instilled in her children a love of God and an awareness of the beauty of this earth. May you find that here within these pages.

With gratitude,
Sarah

1897

In March of 1897, William McKinley was sworn in as the 25th President of the United States, while Victoria was celebrating her sixtieth year as the Queen of the United Kingdom of Great Britain. Amelia Earhart entered the world on July 24, 1897, as Thomas Edison was receiving a patent for the movie camera, known as the kinetograph.

May 10, 1897: Paid 25-cents for lodging.

May 11: I arose at 3:20 a.m. and walked to St. Mary's, Ohio Depot and bought a ticket to Paxton, Ill. Started at 3:50 a.m. on train. I passed through Indiana; Redkey, Portland, Muncie, Elwood, Frankfort, Tipton, Lafayette and many other smaller towns. The country east of Lafayette is similar to that at St. Mary's, so far as crops are concerned but the land is in places quite rough especially around Lafayette, where the Wabash River runs near. The Wabash is about 300 ft. wide there. There is considerable new land east of Tipton. The country around Paxton, Ill. is settled about 1 house to ½ mile. Nearly half of Paxton is Swedish, as also the farmers around the town, for several miles.

Most of western Indiana and eastern Illinois is rather thinly settled and not the very best land. I arrived at Paxton at about 12:30 p.m. and wrote a letter to home. Then started north of town to look for a job. I walked about 15 miles, northwest of Paxton, inquiring for work of many farmers. Then stayed all night at a Mr. Wright's, a religious but rather odd man. Most of the farmers have all the help they need now, but some will want more help when corn plowing commences. I did not want to stay at Mr. Wright's on account of small house and many children, six of them. Weather about 75 degrees. All roads are common soil, none of them being graveled.

May 12: I started to walk about 7 a.m. and after walking about 20 miles around the country, I came to Stawn, Illinois, having not found work for now. I wrote home and then walked and rode in spring wagon to Forrest-7 miles from Strawn, where I paid 15-cents for supper and 25-cents for lodging. I also purchased an orange for 10-cents.

At Strawn the Wabash Railroad runs through and the Wabash and Toledo Peoria and Western railroad runs through Forrest. The Wabash has round shops at Forrest, a town of about 2,000 people.

Nothing hindering, I will go to Chenoa in the a.m. of the morrow. Weather is about 60F and somewhat cooler in the eve. Slightly cloudy. God has been good to me in giving me health and strength and cheerfulness. Oh may it continue though to a failing son.

May 13: I took the train for Chenoa at 5:40 a.m. and arrived there at about 6:10 a.m. I paid 49-cents for carfare. I ate breakfast, 25-cents, in Chenoa restaurant. Proceeded southwest to look for work. I inquired among the farmers and found a place about 5 miles, southwest of Chenoa at a Mr. Ino Peck's, where I am to receive 50-cents per day until corn plowing commences. Then I will get between $15 to $17 dollars per month. In the p.m., I rode a horse to Lexington, a 1,500 town, 4 miles south to head cattle that Mr. Peck was taking there.

I purchased a canvas jacket for $1.50 and paid 5-cents for postal cards. I wrote a card to ma and pa, and then headed back to Peck's. It rained all afternoon and I was wet and had to change attire. God bless the Smith's for their kindness to me.

MAY 14–15: I worked today rubbing corn ground and harrowing. Set fence posts.

MAY 16: I read and visited in a.m. Went to church in p.m. Sermon was about hope as an anchor to the soul, a very good sermon to those who would hear. Weather clear and temperate.

MAY 17–18: I harrowed corn fields.

MAY 19: I helped set wind pump up today. Weather about 75 degrees. Sister Cora's birthday anniversary. God guide her and all.

MAY 20–31: I helped repair well curb. Hauled corn for Henry Peck. Two loads to a small station. Meadows on Toledo Peoria Western Railway and one to elevator on Chicago and Alton Railway. I hauled gravel and a load of corn to Chenoa. Got a haircut and ate lunch at Grandpa Peck's. I hoed strawberries and gardened. Replanted corn. Much welcomed letters from home.

JUNE 1–5: Plowed corn

JUNE 6: I read and chored. Made an agreement with Ino Peck to work for $17 per month, dating from June 3, 1897. Weather warm. Sent letters to William Smith and St. Mary's Postmaster.

JUNE 7–11: Plowed corn, cut thistles, grubbed gritch grass in corn fields. I trimmed hedges. Weather about 105 degrees in the sun.

June 12: I chored today. Went to Lexington in evening where I paid $1.25 for plow shoes, 15-cents for a hat, 5-cents for a letter tablet and 5-cents for peanuts. Lexington School House is a new brick building, taller but not as large as the Waterloo School House, which is my alma mater.

June 13–24: Worked pasture on gopher. Bored post holes, cut hedges and plowed. Received letter from home.

June 25: Plowed corn till 9 a.m. when wind and rain storm came. Wind blew about 50 miles per hour or more. Several inches of rain received. Sent letter to Charles at home.

June 26–30: Plowed corn. Weather 90 degrees to 105 degrees. Went to Church and Sunday School (27th). Went to Lexington and sent letter to William Smith. Bought a new shirt for 50-cents.

July 1–3: Plowed corn. I rode to Lexington in a.m. on the 3rd and remained in town until 11:40 a.m. when I went to Bloomington. Bloomington is a town of about 40,000 people and a number of fine business blocks. 3 or 4 paved streets, 3 railroads, a streetcar line, but few manufacturing plants. Bought bananas, 5-cents and 5-cents for peanuts, $1.00 for hat, 5-cents for streetcar fare, 20-cents for supper, 5-cents for gum and 5-cents for a pair of socks. Remained in town until 4:55 p.m. when I returned to Lexington. Got supper and remained until about 9:30 p.m.

July 4–31: Scooped corn for Mr. Hotsenpiller. 25-cents. Mowed and helped Philip Peck haul hay. Hauled manure, cut hedge and shocked oats.

Aug. 1: Gave C. Peck $2.00 and he got me a pair of overalls, for 75-cents, a shirt for 50-cents and a baseball for 15-cents, leaving 60-cents due me. Weather 90 degrees

Aug. 2: I pitched oats in field at John Andrew's threshing. Read.

Aug. 3: Pitched oats in field in a.m., when engine was taken away to be repaired. Today ended 2 months work for John Peck.

Aug. 4–20: Pitched oats for H. Andrews. Scooped oats and cut bands for J. and H. Peck. Worked for J. Wether's, J. Shenybrook, T. Shine and J. Hutchinson. Helped Mr. Allison and Mr. Popejoy thresh.[1]

Aug. 21: Weather about 85 degrees. I am 21 years old today.

Aug. 22: I walked to Chenoa in a.m. and heard Rev. Robert McIntyre preach the M. E. dedication sermon. His theme was that anyone could be a Christian anywhere on account of nature of religion, the freedom of man and the certainty of God's help. A very sound and well presented discourse.

Aug. 23–25: Hauled gravel. Hauled corn for H. Peck. Took 4 loads to Meadows.

Aug. 26: Rode to Lexington in a.m. to picnic in timber. A large crowd of 2,000 people or more. Hundreds of woodsmen present. Gave 5-cents to Negro performer who bent 5/8" bars and 7/8" gas pipe over his arm and carried 190 lbs. in his teeth. The baseball game was quite interesting. El Paso winning over Lexington. I walked home in evening. Sent $10 to family.

Aug. 27–31: Received letters from home, J. H. Plummer and St. Mary's. Hauled gravel. Read.

Sept. 1–3: About 85 degrees. Pulled burrs out of corn and hauled straw.

Sept, 4: Weather hot but wind most of week. Peck and family returned today from Nebraska.

Sept. 5–14: Attended church and read. Helped examine colt's hoofs. Hauled gravel.

Sept. 15–26: Cut corn on 15th. 40 shocks, 10 hills square. Picked up potatoes and sowed grass seed in 10-acre field. Hauled gravel.

Sept. 27: Received "Press" from home.[2]

Sept 28: Husked 60 bushels corn today.[3]

Sept 29: Husked 56 bushels

Sept 30: Husked 52 bushels today. Rode to town, paid 25-cents for horse care, 25-cents for a haircut. Will go to Springfield on 12:55 a.m. train.

Oct. 1: Arrived at Springfield around 3:30 a.m., about 80 miles south on Chicago and Alton Railroad. Walked to town then to the depot and sat down until about 5:00 a.m., where I got my breakfast. Went to Court House, then took the streetcar for Lincoln Monument. The monument is of marble, the base or pedestal is about 50 ft. square and 20 ft. high, upon which is a hollow shaft about 40 or more feet high and 10 ft. square base. Flowers were kept on the casket though his bones are buried 20 ft. below the monument. A statue of Lincoln and of soldiers surrounds the pedestal.[4]

I went to Fair Ground and visited the various halls and stables all most were well filled especially the cattle, horse and chicken departments. I attended the races in the evening. Thousands were in attendance. Saw Star Pointer and Joe Patchen race.[5]

A very memorable time.

Oct 2: I made some purchases. Visited the State Capitol and walked around town, ate dinner, then went to depot and came home.

Oct. 3–29: Husked corn. Ino Amos and Ino Peck paying me 10-cents a day to shovel and load corn.

Oct. 30: Husked 2,150 lbs. corn in a.m. and 2,540 lbs. minus 1,060 equals 1,480 lbs. in p.m., making 3,630 lbs. or 45 bushels and 30 lbs.

Oct. 31: Read and went to church

Nov. 1: Husked corn. 1,850 + 2,190 lbs. at 80 lbs. per bushel. Weather rainy and cold.

Nov. 2: Husked corn. 2,450 + 2,680 lbs. today. Shoveled corn for P. Peck to receive 25-cents for it. Weather warmer than yesterday. Clear.

Nov. 3: Husked 3,000 + 2,410 lbs. today. Rec'd 25-cents for unloading corn for Peck.

Nov. 4: Husked 1,180 lbs. corn in a.m. and settled with J. Peck for work. Rec'd $26.94 for husking and $78.06 for work. Rec'd check for $105.00 that canceled account with J. Peck. Went to H. Peck's in p.m. and husked 25 bushels of corn.

Nov. 5: Husked corn in p.m. 38 bushels. I went to town in a.m. and cashed the check and deposited $55 in bank. Loaned H. Peck $100 with interest at 5% for 30 days or longer at my option. I purchased 2 shirts for $1.25 and 1 yard canton flannel (a plain or twill weave cotton fabric, with a long fleecy nap) for 25- cents. Rec'd 10-cents from J. Amos for my unloading corn for him.

Nov. 6: Husked 38 bushel of corn in morning and 25 bushels in afternoon. Weather quite cold. Fingers sore from chaps on them.

Nov. 7: Read and played dominos and went to Noel Shaffer's. Cool out.

Nov. 8: Husked 50 bushels of corn in sleet. Very wet on feet.

Nov. 9–17: Husked 68 bu., 72 bu., 61 bu. Husked 7 rows of corn for Garnet Brower. Husked 8 rows. Read and did chores. Husked 9 rows of corn. Wrote home.

Nov. 18: Husked 8½ rows today. 350 bushels in all for Mr. Brower and received $7.

Nov. 19: Walked to Lexington in a.m. Paid 10-cents for shave, sent letter and postal to home. Paid $1.50 for pair of shoes, 75-cents for overalls, 65-cents for gloves and 10-cents for socks. Walked to Noel Shaffer's, ate dinner and hired to him for 8 months. Next year from April 1 to Dec 1-1898 will receive $150.00.

Nov. 20: I plowed today for Henry Peck. Receiving 50-cents per day for plowing or other work.

Nov. 21–24: Plowed, Chopped wood, packed water tank.

Nov. 25: Thanksgiving. Heavy rain last night. Chored, sewed and read today.

Nov. 26: Went to Lexington in a.m. and purchased pair of felt boots for $2.50. Plowed in afternoon. Weather misty, slight snow with a northwest wind. Rec'd $1.60 for 3 days work plus 32 days pumping water.

Nov. 27–29: Chored, plowed. Ground is frozen. 1½" snow Rec'd letter from home.

Nov. 30: Went to Chenoa in a.m. Purchased pair of mittens.

Dec. 1–22: Plowed almost every day. On 14th went to Noel Shafer's and went hunting. Snowed 3" on 18th. Weather cold and freezing fast. Made total of $1.35.

Dec. 23–25: Chored. Scooped corn. Nice Christmas dinner at Noel Shaffer's on the 25th. Weather growing warmer.

Dec. 26: Went to Disciple Church in morning. Excellent speaker from small place. Went to Olivet in the evening and heard a holy man from Los Angeles, California.

Dec. 27–31: Chored Scooped corn for J. Peck. Went to Chenoa and rec'd two books from the post office that I had written for. Colder with snow on the 31st

Paxton, Illinois Depot-Arriving on May 11, 1897.
Picture courtesy of Forrest, Illinois Historical Society

Forrest, Illinois - Main Street, late 1890's,
where WBH dined and found lodging.

Chenoa, Illinois Depot 1897-1918,
when it was destroyed by fire.

Façade of building in Lexington, Illinois, that
is still in existence. *Picture taken in 2015*

Waterloo School was built in 1872, at a cost of $20,000. It served one to twelve grades until 1925. *Postcard among SED's possessions.*

Lexington School was built in 1896 at a cost of $20,750. *Picture courtesy of Lexington Historical Society, The Fort*

Lexington Depot was relocated and has been converted into a home/flower shop *Picture taken in 2015*

Springfield, Illinois, Union Depot, City Hall and 5th Street, *Postcard among WBH's possessions.*

1898

The Spanish American War begins and ends in four months. "War of the World's" was first published in hardcover in 1898, written by the prolific author, H. G. Wells". The Winston Motor Carriage Company publishes the first automobile ad, using the headlines, "Dispense With A Horse". Heroin was being marketed as cough medicine.

January 1, 1898: Weather about 15F Chored today.

Jan. 2–7: Doing little of special things. Weather changeable.

Jan. 8: Went to Lexington in afternoon. Received a welcome letter from home and from St. Mary's, Ohio. Bought a shirt, 75-cents and 5-cents for copper.

Jan. 9: Attended church in a.m. and ate dinner at Willis Shaffer's.

Jan. 10–14: Worked 2 hrs. plus 1 hr. on ditch and received 30-cents. Attended preaching the evenings of 10th and 14th. Haircut 25-cents.

Jan. 15: Rec'd pay for $25.00 note of H. Peck with 15-cents interest. Loaned $25.00 to A. Slagel for 6% for 6 months or longer.

Jan. 16: Sunday. Attended United Brethren Sunday School and preaching

Jan. 17–27: Chored and read Weather quite cold with 5 inches of snow. Rec'd 60- cents for scooping corn for J. Peck a month or so ago.

Jan. 28: Went to woods today and cut a sugar tree of which we took the limbs for wood. Weather about 10 degrees.

Jan. 29–31: Chored and attended church

Feb. 1: Hauled straw most of the day. Weather 6-25 degrees. Damp.

Feb. 2: Chored, etc. Attended church and Sunday school in morning at Disciple Church. Weather increasingly warmer.

Feb. 7: Cut a load of pole wood, 3 miles southwest of Lexington.

Feb. 9: Ditched 4 hours in afternoon, earned 40-cents. Brother, Charles birthday anniversary today. He is 20 years old.

Feb. 10–28: Received letters from home. Chored. Attended church, excellent sermon on practical duties of a Christian. Hauled, shoveled, and shelled corn. Weather breaking so roads soft, prohibiting hauling after late afternoons.

March 1–3: Five to six inches of snow on the 1st. Butchered hogs on 2nd and 3rd . Loaned S. Shafer $100 for one year at 7%.

March 4: Received prices from A. M. Ward Company for Waltham, 17 jewel – Crescent St. movement watch, number of watch movement 6019809 = $18.00. Silverine Case - $1.50.[6]

March 5–6: Chored. Paid 85-cents for half soling rubber shoes. Attended church on the 6th. Gave 5-cents for heathens. Weather clear, warm, delightful, safe under feet.

March 7: Sent to A. M. Ward for watch. Crescent St. Movement. And silverine case = $19.50. *(A silverine case wears as well and is stronger than solid silver. They are made only in weight about 3½ oz.)* Dust Protector = 90-cents, Handkerchiefs = 75-cents, Socks 75-cents, Necktie = 20-cents, Overalls = 90-cents less 2% for cash. Paid 12-cents for money order to send home. Loaned $10.00 to Albert Slagel for 2 or 3 weeks. Drew $25.00 from S. Bank of Lexington. Leaving me $5 in the bank. Weather clear.

March 8–11: Chored. I received the watch, 2 yards of shirting. I paid 50-cents for express on the goods. I also received 36-cent treasurers note on A. M. Ward and Co. for return of value to me. Watch will certainly suit my needs. Muddy roads.

March 12–13: Chored. Attended church on 13th.

March 14: I began work by the month, today. Worked in garden. Ground drying rapidly.

March 15–19: Fixed stock rake. Harrowed, raked and burned stalks today. Plowed garden and drove colt to town. Chopped wood, trimmed hedge and rolled wire.

March 20: Attended church today at the Baptist church. A moderately good sermon on necessity for earthly goodness.

March 21–31: Set out peach trees in east orchard, greased harness. Hauled brush out of orchard. Ditched for 2 days. Made hog pens in hay barn. Raked and burned corn stalks. Cleaned oats and repaired fences. Hauled hay.

April 1: Trimmed hedges. Piled and burned hedge brush in p.m.

April 2: Raked cord stalks today. Received Mother's and sister, Cora's picture today, a very natural one.

April 3: Attended church on 3rd. Sermon about Jude's letter.

April 4–11: Disked in oats in south field. Broke stalks and cultivated oats. Harrowed in south field. Drove team on rougher ground, trimmed hedge on north side of road. Much warmer.

April 12: Planted potatoes and artichokes today. The bay yearling colt was very stiff this morning and Veterinarian Bannet pronounced the infection to be lockjaw. The colt grew rapidly worse, suffering terrible pain. He gave it ½ drop of belladium every 3 hours, which afforded but passing relief. His muscles contracted with great tension rendering them like India rubber. No better at 10 p. m.

April 13: Did little work today on account of almost continual rain. Colt after suffering unconceivable pain died at 7 p.m. It seems pitiful that animals often cannot acquaintance us with the causes of their suffering. A model for stoic surety.

April 14: Built fence in orchard. Buried colt. Nothing of cause of the colt's malady was found.

April 15–16: Finished pig shed. Raked corn stalks and plowed 55 degrees

April 17: Attended M. E. Church in a.m. and attended Mr. William Hotsenpiller's funeral in p.m. Mr. Hotsenpillar was an exceptionally kind, friendly and good man. He is held in high esteem as was evident by the hundreds of people who attended his funeral.[7]

April 18–23: Plowed fields (4 days) Sawed wood and built fence

April 24: Read and slept today. Attended preaching at Olivet in evening, a United Brethren man. Shots were fired in Lexington, announcing war between the United States and Spain.[8] A few have enlisted from Lexington or rather offered their names for enlistment. Rec'd a good letter from home.

April 25–30: Continue to plow. East and West fields completed. Went to Chenoa and got a haircut and a straw hat. Weather quite warm.

May 1: Read and chored

May 2–7: Disked east and west fields. Harrowed east field, hauled rails and hay and drove colt. Worked in garden and set corner posts in south field.

May 8: Attend church and Sunday School in a.m. and gave 5-cents. Read the Chicago Sunday Times. Official news of Dewey's victory in Manila.

May 9–21: Disked, mowed in yard. Harrowed in west field. Killed 2 bull snakes, 4 ft. long, first site of them this year. Repaired fence, trimmed hedges, chopped wood. Sunday when out, being very hot. Rev'd letter from home. Purchased a suit for $3.50 and 36-cent note to A. M. Ward and Company for 1 necktie, pair of pants and coat.

May 22: Attended preaching in morning. Read in afternoon, at home. Paid 15-cents for freight on goods.

May 23–28: Repaired fences, Hauled 8 loads of corn for Hotsenpillar family. Scooped corn for H. Ellis, N. B. Shaffer, hauled 3 loads for J. Ellis and 2 loads for P. Peck.

Paid John Ellis 50-cents for Shaffer to be repaid to me by Shaffer. Hauled cobs and shingles. Hoed vines in corn.

May 29: Attended preaching in school auditorium. Memorable sermon.

May 30: Hauled shingles and shingled the barn. Many went to Decoration Day exercises in Lexington.

May 31: Cultivated corn in north field. Weather continues to be very warm. Received the 50-cents from Schaffer.

June 1–11: Cultivated corn. Ground so very hard and weedy. On 5th rheumatism in left foot, so went no place. Then finished plowing corn first time on the 6th. Some rain and many clouds.

June 12: Attended Presbyterian church in morning. Minister has fair delivery though weak voice. Talked on kinds of Christians. Weather hot, cloudy. Paid 5-cents for paper.

June 13–18: Cultivated corn. Stemmed good berries and cultivated millet. Plowed turnip patch and corn. Hoed potatoes. Received letter from home and Waterloo Press paper from home.

June 19: Attended Disciple church in a.m. M. E. Olivet in p.m. and a children's exercise in the eve at the Disciple Church. Young preacher at M.

E. Olivet is U. B. country boy and not yet highly educated but earnest. 5-cent paper.

June 20–30: Hoed potatoes and artichokes. Cultivated corn, made hay. Sent letter home on 22nd.

July 1–2: Finished cultivating corn for this year. 25 acres, 4 times plowed. Weather very hot.

July 3: Attended church at Olivet in afternoon. Young preacher improving.

July 4: Went to Lexington, rode with J. S. Amos.. Heard Colonel Isaac Clanus of Normal, a very forceful talking speaker. 10-cents for dinner and 25-cents for ballgame. Also, went to races.

July 5–23: Repaired hay loader. Picked gooseberries, hoed potatoes. Cut hay, repaired orchard fences and hay rack. Picked raspberries, hoed weeds. Painted buggy and set tires. Shocked oats. Went to town on 9th and sent $5 home to folks. Purchased stamps, money order and stamped envelopes. $1 for 2 shirts.

July 24: Attended church at Prairie School. A very good talk by disciple preacher. Hottest day of the year.

July 25–26: Pitched oats at Ragon's. Repaired rack. Stacked straw here. Ragon's oats equals 27 bushel per acre for 65 acres.

July 27: Scooped oats here, 1,474 bushels for 35 acres. Scooped oats for O. Siren

July 28: Scooped oats for O. Siren 30 ½ bushels for 40 acres.

July 29: J. Holt oats avg. 43 bu. for 24 acres. Ellis oats avg. 27 bu. for 40 acres.

July 30: Pitched oats in sheaves at L. Liren's from 10a. to 6p. Oats straw long and tangled by far the most wooly of any I ever handled.

July 31: Attended church in town in a.m. and at Olivet in p.m.

Aug. 1–20: Hauled oats at L. Birlingmair, P. Kennedy's, J. Peck, J. Schope and E. McCurry. Repaired fences, Mowed and cut thistles in pasture and dug potatoes. Staked fences and shingled barn.

Aug. 21: Attended United Brethren Church in a.m. Shuey, an agent for Westfield College preached. Average sermon. Hot. I am 22 years old today. Time recedes as age advances. Purchased Sunday paper.

Aug. 22–27: Re'vd Waterloo Press. Sad news of drowning of former acquaintance and classmate, Miss Lena Rempis and a Mr. Roby.[9]

Aug. 28: Attended M. E. Church. Heard the Chancellor of Illinois Wesleyan University. A very good speaker.

Aug. 29–Sept. 3: Cleared timber land about 2 miles south, southwest of Lexington on M. Harness place. Hot very – all days. Slightly poisoned with ivy. Received letter from home.

Sept. 4: Remained at home all day and doctored for poison ivy, which I killed.

Sept. 5–7: Chopped, hauled and sawed wood in timber. Quite cool and breezy. Paid 10 cents for sweet oil.

Sept. 8–10: Plowed in west stubble field. Sent $4.68 to M. Ward and Co. for coat and vest and a pair of suspenders.

Sept. 11: Read and attended church at Olivet in p.m. Rev. Frank Stewart preached his last sermon. Gave 20-cents to preacher.

Sept. 12: Hauled 2 loads of wood from timber today. Rev'd suspenders by mail.

Sept. 13–17: Gathered and peeled peaches. Plowed hauled wood from timber here. Hauled wood to Chenoa. Trimmed hedge and gathered corn. Cut corn and my leg at J. Holbs.

Sept. 18: Read and visited with neighbors. Attended preaching at Prairie School. Good sermon on "Opportunities for Salvation". Very warm.

Sept. 19: Leg looking better. Plowed today. Received Waterloo Press and postal from home. Still heavy and hot.

Sept. 20–21: Plowed Eve of 21st went to town and sent treasurer's draft of Ward and Co. for $4.40 and money order for $2.25 for a suit of clothes.

Sept. 22: Rained intermittently till 2 p.m. Plowed most of the time.

Sept. 23–24: Plowed Weather avg. about 75F. Clothes sent to Lexington but did not get there.

Sept. 25: Read and visited with J. S. Amos and R. Riley.

Sept 26: Plowed. Walked to Lexington and paid 30-cents for express on suit which I received. Cloth of suit heavier than average, nearly black in color.

Sept. 27–30: Plowed. Rev'd letter from home. Sister Cora starts on vacation tour next Monday. Will be here in probably a week after. J. S. Amos and Simon Shaffer here part of the day on the 30th.

Oct. 1–5: Chopped wood, separated hogs, and gathered corn. Plowed in sod and all of stubble ground. Quite warm for October. Dug potatoes and gathered them all day on the 5th.

Oct. 6: Cut and gathered corn. Trimmed hedge in p.m. Attended Republican Rally in Lex. In evening, heard M. B. Madden and Pat O'Donnell of Chicago. Also a Negro quartet from Bloomington sang. O'Donnell a very forceful speaker.

Oct. 7: Hauled straw. Mulched black berries. Went to Lexington in evening and received a letter from Cora.

Oct. 8: Hauled straw, manure and gathered corn. Rec'vd card from home.

Oct. 9: Read Walked two miles north and returned. Most of all plowing done. Lots planting good. Early planting poor.

Oct. 10: Plowed in corn ground in morning and chopped wood.

Oct. 11: Went to Bloomington at 11:40 a.m. Walked around town and through Court House then to Lake Erie and Western Depot. At 2:30 p.m. Cora came. Walked about town and to Union Depot. Then we came to Lexington and drove out home. Cora somewhat heavier though otherwise much the same as ever. Paid 25-cents for horse care, 41-cents to Normal, 5-cents to Bloom. L. E. & W. Depot, 98-cents for two to Lexington. Gave 10-cents to cripple person on train.

Oct. 12: Walked around farm in a.m. and shoveled corn for 2 hours for J. Holt. Visited and chored.

Oct. 13–14: Remained indoors in a.m. and drove to Lexington in the evenings. Showing Cora around.

Oct. 15: We rode to Chenoa in morning and left for Chicago on 9:30 express. Arrived in Chicago at 1 p.m., where we met Charley. Walked a few blocks and ate dinner after which we went to McVicker's Theater, where we saw a comic opera. Good to be with family. Took an I.C. train and went to South Chicago, then the streetcar to 9921 Ewing Avenue. Ate supper and then went to a Thomas Concert at the auditorium. Heard some fine music. Returned to South Chicago at 12 midnight. Weather clear and warm.

Oct. 16: Went to S. Chicago shipyards. Saw several yachts, some steamers, fire boats, etc. New machine shop 100 x 14 ft. sides and roof of glass. Much of it is corrugated make it light and cool. Shop about 80 ft. high contains two 40 ft. lathes, large drills, melting, cutting, planing machines. A very fully equipped shop. Docks are about 300 or more feet long and 100 ft. wide. Much of work consists in building boats and making necessary machinery for them and a lot is outside work for Illinois Steel Company and similar concerns.

In p.m. we went to Field Columbian Museum, where we saw statuary. Went through the Zoological, Archeological, and Ethnological departments. Walked through rooms containing the types of locomotives from the first to present. Went along lakefront to German building. Then back to South Chicago. 5-cents for street fare.

Oct. 17: Went to S. Chicago with Cora. Went to L.S. & M. S. Depot and Cora left at 11:05 a.m. for home. I went to 63rd street, got dinner and then returned to Charles's room. Reading book, "The Jucklins"[10]

Oct. 18: Went to ship yards in a.m. and downtown in p.m. Jubilee being celebrated here this week. Our President McKinley here. Some very nice decorations on the streets, though many were spoiled by the rain. 5-cents for apples.

Oct. 19: Went back to ship yards, then to town in 9 a.m. Got to Union Depot 10 minutes late for 11:08 Limited, so saw the Peace Jubilee Parade.[11] Large crowd and patriotic. Ate dinner then came to Lexington. Pd. 10-cents for street fare, $3.07 for car fare (train) and 34-cents from Chenoa to Lexington and a card for Cora. Walked out to Shaffer's. 5-cents for bananas.

Oct. 20–24: Commenced to repair cow stable but rain stopped work on the 20th. Refilling cow stalls with dirt and plowed sod. Gathered corn. Shucked corn. Corn in spring plowing and early planting not very good. Fall plowing just fair.

Oct. 25: Cleaned crib and repaired for corn in morning and cleaned chicken house and commenced addition to chicken house in p.m. $1.00 for 5 yards of cotton flannel. Received $1 from Shafer for work and 50-cents from J. Holt for scooping corn. Received Cora's picture and one of the telephone switchboards at Waterloo. Very fine pictures.

Oct. 26: Finished addition to chicken house and moved potatoes to cellar. Very cool, snow slow to leave.

Oct. 27–29: Shucked corn. Received letter and Press from home.

Oct. 30: Attended church in a.m. Heat little – no preaching.

Oct. 31–Nov. 5: Shucked corn Received letter from Cora and Press from home.

Nov. 6: Read Cool, freezing nights.

Nov. 7: Shucked corn. Received $100 from N. B. Shaffer for work. Loaned $100 to A. E. Slagel till January 1st 1900 at 7% interest.

Nov. 8: Shucked corn. Ate dinner at Willis Shaffer's then rode to Chenoa and voted for some state and county officers. Pd. $2 for two suits of underclothes, 50-cents for jacket, 5-cents for writing tablet and 22-cents for stamped envelopes. Arrived home at 3:10 p.m. Then cleared driveway and corncrib.

Nov. 9–Dec. 3: Shucked corn most of the time till Dec. 1st after which I shucked 107 bushels at 2 ½ -cents, finishing at N. B. Shaffer's. December 3rd weather very changeable. The last week of Nov. being very cold, growing warmer toward December. Paid 5-cents for shoe nails. Settled account with N. B. Shaffer and rec'vd $40.67 in full of acct. Rode around country in search of a shucking job and sighted one at L. McCarty's, 2 miles south of Chenoa.

Dec. 4: Attended church in morning and went to L. McCarty's in afternoon, where I got the job of shucking corn at $1.10 per day. Returned to Shaffer's and then back to McCarty's. North wind cold, 15F

Dec. 5–9: Shucked corn. Corn very good here. Weather avg. 0 to 20F

Dec. 10: Received pay $5.50 for shucking corn and then walked to H. Peck's then walked on to Shaffer's. North wind cold 15F

Dec. 11: Remained at house Very cold.

Dec. 12–13: Helped Shafer butcher

Dec. 14: Came to H. Peck's Took load of corn to Meadows.

Dec. 15–18: Chored. Got clothes from Shafer. Weather warmer at 18F

Dec. 19: Went to Lexington in a.m. Sent watch to A. M. Ward and Company in Chicago for repairs. Paid 25-cent for express.

Dec. 20–23: Chored. Went to Lex. Pd. 25-cents for pair of silk mittens for R. Shaffer for Christmas.

Dec. 24: Went to Chenoa. Sought for sermon textbooks which could not find. Sent $5 home. Rec'vd from home a collar, necktie and 2 handkerchiefs for Christmas.

Dec. 25–26: Remained at home. Chored and read

Dec. 27–30: Chored Purchased candy 5-cents

Dec. 31: Rode to Lexington to see about purchasing hay for H. Peck of his brother. Received 10-cents for the trip. Sent "The Jucklins" to Cora. Wrote Ward and Company about watch.

Hand-addressed Montgomery Ward envelope.
WBH's possessions. (Note: the 2-cent stamp)

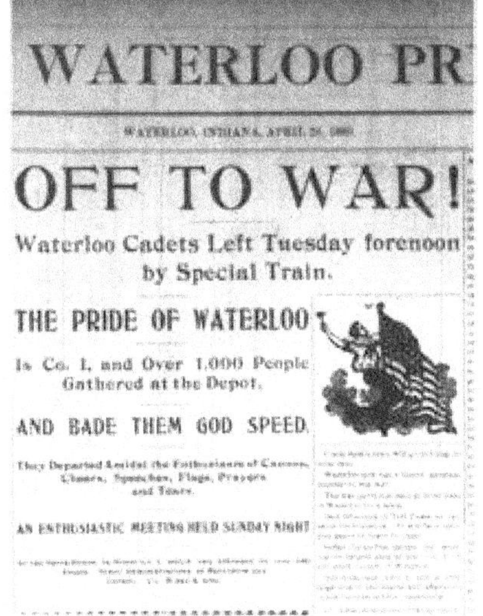

WATERLOO PR

OFF TO WAR!

Waterloo Cadets Left Tuesday forenoon by Special Train.

THE PRIDE OF WATERLOO

Is Co. I, and Over 1,000 People Gathered at the Depot.

AND BADE THEM GOD SPEED.

AN ENTHUSIASTIC MEETING HELD SUNDAY NIGHT

Waterloo Press – Front page reads OFF TO WAR! The editor provides the reader a sense of excitement and patriotism, ignoring all risks. Every eligible man in DeKalb County, Indiana was packed and ready to join the fight.

1,011,068 The World. 1,011,068

DEWEY SMASHES SPAIN'S FLEET

Great Naval Battle Between Asiatic Squadron and Spanish Warships Off Manila.

The World newspaper headlines read, "Dewey Smashes Spain's Fleet" Notice the dramatic renderings of Dewey, Montojo and the Spanish cruisers that were destroyed.

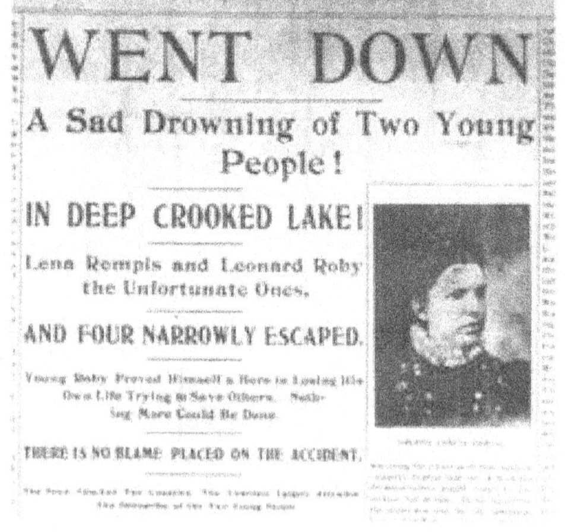

WENT DOWN

A Sad Drowning of Two Young People!

IN DEEP CROOKED LAKE!

Lena Rempis and Leonard Roby the Unfortunate Ones,

AND FOUR NARROWLY ESCAPED.

Young Roby Proved Himself a Hero in Losing His Own Life Trying to Save Others. Nothing More Could Be Done.

THERE IS NO BLAME PLACED ON THE ACCIDENT.

Front page of Waterloo Press reporting on tragic accident of WBH's friend, Lena Rempis.

McVicker's Theatre, 25 W. Madison Ave. Chicago, Ill. The original theatre was built in 1857. Two fires later, in 1890, Louis H. Sullivan's graceful stylized floral stencil-work decorating the theatre was quite modern for the day. "Form follows function" is attributed to him. He was a mentor to Frank Lloyd Wright and the Chicago group of architects who have come to be known as The Prairie School. Sadly, in 1985, the theatre was demolished.

Elmo Hotel 9921 Ewing Ave. Chicago, Illinois. Charles Hill rented a room here, where brother Bert would visit and stay. *Postcard among WHB's possessions.*

Illinois Steel Company, Chicago, Ill. Located in south Chicago shipyards. *Picture among WBH's possession.*

Light House, with Illinois Steel Company in background. *Postcard among WBH's possession.*

1899

WILBUR WRIGHT, Ohio bicycle mechanic, wrote the Smithsonian in 1899, affirming his belief that human flight was possible while Claude Monet was painting his first "Lily Pond" series.

JANUARY 1, 1899: Chored and read. A cold 15 degrees.

JAN. 2–8: Hauled corn for A. H. Acrogin to receive 40-cents. Freezing rain then a few inches of snow on 6th. Went to Lexington and received repaired watch. Attended a combustion sale in Lex. Most articles sold cheap. On 8th remained at home. Chored and read.

JAN. 9: Helped to prepare machinery for sale.

JAN. 10: Helped at sale of H. Peck. Took the clerk to Chenoa in evening also went to Lexington and got 25 I. R. stamps in p.m.

JAN. 11–12: Saw Ino Hutcheson concerning work made no agreement, except to meet again in a week and 2 days. Received $1.60 for work of H. Peck sale.

Jan. 13: Went to Chenoa with load of vinegar. Paid 4-cents for spool of thread.

Jan. 14: Chored, etc. Went to Lexington with H. Peck and stallion. Stallion quite nervous most of time. Saw George Boyd who offered me $20 per month from 3.15 after corn shucking. Have until next Saturday to accept or reject.

Jan. 15: Went to Lexington for Dr. Covey for Mr. Newbanks, who has la grippe.[12]

Jan 16–20: Put corn in crib. Saw F. Miller about work. Went to N. B. Shafer on 19th. Newbanks quite poorly from la grippe. On 20th went with Peck to Lexington, sold stallion. Saw Si Biggs about work but he has another man to consider first.

Jan. 21: Saw J. Hutcheson about work but made no contract with him. Walked to Lexington and saw Ino McColm about work. Will see him soon again. Wrote card to home. Warm and cloudy with northwest wind.

Jan. 22: Read and visited sick at Birlingmair's

Jan. 23: Went to Lex. Virtually hired to J. McColm for $20 per month for 8 or 9 months commencing on 3/1/99

Jan. 24: Went to Jos. Wethers to stay for a time. Jos. Wethers expectant of increase of family. Hauled jag of straw in p.m.

Jan. 25: Scooped corn for J. Schopp, at A. H. Scroggin in p.m.

Jan. 26–27: Chored at Wethers and scooped corn at N. B. Shaffer's and H. Peck's. Informed that McColm desires me to commence work soon. Rec'd $125 for work.

Jan. 28: Arose at 4:00 a.m. dressed, walked to H. Peck's. Walked on to Lexington and got a week off from McColm. Drew $40 from bank and took note to bank at Chenoa to be paid there. Paid 25-cents for haircut and shave, 2-cents for stamp on check and 24-cents to Chenoa. Bought overcoat, pair shoes and gloves, $11.00. Ate dinner 25-cents, $1.50 ticket to Chicago. Arrived at Chicago at 5 p.m. Went to South Chicago on I.C. Railroad, then to St. Elmo. Went to ship yards, testing an old boiler at shipyard till 11:00 p.m. 20-cents streetcar fare to Charles home.

Jan. 29: Went back to shipyards till 1 a.m. then took train home to Waterloo. Surprised the folks. Home place is little changed, though Waterloo is much improved in buildings. It's been a several years since a visit home.

Jan. 31: Visited family and friends. Shave for 10-cents

Feb. 1: Visited in a.m. and went to Auburn at 10:23 a.m. Saw Lester Till, now running a restaurant. Ate dinner at Aunt Lavina and Uncle Wm. McCrory's who now runs the engine at the power plant. Went to Kimmell thence to Wolf Lake with Bert Mayfield. Folks well as commonly and place familiar. Remained at Grandma Shambaugh's all night. 25-cents return fare to Auburn, $1.35 to Kimmell and 25-cents to Wolf Lake.

Feb. 2: Visited with the folks till 8:30 a.m. then returned to Auburn via Kimmell. Ate dinner at McCrory's. Went to town powerhouse at 2:38 p.m. to Lester Till's restaurant, then home to Waterloo. 25-cents for cigars.

Feb. 3: Stayed home in a.m. with folks. Went to Grand Crossing, Chicago. Left Waterloo, 4:40 p.m., arrived at 8:30 p.m. Streetcar to South Chicago thence to 99th Street and Ewing Avenue. Then turned in at Charles's room at 10:30 p.m.

Feb. 4: Ate breakfast with Charles. Then took Pem. Car to W. Depot then train, C&A to Chenoa. Ate dinner and got clothes left at store and walked to H. Peck's. Took suit of working clothes and walked to Lexington. Purchased boots and rode to Ino McColm's place. Pd. 10-cents shaving cup, $1.98 felt boots.

Feb. 5: Read, chored and acquaintance myself with place.

Feb. 6: Began working by month for Ino McColm. 10 cows are milked now. He has 5 horses, 75 sheep, 160 acres of land and good buildings. Cut wood and chored.

Feb. 7–18: Worked on wood. Went to town and helped distribute milk, chored, cut down trees. Went to town on 13th to H. Peck's for my clothes. Average temp 10F

Feb. 19: Read and chored. Studying German.

Feb. 20–26: Cut wood in timber. Cleared chicken coop, hauled manure and shucked corn. Read and chored. Weather cool, damp disagreeable.

Feb. 27–March 3: Went to Lexington, Chored Pd. $1.25 for 2 pair of overalls. Snowstorm from northeast. Note of Simon Shaffer of $100 at 7% due today to be paid at State Bank of Chenoa.

March 4–19: Went to Lex. with milk. Uncovered straw stack. Charles Jones of North Carolina now here for a time to work. Tending stock.

March 20–25: Stock work and wood cutting. On Wed. 22nd agreed to loan A. E. Slagel $50 till Dec. 1 – 99 at 7 % interest. Calvin Smith here till 25th.

March 26–28: Read and chored. Worked mostly with stock, some wood-cutting. Ira McColm arrived the 28th from Manchester, Adams County, Ohio to work for his Uncle Ino McColm. Weather stormy and cool. Snow

March 29–30: Snow storm all day and into the night. 6 inches snow fell with northeast wind. Attended to stock.

March 31: Hauled straw, fodder and cut wood. Stiff west wind.

April 1: Attended sheep in morning. Chored and hauled wood from Franklin.

April 2–15: Hauled, cut and sawed wood. Cleaned chicken houses. Went to town on the 8th. $1.25 for pair of shoes. 10-cents for horehound candy for cold.

April 16: Chored and read, etc. Cal Smith and John McColm visit here. 25-cents for straw hat. Sent for flower seeds.
Hauled rails of cornfield fence to corner of pasture. Cultivated oats ground.

April 17–18: Harrowed oats ground, dry and ground to same extent caked on top.

April 19: Harrowed oats ground Clear and warm

April 20: Rain last night. Shucked corn in a.m. to sow 10 pks. Equally mixed clover and timothy seed, on 9 acres.

April 21–30: Sowed grass seed and harrowed the grass sown ground. Broke corn stalks and plowed in oats stubble field. Plowed oat stubble field. Ground breaks well for most part. Quite fine and loose. Rode to town in eve of 27th. Paid 15-cents for a haircut and 5-cents for a fishing line and hook. Went fishing in the evening of the 29th – alas no fish. Hot and clear.

May 1: Finished plowing oat stubble ground and cultivated fall plowing.

May 2 - 19: Southeast corn field dry and dusty. Harrowed north field. Fall plowing dried, 3 inches deep, cloddy and hard. Castrated buck lambs. Planted potatoes. Planted corn and plowed on 6th. Lost the fork of checker on planter necessitating discontinuance of planting for this day.

Finished it: 25 acres planting of corn in north field. Rolled corn ground for days. Split wood and trimmed sheep on the 19th.

May 20: McColm gave us a holiday! I went to Lexington in the morning. Got a 10-cent shave and $3.00 for 1 dozen cabinet sized photos of myself. Went fishing in p.m. No bites, no fish, nothing but fun!

May 21: Read etc. 50 F

May 22: Split wood. Finished splitting maple, commenced on oak.

May 23: Split wood, burned brush in Franklin's pasture 2 stray, 6 day old pigs brought in.

MAY 24–27: Spade around trees in orchard. Made fence, west of chicken house and repaired fences around straw lot and in pasture. Went to Lex. on 26th with milk. Cut weeds in potatoes. Repaired fence in northwest pasture. 80F

MAY 28: Attended Memorial Service at Lexington High School Auditorium in morning. A good sermon by Cannon of Christian Church. Slept and visited in p.m.

MAY 29–31: Cut wood and thistles. Thistles very plentiful on hillsides in pasture. Went to Lex. on 30th to hear fine talk by Mr. Scringer of Bloomington. Fine weather
Corn is 4 inches high. 80-85 degrees

JUNE 1–10: Cleared garden, plowed corn, Many running vines in corn hills. Ground very loose causing cultivator shovels not to scour well. On 6th went to Lexington to high school commencement exercises. President Ino Cook of Normal made a good talk on education of civilization. Received 1 dozen photos of myself.

JUNE 11: Spent a.m. as usual and in p.m. went to Dunker Church in Clarksville, attending a township Sunday School conference. Large crowd.

JUNE 12–17: Plowed and thinned corn. Wool was sacked and delivered today. 9 1/3 lbs. per fleece, 7 fleece at 18-cents per lb. 80-90F Received Waterloo Press.

JUNE 18: Read and attended Sunday School and preaching at Heffner's School House in p.m. United Brethren denomination. Gave 5-cents to S.S.

June 19–24: Plowed corn, west and southwest fields. Ground is wet as should be worked in morning. Hoed vines in cornfield. Picked 20 gallons of cherries and 5 quarts of raspberries on the 23rd. Early Richmond cherries – very full and ripe. Sowed and raked seed. Cultivated corn. Heard from home and Wolf Lake.

June 25–30: Plowed corn every day. Completed plowing corn for this year. Hoed some corn. Some poison appearing on face. HOT 98 degrees

July 1: Hoed and pulled vines.

July 2: Spent day at home. Poison ivy prevents me from shaving face.

July 3: Pulled vines from corn. Put up small jag of hay in afternoon. Rain 1 inch.

July 4: Spent most of day at home. Frank McColm and family from Chicago, B. F. Robinson and family from Colfax and George Flesher's family were here for a visit.

July 5–8: Cut thistles. Pulled and hoed vines from corn. On the 8th went to Lex. in evening and listened to band music and saw the fireworks. Very fine.

July 9: Read and slept. Poison ivy still preventing me shaving but is less active in eruptions.

July 10–20: Hauled 2 loads of straw to Dr. Welch's barn in Lexington. Cut thistles, put corn and 1 load of hay in barn. Pitched hay, 10 loads in barn on 11th and 12th Hauled hay, 4 loads and 7 loads of hay from northwest meadow. Stirred, hauled and pitched hay and had 7 loads of hay from southeast meadow.

Hauled wood and made and set fence posts. Strung wire on fence. Very hot these last several days. 98-100F

July 21–31: Shocked oats today 9 acres. Rode 3 miles in evening to B. France's place Helped in hay at Brown's and Pott's on 25th. Ira McColm commenced to run the blower on Brown's threshing outfit. Hauled load of oats from William Brown's and repaired granaries, etc. preparatory to threshing. Hauled oats from field at Wisner's. McColm's oats – 1,459 bushels on 25 acres. Hauled oats to granary at Pott's. Have got a cold and headache today.

Aug. 1: Rain in morning. Hauled corn to barn crib. Drove calf from Mahan's pasture back home and loaded corn for pig lot.

Aug. 2–16: Mowed weeds and then helped J. Smith, F. Brown and J. Biggs thresh oats. Cleaned up and topped out straw stack. Hauled rails to start a 5-rail lamb fence. Completed fence on 8th. Threshed for days. Very Hot! Hauled oats from Charles Hall's to Lexington. Repaired ram lot.

Aug. 17: Helped bring cow from Lex. to farm. Helped M. Adreon thresh oats. Answered letter from brother Charles.

Aug. 18: Helped thresh and hauled oats to town. Hauled coarse gravel to farm. Still 100F

Aug. 19–25: Picked apples Took lambs from Jos. Beasly's, 19, 14 lb. lambs all healthy. Continues hot and dry. Brought 17 lambs from M. Adreon's farm. Hauled corn into barn and spread manure on the fields. Cut cockle burrs and butter privet .

Fleeting clouds. The anniversary of my birth passed without notice.

Aug. 26: Went to Lon Flesher's, 6 miles northwest from here for 12 lambs, avg. 6-8 lbs. Helped rinse cistern. Hauled sand to repair cistern. Went to town in evening. Paid $1.00 for shirts and got a haircut.

Aug. 27: Spent the day reading and visiting with neighbors.

Aug. 28: Hauled lambs to Lexington. McColm shipped lambs this evening to Chicago. Some lambs dying from scours which is cause of his selling them now.[13] Received $25.00 from McColm. Sent $15.00 money order home to folks.

Aug. 29–31: Hauled stone and sand. Hauled corn for Wm. Brown. He stores about 16,000 bushels at Lexington. Cut corn, 14 shocks – to green to cut. Hot and dusty.

Sept. 1: Dug trench in ditch. Burned cobs, hauled sand from house yards and cut corn. 100F

Sept. 2: Spend day cutting corn in orchard.

Sept. 3: Sundayed quietly

Sept 4–7: Hauled water to house. Dug holes and set posts on south side of meadow. Made fence and put wires on east meadow fence. Sent watch to A.M. Ward and Company to have it cleaned. Finally some relief from heat, thunderstorm.

Sept 8–9: Cut and tied corn. Helped ring hogs. Received letter from home and the Waterloo Press newspaper. Weather is more pleasant.

Sept 10–15: Reset and cut and tied corn in stack. Also gathered small load of corn. Cut butter privets and dug potatoes. Excellent weather for working 85F Shelled corn for C. F. McColm. Hauled old corn into barn and rail crib in hog lot. Sowed timothy seed on 9 acres oat stubble field. Harrowed grass and sown field. Sent A. M. Ward and Co. $1.56 for watch repairs.

Sept. 16: Went to Lexington to hear Rev. O. W. Stewart make a temperance lecture on "Christian Citizenship" Spoke well. Fair speech. 10-cents for a shave.

Sept 17: Rested and read and visited. Rain and cooler.

Sept. 18: Sowed more timothy seed on same field. Went 4 miles after to get a good Jersey cow.

Sept. 19–30: Hauled straw to barn, Hauled manure. Trimmed sheep's feet. Few of their feet lame from rot. Dug potatoes and gathered corn. Frost on 28th

Brought 34 ewes from M. Adreon's and trimmed their feet. 1/3 lame from foot rot. Finally received watch. Runs all right. Dug potatoes 30 – 60F

Oct. 1–7: Very cool and cloudy. Dug potatoes and made rail pig pen. Shoveled gravel and hauled it to F. Mahan's pit to road.

I must pay one day's work for poll tax, which I did on the 4th.[14] Shoveled gravel in pit.

Oct. 5: Completed the present road repairs. Cleaned chicken coop of summer accumulation. A few places had lice. Whitewashed chicken house and husked corn.

Oct. 8: Went to N. B. Shaffer's in morning. N.B.S. has prospered this year Returned in evening.

Oct. 9: Shucked corn. Heard from home. McColm closed out his dairy business today. 15 cows in all are to go. 13 left today.

Oct. 10–14: Hauled manure Retrimmed sheep's feet and commenced building rail fence. Completed fence and shucked corn. 85F increasing to 100F in sunshine. Received $100 to my credit at State of Lexington and $3 in cash from Ino McColm in full for work "till Sept. 1 – 99"

Oct. 15–21: Shucked corn. Charles McColm helps most of the time. We shucked about 100 bushels per day. Corn makes 45 bu. per acre. Uneven quality, mostly sound. On the 16th I paid 30-cents for having 12 pairs of mittens made.

Oct. 22: Sundayed as usual. Very warm for October. 82F

Oct. 23–31: Shucked corn. On 27th rained all day. Read and sewed. Sent $8.50 to A.M. Ward and Co for black enameled iron covered bureau trunk. Plowed stubble ground.

Nov. 1: Shucked corn. Some mist the most of afternoon.

Nov. 2: Shucked corn till 9:00 a.m. Snow commenced falling at 8 a.m. constantly increasing for 1 hour and continued remainder of the day. Melting as fast as it falls.

Nov. 3: Snow 3 inches deep on ground in morning. Hauled manure in p.m. from sheep shed. Sunset all clear.

Nov. 4: Shucked shock corn today.

Nov. 5: Walked to Shaffer's in morning. Had a visit with all the families. I agreed to go to Arizona, with N. B. Schaffer between now and December 10th. He is to pay all expenses except railroad fare until we return or till he returns or till a find is made that is worth working. Weather pleasant.

Nov. 6–11: Shucked corn. Corn is yielding from 50-60 bushels per acre. Weather for most part is favorable for husking. Received trunk Tuesday for which I paid 25- cents for freight. Wednesday, I sent 90-cents for a money order for book entitled, "ABC of Mining" by Charles A. Bramble. Received the book on Friday, the 11th.[15]

Went to Lexington in evening and paid 25-cents for galluses, (suspenders) 5-cents for needles, 5-cents for candy and 4-cents for a spool of thread. Sent inquiries to railroad companies for rates and western points.

Nov. 12: Read and visited.

Nov. 13 – 14: Shucked corn. Finished husking corn on stalk for McColm. Received 5- cents in stamps from A.M. Ward and Company as return of extra amount I paid.

Nov. 15–18: Hauled the manure, gathered turnips. Helped Frank Wisner shell corn, cut rails, cleaned chicken coops. Reset fence on west side of hog lot. Letter from home. Always welcome.

Nov. 19: Passed Sunday as usual.

Nov. 20: Shoveled corn for Frank Wisner who shelled his corn in morning. Put corn-fodder in barn and repaired fence. Wrote notice to A.E. Slagel and G. E. Slagel that note was due, December 1, 1899.

Nov. 21–25: Cut wood today and put new chicken boxes west of original chicken house. Cut wood, hauled broken rails and shocked corn. Lon Flesher's, Jr. went to Chicago. Hauled gravel to barn lot. Received pictures from home.

Nov. 26: Went to N. B. Shaffer's in morning. Conversed with regard to our Arizona trip. Spent the day.

Nov. 27: Hauled gravel from N. Franklin's creek bank to barn lot. Attended to sheep's feet.

Nov. 28: Went to Lexington in a.m. then to Chenoa. Drew my money $57 from bank. Went to H. Peck's and saw his new $3,600 house, nearly ready for occupancy. Finely finished in oak, the most of it. Furnace and electric lights! Purchased key ring, 4- cents, 5-cents for a mirror. Fishing tackle, 15-cents. Purchased second-class fare from Chenoa to Phoenix, Arizona it's $52.25 via Denver, or Kansas City. From Lexington cost $51.50.

Nov. 29: Hauled gravel all day.

Nov 30: Loafed around plantation. Fine turkey dinner. Clear and pleasant.

Dec 1–3: Hauled gravel. Hauled in feed. Rain and more rain.

Dec. 4: Loafed and went to Lexington. Went to A. E. Slagel's to see him about note but he was in Chicago. Purchased a fine hat $1.00 and 15-cents for collars. Growing colder.

Dec. 5: Brought effects to Shaffer's from McColm's. Saw Slagel who is to pay interest on both notes tomorrow and send the $50 to me in Arizona, when I write for it.

Dec. 6: Went to Lexington. Got a note from A. E. Slagel dated Dec 6, 99, and due January 1, 1901 given him the former note of same amount, which is due Jan. 1, 1900 and received $5.99 interest. $2.40 and $1.60 is yet due on that note and another one of $50 is due on Dec. 1, 1899. Packed trunk. Got $69 from S. Bank of Lexington. Went to depot in evening. Paid 49-cents for my ticket to Bloomington. Started at 6:51 p.m. Purchased ticket to Phoenix via St. Louis on the Iron Mountain Route. Leave for St. Louis at 1:30 a.m.

Dec. 7: St. Louis, Mo. Came here from 1:30 a.m. to 7:30 a.m. Ate breakfast then went uptown. Union Depot is a very large and finely finished building. Sent card home. Purchased a steel colt, single-action 38-caliber pistol for $9.50. Paid 40-cents for cartridge belt, 75-cents for scabbard and 60-cents for 50.38 long central fire cartridges. Went down on wharf and watched passing ships. Paid $2.50 for berth in tourist sleeper from here to Maricopa. Left St. Louis at 8:15 p.m. on the St. L&M &Sky.

Dec. 8: Arose at 7 a.m. Pass most of my time watching countryside. At 1:15 we were switched to the Texas and Pacific Railroad, which we will go to El Paso. Got to Texarkana over 1 hour late. Passed Marshall, Dallas arrived at Ft. Worth at 10 p.m. Dallas and Ft. Worth are good size towns with streetcars. Purchased apples, 5-cents. Remained in Ft. Worth and retired at 10:30 p.m. Sent postal home.

Dec. 9: Arose at 7 a.m., ate breakfast. By 10:00 a.m. at Big Springs, a ranch town of 1,000 or more. Passed through grazing country, red sandy soil, closely cropped grass, many mesquite bushes, a large number of prairie dogs, some cattle and mules, a few horses, and a number of water ponds. Country rolling, no trees. Passed Red River, 300 ft. wide, where crossed. Arrived in El Paso at 12 midnight, after stopping for supper at Sierra Blanco.

Dec. 10: Arose at 7 a.m. central standard time, went uptown ate breakfast, walked around town for an hour. Got a shave. El Paso = 23,000 population. Business and houses are modern and almost entirely made out of brick. Terminal building is a 3 story structure with a 5 story dome about 130 ft. X 100 ft. or more. Stayed here from 12 last night till after 7:40 a.m. A change of 2 hours in time between Central and Pacific Time. Sent letter home. Purchased candy.

Dec. 11: Arose at 4 a.m. Got a cup of coffee, waited 1½ hours then started on road to Phoenix. Phoenix = 20,000 people. Arrived there at 7:45 and went to Gregory House where Shaffer and I took a room for 50-cents per day. Ate breakfast downtown. Hunting for burros among the different corrals. Got on track of some burros, which Shaffer went to see in afternoon, 4 miles south of town. He also purchased some mining tools. Got trunks from depot for 50-cents. Half which Shaffer will pay. Paid 5-cents for good peaches.

There are two public buildings here with courts surrounding them. Courts are decorated with trees, palms, cacti and flowers. One is the capitol and city hall the other is county court house. Got copy of acts of last legislature at secretary of territory office. Sent letter home. Weather clear and temperate.

Dec. 12: Got drills and other tools ready in morning. Saw a fire consume 4 store rooms in heart of town. Took burros to Gregory House and packed them and started toward Tempe at 3:30 p.m. Went about 3 ½ miles east and remained over night at a farmer's old house. He is a former Illinois farmer named Wharton. A very kind and obliging man. Dry and pleasant and night cool.

Dec. 13: Cooked breakfast and started from camp at 8:00 a.m. Passed through Tempe, a town of 2,000 at 9:45 a.m. Waded Salt River, only

50 ft. width of water and 1 foot deep. Railroad bridge spanning Salt River = 1,000 ft. long or more. Stopped for 1 hour dinner. Unpacked and repacked our 2 burros. Started at 1:15 p.m. to Mesa, 19 miles from Phoenix. Stopped at corral in town at 3:30 p.m. Passed many irrigation ditches, fruit farms, and alfalfa and barley fields. Shaffer purchased oranges of farmers along the way. Tasted very good. Sent letter to home. Water physics me and makes me somewhat weak. Pleasant but very cool at night. Lord bless home and everyone!

DEC. 14: Mexican ranch 17 miles northeast from Mesa, AZ. We had our breakfast in Mesa, then made ready and started northeast from Mesa. We missed the right road and 1 mile too far east making 3 miles unnecessary walk. Crossed some large canals and struck across level country for 2 or 3 miles. Country then became slightly rough, till 8 or 9 miles out, when we crossed an abrupt granite butte. Valleys and hills from 10 -40 ft. high. The country gradually leveled till within 4 miles of ranch. This applies only to valleys. Passed along Salt River Valley, most of way. Passed a large red limestone mountain about 2/3 of the way from Mesa. Stopped for a short time for dinner, then resume journey. Legs very tired. Checked wrong trail near ranch and went ½ mile or more out of way again. Went up river for 300 ft., scaled a 60 ft. hill, very steep and covered with rocks. One burro fell and had to unpack him and carry pack up. Continued east for ½ mile, then struck ranch. Ate supper after getting feed for burros, then retired. I was quite weak and tired all p.m. Carried shotgun till 4 p.m. when Shaffer took it. Feeling quite good now with a little rest.

DEC. 15: Arose at 7 a.m. Prepared breakfast = Dutch oven = bread, potatoes, bacon and steak, also coffee. Started from Mexican ranch and headed northeast direction crossing many and various sized hills and gulches, along Salt River Valley. Waded river which was ice cold. Width of ford 150 ft. Continued till 12:30 p.m. when stopped for dinner. Shaffer bothered with sore knee from cacti prickers yesterday. Ate in large cannon box about ½ x 1 ½ miles. Kept winding around the river for a few miles, then took across hill and gulches following trails of horses. Most of way for 8 to 10 miles, when we began to descend the canon (Spanish spelling for canyon) in which are the Hidden Springs. Arrived at Springs at 6 p.m. Ate supper and retired. We are in a very picturesque spot and will sleep under a large projecting rock. Opposite hill over 300 ft. high, straight up. I am feeling well. Poor burros will have to wait for feed until tomorrow. Continued pleasant weather with bright moon-lite night.

Dec. 16: Arose at 7 a.m. and packed burros, climbed steep stone bluff under which we slept. Up 500 ft. for 1½ miles, where we prepared breakfast and let burros graze. Repacked and continued toward four peaks. We continued 4 or 5 miles, making up and down grades till we arrived at Cain Springs, 1 mile up a long gulch. Here we camped, prepared and ate dinner. Quail for dinner that Shaffer shot. Hobbled burros on grassy hillside south of camp. Washed dishes, then we put up tent. Had beans for late supper. Hazy all day and quite cloudy. Will remain here over Sunday. Feeling well.

Dec. 17: Arose at 8 a.m. Quite a strong wind for most of the night. After breakfast we walked ¾ mile east, where Shaffer and partner had sunk 30 ft. shaft and quartz formations here. Spent remainder of day lying in camp tent. Quails very numerous, coming close to camp. 3 shots failed to bring any quail down. Beans, apricots, raisins, salmon, bread and coffee for dinner.

Dec. 18: Arose at 6:40 a.m. Sprinkling as we were dressing, after breakfast we packed burros and came in northeast course about 8 – 10 miles to within ½ mile of the peaks. Here we found the claim, Shaffer and partner had located in '93 was taken by another man, who had done his assessment work for 1898 and assessment had till January 1900 before doing any more work on it would be necessary. The claim has located phosphorus and quartz rock. Water of poor quality and small quality and small quantity. Here we camped and tested prickly brush. Some juniper trees and pine about peaks. Warm during noon hours but very cold in evening. Snow at peaks in morning, clouds obscuring them for a time but few scattering clouds in evening. Wind blows up gulches and canons in daytime and down at night. All is well.

Dec 19: Arose at 8 a.m. after a cold nights sleep. Wind blew at 30 miles per hour. Prepared hasty breakfast and started ascending at 9 a.m. We went on the wrong side of ridge and our assent was slow and at times perilous. Forced to cut some of way through brush and weave back and forth to get on top. Each burro had to be repacked twice. Wind kept blowing 40 miles per hour and very cold. Steady trip for 9 hours. We went 1½ mile and arrived at the top of pass, 1000 ft. over the peaks. Some pine on west and north side of peaks and oak of 1½ diameter. Pine is 3 ft. diameter and 80 ft. high. Many hills covered with Manzanita scrub oak with many prickly bushes. Saw several deer tracks and Shaffer shot at 2 does but missed both. Took southeast course down and after 1 hour decent we came on to trail leading to Sycamore Creek. Filled canteen at spring in peaks, then descended 2,500 ft. or more in 2 miles down to the creek. Many places being simple slides. At the creek we camped and the water is very good, cold and pure but only a small stream.

Shaffer killed a hydrophobia skunk after dark at camp. We passed for about 1 hour over frozen ground in peaks and drank water on which was ice. Wind very cold and strong till 2 p.m.

Dec. 20: Passed a comfortable night and were ready to start at 9:20 a.m. Went 4 miles, within 1 mile of Sycamore Creek, then took a northeast direction for a 3-hour journey. We struck Tonto Creek crossed it and ate a 3 o'clock dinner. Repacked and came down on wagon road. Gradually walked away from Tonto Creek till 5 p.m. when we camped. Most of the day travel was gradual decent of 1 to 15 feet, with sandy paths though well grassed country.

A Mexican man came along road and stopped over night with us. All is well.

Dec. 21: Very cold morning but soon warmed and so continued till evening. Took east by north course for 15 miles. Kept within sight of Tonto Creek for 4 or 5 miles, then soon came to Salt River. Continued the remainder of the day. Crossed Salt River at 12:40 p.m. Crossed where it was 120 ft. wide and 1 ft. deep. Water very cold, upper Salt River valley is well-settled and large crops of alfalfa and some wheat and barley are grown. Only saw one field of corn. Irrigation is in force here. We kept on Pason road all the way. Many cotton wood trees all along the valley. Ground slightly sloping and for most part even. Sent letter home from the only one store/post office called Livingstone. Here we camped and will stay over till tomorrow, noon to await mail delivery. Four miles below here is where Shaffer used to work on farm ranch. All is well.

Dec. 22: This morning commenced the shortest day of the year. We remained in Livingstone until 1:30 p.m. to await mail. Then took north-east course until 5:45 p.m. Crossed Salt River and gradually ascended and crossed the first high passes in the foothills of the Surra Anchis (Sierra Ancha) Mountains. Just below the first real pass, we camped behind some oak bushes and cacti. The warmest place we have yet stopped. Took but small canteen of water so no dishes were washed. Plenty of grass on hillsides.

Dec. 23: Arose at 7 a.m. breakfasted and started and made a general southeast course, rather east by south. We made Coon Creek at morning and ate dinner then made Cherry Creek at 2 p.m. down which we went for 2 miles. Coon Creek = large ditch, big fall, cool water. Cherry Creek is 3 times size of Coon. Camped at 3 p.m. and put up tent. Tried pistol, works well. Large limestone and red stone. I think it is cyanite (sometimes spelled Kyanite) mountains along Cherry Creek. Little grass where we stopped. Coon to Cherry Creek equals 1¼ mile straight where we crossed. All well. Warm and clear with little winds. Will remain here over Sunday.

Dec. 24: Sunday Christmas Eve. Arose late after a warm sleep, breakfasted and then went about 4 or 5 miles southeast of here, where we came upon Salt River. It is a muddy looking rather sluggish stream and small. We ascended fully 1500 ft. in the trip up. River there was fully 500 ft. below side hills or mountains, whose sides were quite steep on west side and abrupt on east. We are camped only 2 or 3 miles from mouth of Cherry Creek. When we first reached top hills, we took southwest course for ½ mile on tops of some hills. Here we saw a deer with bunch of cattle. I shot 2 quail. Returned to camp at 1 p.m., ate dinner and worked about camp, remainder of the day. Object for walk was to find course to be taken. Warm and a little windy.

Dec. 25: Anniversary of Christ's birth. We took a 2-hour journey south, inspecting hills and rocks. Went to Salt River and fished a short time but got no bites, much less fish. I shot 2 quail. We returned up Cherry Creek bottom, a distance of over 2 miles. Ate dinner then I went a mile or more north in evening. Very much limestone and porphyry. About here, also granite. Beautiful scenery here, especially along Salt River. Will try to make Canon Creek tomorrow. Northeast of here the mountains are several hundred feet high, on each side of creek, many of them too steep to ascend. The warmest Christmas I ever passed.

Dec. 26: We broke camp at Cherry Creek in the morning and took northeast direction passing between Cherry and Salt Rivers. Passed over mostly ground covered with volcanic stone and gravel. Little grew on volcanic ground. We made an almost continuous ascent until morning and after. Dined on jackrabbit. Continued on course till we had passed a long range of hills. About 3 p.m. we began to descend which we did until 5:15 p.m. We arrived on Salt River bottom, were we camped. Had 4 quail, which I shot and jack rabbit for supper. Made about 7-hour journey. A fair number of cattle and some horses in country. Saw a number of geese along the river. Had a well beaten trail after 11 a.m. to follow.

DEC. 27: Started at 9:15 a.m. up the Salt River bottom which we kept for a couple miles. Indians have some farming ground here, though off the reservation. We went nearer north on another ascending range of hills, until mountains, where we ate a cold dinner and let the burros rest. A spring below us on the west is about a mile away. We repacked and descended after 1 p.m. in a northeast course for 3-hours, when we struck Canon Creek. Here we camped probably on Apache Reservation. Creek has very big fall and pretty granite bed here and it joins Salt River, ½ mile below. A rather gloomy place to camp.

DEC. 28: Passed a warm night. Gathered wood for fire, ate breakfast, then went up Canon Creek, a short distance thru west for 2 miles then back to camp. Climbed many high hills in our walk. Country does not resemble the one looked for, so decided to make way back west to camp on Salt River. Left camp at 12:15 and took shod horse trail along river bottom. Passed Indian farm plots, on up river 3 or 4 miles. Good walking, most of the way. Here we camped on Salt River, changed clothing and washed dirty ones, a cold job. Grass is close by us also water and we have a warm place to stop. As cheerful a place as we have yet to camp. Saw some ducks but got none. Canon Creek runs in several southern directions. Ate hearty supper of bacon, gravy, bread, beans and tea. Mesquite makes good fuel. Sat about the fire till late bedtime of 8:00 p.m. All well.

Dec. 29: After breakfast took a walk north and west, up and down canons and gulches: returned at 11 am. Shot 3 quails. After dinner of quails, beans, etc. we took fishing tackle and went to river. Saw some ducks and shot one. Took all clothes off but shirt and waded for duck but could not get him. Then went down river ½ mile to ford and crossed river. Water cold and thigh deep, slippery, stony bottom. After ½ hour trying I got him to shore. I recrossed ford and fell in water. Took shirt off and put Shaffer's and my waists on together, with other clothes and stayed to fish. We caught 8 lb. of suckers. Cleaned duck and fish. Put up tent, cleaned remains of fish and retired. Weather cloudy with rain after 4 p.m.

Dec. 30: Light desultory sprinkling during night and morning. Cleared with few cumulous clouds. Took canteens and shot gun and went to river. Saw a flock of geese on water and attempted to shoot them while sitting but they raised and came towards me. I got 3 with one shot! They will weigh 15 lbs. or more each.. Ate breakfast of fish, cleaned geese, had duck for dinner. Duck too fat. Then cleaned up and packed and at 2 p.m. started for Cherry Creek. Arrived at 6:40 p.m., put up tent, ate supper of duck put stock of goods in tent, soon retired. Forded river in morning for geese, some are very fat. Country we crossed was mostly hills of solid formation and rolling country. Feet tender from yesterday's run after duck. All well.

Dec 31: Arose late. Ate fish for breakfast, cleaned about camp, put goose to cook and its meat was excellent for dinner. Loafed about camp remainder of day. Goose and dumplings with apricots for supper.
This day, Sunday bids good-bye to the eighteen hundreds.

A new depot, Union Station, in Waterloo, Indiana was built in 1884. In 1882, L.S&M operated daily 4 trains east and 4 trains west to Chicago. The Ft. Wayne & Jackson operated 3 trains north and 3 trains south daily. The depot remains and serves as a community gathering space and historical museum. Note: So many communities had a "Union Station". The reason; it was an attempt to consolidate rail traffic into one terminal instead of having each railroad build a separate station and approach-track system.

The Waterloo Interurban Station was located in a section of the Waterloo Cigar Factory, which was south across the tracks from the depot. Interurban travel was quick and inexpensive and was also used to ship produce. The cars were operated by electricity, which was generated by the companies themselves. From Waterloo, Indiana, passengers could travel as far south as Louisville, Kentucky. Service was provided until 1937.

Historic map of Phoenix AZ. in 1885. The city was founded in 1868 near the Salt River and incorporated in 1881 and became the state capital in 1912.

References

1. County Court House.
2. Baptist Church.
3. Washington St. Methodist Church.
4. Public School House.
5. Centre St. Methodist Church.
6. Salt River Valley Canal.
7. Residence of J.T. Simms.
8. Gazette Printing Office.
9. Kales & Lewis' Bank.
10. Valley Bank.
11. Herald Printing Office.
12. J.Y.T. Smith's Flour Mill.
13. Public Plaza.
14. Irvins Building.
15. Phoenix Swimming Baths.
16. Phoenix Hotel, Chas, Salan, Prop.
17. Gregory House & Lumber Yard.
18. Hotel Lamon.
19. Catholic Church.
20. Dutch Ditch.
21. Maricopa Canal.
22. Grand Central.
23. Arizona Canal.
24. Residence of H.H. McNeil.
25. Residence of M.W. Kales.
26. Property of E.B. Kirkland.
27. Lount Bros.' Ice Factory.
28. P. Minor's Lumber Yard.
29. H.W. Ryder's Lumber Yard.

References mentioned in journal: 1. County Court House, 5. Centre St. Methodist Church, 6. Salt River Valley Canal, 10. Valley Bank 13. Public Plaza, 17. Gregory House & Lumberyard, Miss Marie Ferguson Prop, 225 E. Washington St., 23. Arizona Canal

1900

In 1900, the U.S. Post Office issued its first book of postage stamps. Engineer, Casey Jones of the Illinois Central Railroad was killed in a Cannonball Express train wreck, after staying at the controls, in an effort to save the passengers. 1900 marks, Charles Comiskey's purchase of the St. Paul's baseball team, moving it to Chicago, as the White Stockings came into existence.

January 1, 1900: Arose at 6:10 a.m. took rifle and went down to creek about ½ mile, before daylight and waited behind rocks for deer to come to water. None came so I returned at 7:30 a.m., ate breakfast took lunch and went up creek ¾ mile. Then northeast to creek, and 2 miles down to camp. Arrived at 3 p.m. Took burros from water to hill pasture, ate supper of goose, sat about fire and retired. Saw mountain lion's fresh track up creek. Also several deer tracks in hill to northwest. Found many quartz rocks, strong with iron. Many dikes or leads in country traveled to day. Well.

Jan. 2: Started at 9 a.m. in northeast direction, went 7 miles over hills and down gulches but found nothing that we knew to be of value to us. At 12:30 p.m. we headed toward camp at which we arrived at 2:30 p.m. by a short cut over fairly flat malpi, covered hills. After resting and watering burros, I took rifle and went over top of hills on east side of Cherry Creek up water for 2 miles, hunting deer but failed to get any fresh tracks, so returned at 5:45 p.m. Saw 2 rust covered rocks but did not sample on account of making noise but wish now that I had.

JAN. 3: After breakfast at 9:20 a.m., we took west of south direction over and around hills following shod horse trail, most of way to Salt River, which we crossed. Forded river with rolled up breeches. Water cold, river bottom uneven with large and small stones. Took more easterly course, upgrade over and around hills and up gulches until about 4 p.m. We then crossed the divide in east spur of Cannals Mountains. Soon after this we struck a wood packers trail down a gulch which we followed till we struck a wagon road at 5:40 p.m. We kept to that trail to the wheat fields and Globe road, which we walked for a mile so, when we camped for the night at 8:35 p.m. Passed a Mexican wood cutters and packers camp. From which camp = 12 miles to Globe. Traveled 2 ½ hours after dark to get water for burros, which we did at farmers on Globe road. Ate supper of goose and bread and then retired. Our general direction was southeast. Globe being nearly east from our starting point.

JAN. 4: Commenced sprinkling at 3 a.m. at 4:20 a.m. we dressed and ate breakfast of goose meat and coffee. Packed burros and started at 5:40 a.m. for Globe, a 7 mile distance. Considerable rain most of the way, down grade. Arrived at Globe at 9 a.m. 15-cents for shave, 10-cents for envelopes, 5-cents for peanuts, 15-cents for pears and 50-cents for lodging. Wrote a letter home.

Loafed and walked around town and the copper mining plant of Globe. Smelting works are quite extensive but mines are doing little now. Large amount of wood and thousands of cedar are on ground. Large bins are filled with dumped or just above smelter also line to be used as a flux with iron in working copper free. Got room at 7:15 and soon retired. Probably leave tomorrow. Many mines now idle.

JAN. 5: Arose at 7 a.m. Went down town ate breakfast. Paid 50-cents for re-nailing shoes. Waited about town till 11 a.m. then packed burros and started toward wheat fields, northwest from Globe. Lunched 4 miles out then went to wheat fields, 8 miles farther –got water and camped, ½ mile above where grass was fairly abundant. Are aiming to make Coon Creek tomorrow. Saloons do the largest business in Globe. More drinking there than any town I have ever been at before.

JAN. 6: Arose at 6:30 a.m., ate breakfast and started up gulch in north direction at 8:30, continued on shod horse trail until at 1:30 p.m. we stopped for dinner at Salt River banks. Burros very tired. General direction of route about north by west, crossed river, crossed bluff and came on Coon Creek, up which we went for about 8 miles, or just above Patterson's ranch. Here we camped at 5:30 p.m. Got 5 quail with 2 shots. Fair grass here abouts. Hazy last eve but heavy dew last night. Shaffer a little off in health. Am well myself. Learned that the Apache reservation comes to within about 1 mile of Cherry Creek.

JAN. 7: Sunday Ate late breakfast of quail. Packed burros and started at 10:15 a.m. up Coon Creek about 2 hour journey or just about the first barge box. Here we camped. Our water supply is stale, although it tastes very good. Well in bedrock of creek, several feet deep and 4 ft. in diameter. Creek flows underground above a point 1½ miles north of Patterson's ranch. Boiled our drinking water. Good pasture. Range horses numerous here. Passed rivers of Cliff Dwellers[16] on creek side. Seven rooms on side of bluff over jutting rock. Walls of stone with wood frame over 1 room. Rooms ascending stair fashion up cliff side. Went 1½ miles farther north in eve to look at country. Some oak trees, 1½ ft. in diameter, have leaves 3 inches long by ¾ in tapering ore at point than at base. All green. Creek bed here is dry and has many falls, some 8-10 feet bedrock in many places, finely carved by water and stones. Much igneous rock in country. Many small basins in creek bedrock holding water. Juniper trees abundant also mesquite and cactus. Scrub oak along creek bottoms, some Manzanita. Are in foothills of Sierra Ancha Mountains, at base of rolling grass covered hills. Shaffer better.

JAN. 8: After 8 a.m. breakfast we put up tent as weather indicated rain then took guns, pick shovel, water and lunch and went about 2 miles northwest to the second canon from here, which goes into the Salt River. Went down it 2 miles exploring for water and to camp on but found none but that in bed rock basins more difficult of access than this where we are. Beautiful scenery in cannons, high perpendicular, irregular, shaped rocky sides with cacti and shrub trees and plants in various nooks and corners. Bedrock of many different colors, various blend and worn in graceful curving forms. Many trails filled with water. All in all a beautiful site.

We crossed from next canon, west from here and ascended it for a mile or more then cut across to camp. Found falls in this canon 25-30 ft. high though there is no running water in it. Most of rock is igneous. Hills by canons are solid of sedimentary rock. Shot 4 quails. Ditched about tent and finished staking it, at supper sat about fire – retired. Cloudy almost all day with thunder in eve. Shaffer stiff in morning but limbered up during day. Am well.

JAN. 9: Some rain last night. Ate breakfast and at 9:30 a.m. started northwest to first large gulch up which we went for 2 miles and found nothing of value. Found some large pieces of pure iron, which had come from mountains higher up. Came out of gulch at 12 p.m., ate lunch and cut across for camp which we made at 1:30 p.m. Later I took gun to look for quail down Coon Creek but saw but one bunch in a 2 mile walk. I got but one of those. Weather very windy. Snow on mountains last night but melted before noon. Probably move camp tomorrow down Coon Creek, 3 or 4 miles.

Jan. 10: Early and most of night very windy, blowing tent hard but little wind entered and stayed warm. At 10:00 a.m. after a final decision not to go higher, we came down Coon Creek to Patterson's ranch and made camp at 12:10 p.m. We passed and inspected the ruins of some cliff dwellers, just below Coon Creek box. There were once 7 rooms along cliff side and some or all had been 2 stories high with another central room in front. The walls and partitions of rooms were of stone about 1 ft. thick, well cemented with mixture of clay and gravel. Possibly some powdered limestone, each room had a doorway opening into the next about 16 x 20 inches, two rooms the only ones standing complete had door ways opening toward the creek. Rooms also had port holes. Tops were covered by laying 6 inch poles length ways of rooms and covering with ½ inch wood slats. Rooms about 8 x 12 ft. and 6 ft. high. Upper rooms were probably not more than 4 -5 ft. high. So very interesting to explore. Shot 2 quail before dinner and afterwards took quail hunt over to near Cherry Creek thence up to camp. Got 4 quail. All well.

Jan. 11: In morning we packed burros and started up Coon Creek , which we followed to box then crossed and ascended on west side then came northwest up and down hills and across flats for 3 miles along old trail. Went ¼ mile north up gulch and camped. Dug well 2½ ft. deep in gulch and got 8 inches water. Fair feed for burros. Wood plentiful. Got but 1 quail today. Quail scarce up here. We are about 1,000 ft. higher than yesterday or not far from 9,500 ft. Crossed 2 running springs, then passed ruins. All are down except where Indians have rebuilt 2 rooms. Much granite here. Hills covered with burned stone and mostly barren of grass. Flats grow little else but species of cacti and brush. Cool here but have roaring fire from oak log.

Jan. 12: Slept cold last night. Water freezes. At 9 a.m. we took walk east of here, up and down, 2 canons sampling, some gravel. Immense mountains of iron in gulches but found nothing heavier.

Saw 20 ft. falls and many smaller ones in canon. In p.m. we went down gulch in which we are camped for a mile or more then west over hills and flats to camp. Limestone just below granite then burned blanketed hills and rocks. Are well, but short on meat. Plenty of beans and flour. In evening I took a short look for deer but saw none.

Jan. 13: Packed burrows in morning and started at 8:45 a.m. in southwest course over and down the divide of the Sierra Ancha Mountains. We kept on excellent trail down and around mountain side then down foot hills over much grassy country til within a mile of Salt River where hills were of alkali and of some light and barren soil. Looking like mud volcanoes. We came to river just west of Walnut Creek which was dry, came up river bottom, crossed the dry bed of Sally May Creek, at mouth of which river is steamboat rock. Hills being barren of grass and none in river bottom we kept on road for 3 or 4 miles farther were we found grass for burros. Here we camped. Saw no quail today.

Jan. 14: Being far from water, we continued on up road for 3 hours. Were overtaken by cowboy named Armour, who permitted us to turn burros in pasture on Tonto Creek. I got 4 quail this morning. Very warm for winter, just like our clear Spring days in Indiana. In p.m. being short of meat, I took gun and went up creek a mile or so and got 2 more quail. Went up and sat with cowboy in evening and read the newspaper. Small fire in fireplace warmed room up quickly. Cow puncher = a very obliging lad.

Jan. 15: Sunday We came on up Tonto this morning to Cline Post Office, ½ mile southwest of were we camped on creek. Only traveled about 6 miles today or from 9:45 a.m. till 12:30 p.m. Shaffer is waiting here for mail which comes at 7 p.m. I took burros ½ mile west to grassy hills. Shot duck on way this morning. Bottom lands along Tonto are 1¼ mile wide and some of it is irrigated. The flats just above are well covered with grass. Sent letter to home and to A. E. Slagel.

Passed some more Aztec ruins along road this morning. A stone wall about 200 ft. square had been built on flats, 40 ft. above the creek and inside was large pile of stone and dirt, evidently where stone houses had crumbled. Also passed some which had small lots divided off by stone fence or small wall. Some walls are 16 inches. Trees here by creek have been felled by beavers a few years ago. Heard several coyotes barking this morning, a very discordant noise. A combination of dog barking and child wailing. "All well" Clear and warm.

Jan. 16: We started up Tonto at 8:30 a.m. and turned to west – 5 or 6 miles from start, then kept on up large wash toward the low pass in mountains. West and north of 4 peaks 'till we came to old Fort Reno. Here we camped at 1 p.m. by spring below fort. After dinner took guns and pick and went up on the mountains, several hundred feet, looking for a strata or ledge on a hilltop by side of calion. Failed to find it in 3-hour search. Got to camp at 5:30 p.m., slightly cooler here than on Tonto. Granite of fine grain is most abundant rock. All well.

Jan. 17: We packed burros at 5:30 a.m. and passed the old fort house now occupied by cattle rancher. On up and over divide and down 6 miles, on the lower west side to Sunflower Valley. Camped here and after dinner took guns to look for deer. I saw none nor any tracks. Shafer saw one buck and four does but he failed to get any. I got 4 quail with one shot.

From Fort Reno to divide is 4 miles with 1,200 to 1,500 ft. ascent. Wind strong at backs during and for a time after ascent. Warm in valley but cool wind on mountaintops. Many springs on hillsides hereabouts and water in the big wash or creek in some places. Creeks are lined with Sycamore and Cotton Wood trees. Numerous Oak and some Willow with few Elm grows close to here. Granite and igneous rock prevail. All well but being short of flour, we will probably pull for a ranch 20 or more miles below here tomorrow and not remain to get deer.

Jan. 18: In a.m., we took guns and returned to place where Shaffer had wounded deer but could not find her. Returned to camp. During our absence, cattle had eaten up salt sack, dish rag towels, some bread and bacon! Ate dinner and started down Sunflower wash at 1:30 p.m. Our course was nearly southwest and much of the road is rocks and rough. We made Screw-tail hill at 4 p.m., about 6 miles from camp, on Sunflower, about 3 miles further, we came to a small level track of land that was called Round Valley. Three miles further we camped by creek-side at 6:15 p.m. Ate supper of bread, gravy and one quail. Warm camping place. A wagon road from Sunflower to Round Valley is very winding – around and up and down hills mostly granite with some Malpi. Descended probably 500 –1000 ft. from where we were on Sunflower. Clear. All well.

Jan. 19: Left O'Tera's place at 9:20 a.m. and came in west southwest for 3½ hours. Took short cut up creek to cut off 3 miles or road. Sheep man was along most of way, hunting stray horses. Ate dinner of bread and beans. Then came on to Verdi River which we waded at 4:30 p.m. Swift running water and larger than Salt River, which is above its mouth, east Verdi's. Continued down river for 1 mile to Fort McDowell[17] where we found feed for our burros. Here we camped. Obtained some flour of the owner of camping place and ate a hearty supper. Much deep sand on route today as most of road was in washes. Several farms about the old fort which is abandoned but many of buildings and old walls remain. A few settlers live at Ft. McDowell, also a number of Mexicans. Level country, mostly by the fort. Clear and pleasant.

Jan 20: Arose at 4:30 a.m. and started on road at 6:45. Made gradual ascent for several miles then a gradual descent, on level country. Crossed the Grand Canal, 12 miles from Fort McDowell at 10:45. Went 4 miles further and camped for dinner. Had Mexican company for a few miles, continued on course and Phoenix at 7:15 p.m., a walk of 32 or more miles. Passed Nine Mile Mountain. At 4 p.m. first large lateral canal at 5 p.m. Put burros in corral. Paid 25-cents for supper, 50-cents for haircut and shave. Then went to corral to sleep. Loaned Shaffer $5.00. Left foot a little sore, otherwise felt a little tired.

JAN. 21: Took clothes to Gregory House after 25-cent breakfast, where we engaged room. Changed clothes and went to Disciple Church where heard fair sermon by Pastor Ferguson. Paid 25-cents for oranges and 10-cents for candy and peanuts. Went up around square in evening. Heard band concert at 3:30 p.m. Large crowd in town, many transients. Failed to get any mail this morning. Went to M. E. Church in evening, a fair sermon on positive influence for good and right living.

JAN. 22: Arose late. 25-cents for breakfast. Saw mountain lion at corral. Loafed about town. Cleaned and put pistol away. Had supper and 5-cents for peanuts. Listened to M. E. and Salvation people talk then came to Gregory House and retired.

JAN. 23: No mail. Weather somewhat hazy. Loafed around town. Received $5.25 in payment of loan to Schaffer. He closed out his burros and $10 for 2. Then packed trunk in p.m. At 6:30 started on his trip back to Illinois. Paid 15-cents for dinner, 50-cents for room rent, 25-cents for supper and 25-cents for lodging. I packed trunk and stored at Gregory House, then got lodging at station lodging house.

JAN 24: In morning after breakfast, I paid 30-cents for washing clothes. Still getting no mail. I started to Glendale, 12 miles north on A. P. Arrived at 12. Saw Joe Ambrose but he knew of no opening for a job so after inquiring at a ranch close to there, I started to retire at 1 p.m. and arrived at Phoenix at 4:30. Went to the Star Lodging House and paid 25-cents for lodging and 15-cents for supper. Took a bath in evening. Think I'll wait here now till I receive mail then I will try for job again. Hazy with clouds.

Jan 25: Paid 15-cents for breakfast and sat about lodging house for a time. No mail. Loafed around town most of the day.

Jan. 26: Continued loafing about town. Warm and clear

Jan. 27: Paid 10-cents for magazine, 50-cents for 2 nights lodging. Met an English restaurateur of Redlands, California, who was looking for work, but is going back home disgusted. Plenty of ranch work, so he says in southern California. No mail.

Jan. 28: Loafed about Star Lodging House, most of the day. Band concert in evening.

Jan. 29: Cool in morning and clear. Saw bookkeeper at Goldberg's, who said the best way to get a job was to go to Canal Company corral and wait till foreman of ranchers come in. I went to post office and receiving no mail. I wrote a letter to myself to see if anyone else was here, having my name. Also, wrote home. Talked with Montana ranch-hand for 2 hours.

Jan. 30: Walked 4 miles north on Black Canon Road, east to Center Street Extension, then south to town. I inquired for work on route but found none. Saw ostriches on farm. Male birds have quite pretty plumage. Black bodies, light gray neck and head with gray bare legs. White feathers on wing tips. They stand about 2½ ft. from ground. Body about 1 ½ ft. X 3 ft. oval, neck 3 ft. long, head 5 inches broad, nearly flat, but rounded on top. Their bills are about 4 inches long and 1-2 inches at base wide. Large gray eyes, and have 1 main toe, 8 inches long with 1½ inch claw on end of it. Also, have one 3-inch side toe on outside of large toe and at its base. Not much ranch work here nor will there be till rain comes. After resting, started up the Maricopa railroad tracks to Tempe. Arrived there at 4 p.m. Told by carpenter of probable job at a canagrie root farm, 4 ½ miles southwest of town. Walked out there, failed to find the foreman, but idle men were there so I returned to town and arrived at 6:30 p. Very fine country around Tempe and has plenty of water. Paid 10-cents for oranges, 5-cents for coffee and 25-cents for lodging. Tempe = 120 population with excellent business buildings.

Jan. 31: Had breakfast then waited around an uncompleted building for ¾ hr. Then started up Mesa Railroad, inquired for work along route but found none. Had instructive talk with Canadian school teacher, who is renting 40 acres of land for $150. Fine country hereabouts. Mesa = Mormon settlement of 200 people. Stayed at Mesa until 12:30 p. Passed through Tempe and on to Phoenix at 6:15 p.m. Received letter from home. Chinese are raising a great din on account of their New Year commencing on January 30th. They celebrate for 2 or 3 days. Am well.

Feb. 1: Paid 15-cents for breakfast, then went 1½ miles north on Black Canon Road to a dairy farm but they are full handed. Went to creamery of south side but found no jobs. Loafed about town remainder of the day.

Feb. 2: 10-cents for shave and 25-cents for dinner. Went to Maricopa Creamery on south side and heard a farmer, 4 miles from town who might hire help. Came to post office and sent to State Bank of Lexington for $65 and wrote a letter home. Then went and saw the farmer, but he wanted no steady help so I returned up road west, ½ mile and hired to a Mr. Kilpatrick for 1 month for $25 including board and bed. Returned to town and loafed about for 2 hours and then went to Kilpatrick's.

Feb. 3: Dug pomegranates, split wood, set cotton wood posts, hauled manure. Hands very tired and stiff.

Feb. 4: Chored and went with Kilpatrick 3-4 miles NW to a dairyman's place. Sat about and read after return. Hands quite stiff yet.

Feb. 5–9: Sawed and split wood. Sawed wood with a Mr. McKinney. Hauled wood. Helped level ground and clean mud from pond in north fields. Very heavy work. Air full of dust. Received letter from home.

Feb. 10: Hauled stone from river, hauled wood and manure. Split wood. In evening, I rode uptown. Took washing to Chinese laundry. Shave and 10-cents for socks. Cold nights.

Feb. 11–16: Read chored on 11th. Split wood, hauled manure to orchard. Hauled sand on strawberry beds and ran spring-tooth harrow on ends of alfalfa fields. Also went with Kilpatrick 5 miles north and east to get scraper but failed to get it. Several orange and olive groves in that neighborhood. Irrigated until 2:30 in the morning on the 16th.

Feb 17–28: Early mornings. Split wood and harrowed fields and orchards. On the 25th went with Mr. Kilpatrick looking for a mule. Passed through nice country with goods roads, northwest of his place. One balky horse to work is hard on patience. Paid 15-cents for washing, 10-cents for a shave, 10-cents for a tablet and 5-cents for corn plaster.

March 1: Dug holes for trees in orchard, helped put in culvert across road.

March 2–3: Mulched lawn and made hog shelter. Dug holes for trees in lot west of the house. Made furrows along trees in orchard for water to run in. Cleaned ends of furrows and split wood. Working month out here.

March 4: Watched framers put in division box in ditch at the four corners. North of here at 10 a.m. I arranged to help irrigate for a Mr. King. I mended, scrubbed and wrote letters afterwards. Received 40-cents for irrigating.

March 5: Last night I irrigated from 8p until midnight = 50-cents. Split wood all day. Went to town in the evening for a shave =10-cents, washing = 30-cents.

March 6–8: Built fence in barn lot and cleaned it well. Pruned trees in orchard. Clear most of the week and pleasant. Received State of Lexington bank draft for $65.

March 9: Pruned trees in orchard and helped plant trees in afternoon. Captain Hill and wife of Phoenix were out to see me today. Are pleasant appearing people. They invited me to their place. They have 4 boys and 1 girl. Two boys are married. Are all in Phoenix. My father had written them to make my acquaintance.

March 10: Hoed ground here until 9:15 a.m., then pruned trees remainder of the day. Very warm. Went to town in eve and paid 75-cents for overalls and a shave 10-cents.

March 11: Walked to post office in morning. Received letter from home and from A. E.. Slagel, of Lexington, Illinois. Slagel claims to have received but one letter from me and that the last. He said he will pay my note as soon as possible so I'll not sue yet. 90F in the shade.

March 12–14: Pruned trees. Helped repair feed rack and fence in cow lot. Split wood for Mrs. Knox, who is staying here. Mesquite when dead is very brittle and splits easily. Some rain. Later warm and clear with passing cumulus clouds.

March 15: Split wood for Mrs. Knox and for Kilpatrick in afternoon. Work for Mrs. Knox = $1.00 plus board.

March 16: Went with Kilpatrick to get a disk cultivator. Remainder of morning we sawed wood. Split wood in p.m.

March 17–18: Split wood. Walked to town. Received $10 postal order from A. E. Slagel as a payment on note. Wrote letter home and to A. E. Slagel. Hair cut, shave and washing = 65-cents.

March 19–20: Cleaned ditches. Somewhat weak stomach. Got a large sliver in thumb, ½" deep, by throwing stick at a hog. Thumb very sore. Irrigated in eve till 2:15 a.m. Stormy.

March 21: Split wood in a.m. and went to town in p.m. Was offered a job by a dairy woman at $20 for 1 month, then $25, but refused it.

March 22–24: Repaired fences, then clean ditch. Hired to a neighbor on the west of Kilpatrick, but in evening he went back on me as his man who was to leave, remained.

March 25–28: Cleaned ditches from head-gate west. Irrigated for Kilpatrick till 4 a.m.

March 29: Arose at 9:30 a.m., ate breakfast and remained for dinner in order to settle with Kilpatrick for all work done while there. Receiving $46.75. Went to ranch, 2 miles north to look for place but did not get any work. Came to town and looked for work at the creamery manager's place but failed to find him. Pd. 25-cents for lodging at Star Lodging. Put $40 in Valley Bank. Paid 15-cents for supper.

March 30: Paid 15-cents for breakfast, a 10-cent shave and 15-cents dinner. Saw Kale of the Creamery and got a job on a ranch for a week or more at $1 per day plus board. Rode out 4 miles to ranch with Kale's boy. Paid $3.50 for 2 comforters and 2 yards of canvas. I slept over the chicken coop. Stars shining through the roof, cats prowling beneath me, roosters crowing most of the night, chicken lice holding high revels and driving the hens to distraction. I have the ideal sleeping apartment in this garden spot of Arizona. Hale's other man also occupies this princely suite.

March 31: Arose at 4:45 a.m. Milked 8 cows, ate breakfast, then built fence till 5 p.m. Then milked 10 cows and at 7:30 p.m. ate dinner.

April 1: Milked in morn and eve. Lounged around place remainder of time. Warm

Apr 2–3: Cleaned ditches

Apr 4: Arose with a headache, worked till noon, then went to bed and remained till next morning.

Apr 5: Milked Put in tarpon to fill pond. Cut wood. Rain most of the time

Apr 6–7: Cleaned cow stalls and horse shed, fixed fence and cut wood. Harrowed and cultivated fields.

Apr 8: Came to town in a.m. on a milk wagon. Shave, dinner and washing = 65 cents. Walked northeast of town to see if I could get a job of haying. But haying delayed about 2 weeks on account of rain. Found 5-cents on the road.

Apr 9–26: Cleaned ditches on 12th irrigated till midnight. Cut wood, fixed fences, hoofed cattle, took calves to Hurley's slaughter house. Racked and raked hay. Cocked and hauled hay. Weather very hot!

Apr 27: Hauled in hay. Told Kay's that I quit him in the morning on account of too long of hours.

Apr 28: Helped milk in rain then after breakfast, I packed bed and rode to town with milk hauler. Paid 25-cents for room at Star Lodging House then settled with Kay's. Receiving $23.75 in full. Paid 15-cents for dinner and supper. Put $20 in Valley Bank.

Apr 29: Arose at 7:40 a.m. Very pleasant morning. Walked to Capitol grounds building. It is about 200 X 100 ft. front with sides of stone also part of back, remainder is brick. It is a 3-story build, 1 mile west of town.

Apr 30: Saw Rinehart and remained about Goldberg's till noon then went out with Fred Tate to hay at $1.25 per day. Spread hay in p.m.

May 1: Spread and pitched hay

May 2: Pitched hay. Warmer. Extra water is coming in canals on account of rise in river.

May 3: Worked 3 hours in a.m., then stopped on account of hay being too wet to stack. Cocked hay in p.m.. Warmer than common.

May 4: Pitched hay 80F

May 5: Pitched hay in a.m. and cocked hay for Jon Tate about ½ p.m., when rain stopped us. Had a part in strawberry raid at Tate's.

May 6: Lounged about place in morn, observing the branding of some cattle. Came to town in p.m. Paid 20-cents for washing, 5-cents for peanuts and 5-cents for a paper.

May 7: Cleaned out water pond in morn. Put up hay at Tate's in p.m. 100F

May –12: Cleaned ditches, hauled hay, cultivated potatoes. Dug holes and set out trees along road and helped repair header machine. Cut grass for hay. Dug postholes, put up fence. Pitched hay off and on wagons. Helped repair "header" and cleaned out well. Sand storm. I lost a 5-cent bet.

May 13: Helped change cattle to different pastures. Rode to town in eve. Supper= 25-cents. Paid $2.50 for a pair of shoes. 95F

May 14–17: Cleaned ditch along RR tracks. Helped rig up header machine, mowed oats near Kilpatrick's. Oats are good for amount of water they have had. Loaded barley in header beds for the header machine. About ½ time spent in repairing header. Cutting for Gould.

May 18: Loaded header beds, 2 or 3 hours spent in repairing machine Hot!

May 19: Sister, Cora's birthday anniversary. 25 years old. Loaded header beds.

May 20: I was sick part of night but only a little weak in stomach today. Loafed about camp all day. Sand storm in evening. Came for NW, blew about 25 MPH.

May 2–26: Loaded grain at Gould's, Tait's, Edwards, Field's and Stanford's. Tait purchased me a pair of overalls for 70-cents payment. Worked oat fields at Tait's. Oats will make about 30 bushel per acre. Went to town in evening and paid
35-cents for shave and haircut. Lemonade = 5-cents and 60-cents for shirt.

May 27: Went to town in a.m. Returned to camp for dinner. Took bath in canal. Remained at camp and at Kilpatrick's rest of day. Very warm.

May 28: Finished at Tait's oats, then moved to a Mr. Flarity's on Black Canon Road where we put in remainder of day, on wheat. His grain is heaviest of any yet headed. Clear and 100F.

May 29: Commenced work at 10:30 a. on account of waiting repairs on canvas draper. Handle 2 ft. of straw in heavy grain because some is down. 105F

May 30–June 2: Finished heading at noon. Took wagon to Smith's shop then loafed remainder of the day. Went to town in evening and paid 10-cents for a shave and 5-cents for soda, H2O. Was treated to ice cream. Received $1 from Tait.

June 3–7: Drove header barge, heading oats and barley and wheat fields. This completes heading except for 2 days next week. Paid 10-cents for apricots. Settled with Tait, receiving $41.75. 110F

June 8: Came to town in morning and paid $10.10 for draft home. 60-cents for socks and shirt. 10-cents for washing, purchased magazine for 10-cents, 25-cents for dinner and $1.25 for a knife. Lemonade for 5-cents. Walked back to Tait's in even.

June 9–11: Cleaned out well, cleaning yard. Worked at hauling hay to stack for Aton. Received $1.50 for days worked.

June 12: Drove header wagon. Sonora wheat has fuzz which causes acute itching of the skin, especially, when broken out with heat. Came to town in eve and paid 10-cents for a shave, 30-cents for ice cream. Loaned H. Behern's 50-cents.

June 13: Drove header wagon, completed heading grain for this year. 100F

June 14: Loafed around ranch most of the morning. Helped take header beds back to Gould's. Came to town in afternoon. Re'vd $4.00 for work, in full of account with Tait.

June 15: Paid 15-cents for breakfast. Rode across river with Tait, to a threshing outfit where I looked for a job as hoe-down but being no vacancy. I returned with Tait and cocked hay in p.m.

June 16: Mowed and raked hay all day. 100F Loaned H. Behern's $1.00

June 17–20: Worked in hay fields. Through work here at Tait's on 20th. Rec'd $4.25 for work. Came to town, paid 25-cents for lodging, apricots = 5-cents, Dinner, shave and ice cream = 65-cents. Gave a $1.00 to a busted miner. Rested well.

June 21–23: Loafed around town and lodging house. Met a former co-laborer from Kayes, Charles Gruner. Attended rep. jol. meeting . Heard Governor Murphy, Ex-Governor McCord and others.

June 24–28: HOT! 112F Loafed Purchased map of Arizona = 25-cents.

June 29: Loafed around lodging house till 2 p.m. Paid for washing = 25-cents. Soda water 5-cents. $3.50 for having teeth filled. I had one tooth filled with cement and with amalgam. Paid 5-cents for peanuts.

June 30: Remained about the place. Drew $35.00 from bank and had left it there so as to enable me to send for it if needed. Some headache. Very hot.

July 1: Breakfast and coffee, 25-cents for Bromo quinine tablets. A fine lemonade for 5-cents. Attended band concert in evening.

July 2: Gave Gregory House proprietaries $1.00 to send my trunk to me, if I send for it. Paid $15.20 for excursion ticket to Flagstaff. Ticket good for 60 days with stop over privileges.

July 3: Took bedding and started on passenger train for Flagstaff. Stopped over at Prescott at 2 p. Walked around town which is well scattered on hills and hollows, all being on the mountain top surrounded by pine timber, 5,000 people in town. Some street work being done which I will try to get. Very pleasant. 80F

July 4: Breakfast, dinner, supper and lodging. Saw Simon's today. He is working on ranch 20 miles from here.

July 5: Saw the boss of street work and got a job of shoveling in a.m. and drove team to wheel scraper. Paid for board, lodging and fruit = $1.10 ½ day of shoveling = $1.00 with driving team = 85-cents. Very dusty.

July 6: Drove team on street today. Not feeling good. Headache and nose bleed.

July 7: Drove team on street. Feeling pretty weak. Paid for fruit, shave and one week's lodging = $2.20.

July 8: Rested Purchased fruit, Vaseline, and supper = 60-cents

July 9: Did not feel able to work so loafed about place today. Have had but little appetite for a week or more. The dust on road is very thick and injurious to be inhaled. Very warm 98F. Paid 15-cents for envelopes and 25-cents for whisky.

July 10: Walked around town in morning Received $5.25 for work on street. Very hot with numerous clouds.

July 11: Walked to town storage reservoir in morning. Reservoir = stone walls and bottom, 80x120 ft. and 15 ft. deep. Water is pumped into this from below town. No H2O in it now on account of shortage of supply. Paid 55-cents for board and fruit. I am still bilious and weak.

July 12 – 13: Loafed about town and lodging house. Feel about the same as I have for 2 weeks past. Weak and no appetite. 104F

July 14: Paid 15-cents for breakfast, 75-cents for lodging 'till Tuesday next, 15-cents for shave, 20-cents for washing. Very windy. Wind ceased late in eve and I retired at 10 p.m. At 10:45 the fire whistle blew.[18] Fire had started in the Grand View House and with the almost total absence of water, rendered effective work against fire impossible. The wind rose at 11 p.m. blowing a light gale to the NNE. The fire spread across the street and swept whiskey row, with the Burke House, then crossed street and burned both blocks, making in all 3 entire blocks and parts of 2 more blocks. Three or four dozen dwelling houses and 4/5 of the business houses were burned. Powder was freely used in blowing up building, but did little good but to scatter the burning wood. Loss several hundred, thousand dollars.

July 15: I retired at 4 a.m. and slept till 11:00 a.m. Walked around burned district which is swept clean of everything combustible. Swift NE wind blowing sending smoke and ashes in suffocating clouds.

July 16: Arose at 11 a.m. Feeling very bum. Paid 10-cents for crackers. Rested about lodging house. The west and north sides of Plaza are covered with tents and wooden shacks for temporary shelter. It is reported that many of those burned will rebuild much better than before.

July 17: Paid 30-cents for breakfast. Feeling better. At 2:45, I took the train for Flagstaff. Very pretty scenery along route. Uphill trip about all the way to Flagstaff. Arrived there at 9:25 p. Paid 25-cents for lodging. Cool and pleasant.

July 18: Arose at 7 a.m. Walked about Flagstaff. Passed the new Normal School building, a 3-story red stone about 140x160 ft. or more. Feeling some better. Paid 10-cents for doughnuts. Some rain later in the evening.

July 19: Arose at 5:30 a.m. Walked out to the mill and remained in vicinity for 2 hours then return to town arriving there between showers of rain. The sawmill and box factory keep the town up. 3 or 4 locomotives are kept at the mill yards to transfer logs and lumber. Very cool 70F Feel pretty good physically. Sent letter home.

July 20–22: Appetite returning. Saw Rinehart and several Phoenix people. He is working in mill yards at $2.00 per day. Walked to top of hill west of town where an extended view is had to town and some surrounding country. Received a much welcome letter from home.

July 23: Sent check to Valley Bank of Phoenix for $50. Paid 15-cents for stamped envelopes, 50-cents for board and 25-cents for lodging. Remained about town most of the day. Walked 1 mile southeast to stock yards and saw horses being separated and caught. Pleasant, some clouds. 70F.

July 24: At 7:30 a.m. I and a Tennessean started to walk 9 miles southeast to the ruins of cliff dwellers. Arrived there at 11:40 rested then went down canon where we could see the ruins of several dozen rooms built under cliffs. Rooms being from 6-10 ft. high and about 8 ft. wide and from 6-9 ft. deep. Stone walls are 14-16 inches thick, which formed the fronts and sides of rooms. All are now more or less demolished. From 1 to 6 to 8 rooms adjoin under one cliff roof. Canon = 250 ft. deep, 200 ft. across limestone formation. Rested some time and at 2 p.m. we started back taking moderate gait we arrive at 6:40 p. Refreshing breezes blowing. Not very tired.

July 25: Arose at 9:45 a.m. got Waterloo Press newspaper from post office. Lots of news from back home. Scattering clouds and warmer.

July 26: Received draft from Valley Bank of Phoenix for $49.90, which by the aid of Rinehart, I had cashed at saw mill office. Paid 60-cents for board, 25-cents for cigar treat, and 25-cents for lodging. Detachment of soldiers passed through here in evening on their way to Frisco from New York.

July 27: At 9:35 a.m. started for Williams where I arrived at 10:45 a.m. Walked about town, a few miles and saw a friend from Prescott. Left bed at a Chinese restaurant. Pd. 20-cents for lunch. Bought return ticket on Grand Canon Railroad for $5.40. Started at 12:45p and reached the end of the road, of 55 miles length at about 4 p. Paid $4.60 for return fare on stage of 11 miles and arrived at Canon at 5:50 p.m. Paid $6.00

for board and lodging for 2 days, walked along canon a short distance in eve. Canon here is 18 miles wide; from 5,000 to 6,500 feet deep or down to river. River averages 75 yards wide and 60 ft. deep, swift flowing. Top rock is light sandstone, several hundred feet thick under which is red rock becoming darker as decent is made. Warm and dusty during the day. Grand Canon is about same altitude as Williams.

July 28: Ate breakfast and at 8 a.m. took lunch and canteen and walked westerly 4 or 5 miles, along rim of Canon to where the Colorado River can be seen in 3 or 4 places. The sides of the canon are very precipitous. In some places, being a 2,000 ft. straight fall. It bears the appearance of having at sometime sunken, leaving large irregular masses of rock at various depths below the surrounding earth. For the most part these masses of rocks in the canon are covered with shrubbery and some have exclusive Mesa's on top. The river channel is several hundred yards wide on top and about 2,000 ft. deep. The sides are very dark red rock. Returned early. Very warm.

July 29: Went up canon, 4 miles in a.m. View is beautiful and very similar. Returned at noon and took the stage on return to Williams. Arrived in town at 6:30 p. Looked for good lodging house but failed to find any for 25-cents, so slept under lumber pile.

July 30: Arose at 3:15 a.m. Paid 5-cents for coffee. Walked around streets until 5:30 a.m., then paid 25-cents for breakfast. Williams is the toughest small place I have ever seen. Town =1,000 people with 15 saloons and innumerable brazen prostitutes. Many idle men here, the majority not wanting work. No enterprise here but the lumber mill and box factory. Employing 150 men more or less. Comparatively little ranching is done around here. Paid 25-cents for supper, 25-cents for storage of bed. To hard a place to remain in. Purchased a ticket for $1.50 to Flagstaff. Arrived at 8:40 p.m. Paid 25-cents for lodging and after bath, I retired.

July 31: Loafed about town all day. Purchased peaches = 10-cents. $16.05 for a ticket to Albuquerque. Started at 8:50 p.m. Sunshine in morning.

Aug. 1: Rode all last night until 8:05 a.m. Got about 4 hours sleep. Went uptown in Albuquerque. Walked around town all day. I was offered a job of haying, $1 per day. Also a job driving express wagon at $4 per week. Don't believe I'll tackle either. Sent check for $75, all I have remaining at Phoenix. Will probably stay here 3 or 4 days to await money then will go farther north or east. Sent letter home. Warm.

Aug. 2: Loafed about town the most of the day. Walked out across wagon road bridge in afternoon. Bridge spans Rio Grande River bed. It is about ½ mile long. Paid 50-cents for lodging

Aug. 3: Remained in town Purchased apples and newspaper. Clear

Aug. 4–5: Walked to stockyards in afternoon. Remained about town. 100F Very warm. Paid for board, peaches, shave and lodging = 90-cents. Failed to receive mail.

Aug. 6: Received post office money order for $74.73 from Valley Bank of Phoenix, Ariz, which is all I had left in it. I cashed it with but little trouble. Intend to go father east and north tomorrow.

Aug. 7: Went to depot and paid $15.10 for ticket to Pueblo. Train left the station at 8:30 a.m. Railroad follow the Rio Grande Valley nearly 1/3 way to Las Vegas then goes a steeper ascent along foot of mountain tops, in winding path until Vegas is reached. Stopped for dinner at Vegas at 1:30 p.m. Vegas = a summer resort town of 2,000 or more. Rain continued most way till after dark. Arrived at Raton the supper stop at 6:06 p.m. Raton = perhaps 1,500 people, built on a mountaintop with hill protection. Railroad shops are located here. Double header took us up steep grade through tunnel to top of pass after which, engine took the 8 coaches down grade remainder of way to La Junta, Colorado. 36 miles run out of Raton and tunnel = 1 ½ mile run long and run being very slow. Leaving tunnel, we came into Colo. from New Mexico. Arrived at La Junta at 10:45. Walked around town a short time. Had lunch, then retired to depot to await NW bound train.

Aug. 8: Left La Junta at 3:50 a.m. Passed the great melon growing country about Rocky Ford passed on north along valley of branch of Red River for 45 or 50 miles to Pueblo Valley raises besides melon, sugar beets, alfalfa and some corn. Arrived at Pueblo at 5:50 a.m. Paid 20-cents for room and 10-cents for lunch. Walked around town most of the day, a number of very large and fine buildings. Went to steel plant in afternoon. Several smelters are in operation here. Hazy and temperate.

Aug. 9: Viewed Ringling Brother's Show Parade and in evening attended circus. It was very good. They have a good collection of animals including over 20 elephants, 15 of the elephants are excellent performers. 50-cents for entrance fee to the circus. Well worth it. Lodging, shave, haircut lemonade lunch and supper = 85-cents.

Aug. 10: Saw an employment agency and paid $1 for a $30 hay ranch job located 47 miles east on Missouri Pacific Railroad. Will go out this evening. Left at 8 p.m. and arrived at Bradbury at 9 p.m. Retired in large farmhouse on ranch.

Aug. 11: Arose early, ate breakfast and then went with Supt. White to hay camp, where I will get work. Drank some water and threw up my socks and took a number of short journeys to adjoining weeds in afternoon, but all right this evening. 95F

Aug. 12: Loafed about camp today. Ranch = 7,500 acres in pastures, 1,100 acres of alfalfa, 600 in orchards and several hundred in cultivated crops, mostly corn. Corn will make according to present prospect 50 bushels per acre. Water for irrigation obtained from Arkansas River a short distance east of Pueblo. Sent letter home.

Aug. 13: Commenced work on ranch this morning. Am working now as cook's helper or flunky. Work very easy but long hours. Am well.

Aug. 14–18: Flunkyed. Worked at trade today, helping cook, doing errands with team of horses. Hauled in a load of hay. Paid 15-cents for melons. Mosquitoes and flies are very numerous here, owing to the camp's 40 acres weed grown lake. Many water fowls around and upon the lake.

Aug. 19–20: Worked 2 full days 90F Hazy and warm.

Aug. 21: Today = 24th anniversary of my birthday. Worked as a flunky. Sand storm from north in eve.

Aug. 22–23: Worked at hauling hay and grinding sickles.

Aug. 24: Cook quit the camp tonight. Another man here will take his place. Worked all day. Cloudy and cool tonight. Am well.

Aug. 25: Worked all day. Have a new cook, named Shorty. Pretty fair cook. This hay job will probably close in a week or less as water is too scarce to raise a third crop of hay, only a small area.

Aug. 26: Worked most of the day, helping cook, attending horses, etc. Very warm mostly clear. Ate an abundance of small musk-melon in p.m.

Aug. 27: Helped haul and stack hay at main camp all day. Very pleasant man at the main camp. Cantaloupes in plenty. Shorty the cook returned from Pueblo in eve and being "full" kept us all awake till after midnight. Heard from Illinois.

Aug. 28: Worked all day as yesterday. Finished the wild hay crop. Returned to south camp in evening. Cloudy, windy and warm.

Aug. 29–31: Worked on buck rake, 3 days. Very rough ride. Mostly clear 90F

Sept. 1: Finished here last night. Received time check for $17.75. Walked to Manzanola in morning. 6 miles southwest of ranch. Got check cashed. Paid 10-cents for getting check cashed. Crossed the Arkansas River at edge of Manzanola. But little water in it, its water being used for irrigation. There is one artesian well in town; water from it is slightly mineral and about 60F. Got a job with H. Beatty hay outfit. Will help put up hay. Will get $1 per day and board. Weather-cool in a.m. and 85F in p.m. Place near town. Worked ¼ day and received 25-cents. Paid 11-cents for stamped envelope.

Sept. 2: Very windy in morn. Good chuck at camp. Two men went fishing in river by the camp and caught 15 – 4 pound catfish with pitchforks.

Sept. 3 -5: Pitched hay in fields every day.

Sept. 6: Went to Rocky Ford in a.m. Paid 35-cents for return ticket. Paid 50-cents for admission to fair grounds. Today is melon day. A pile of water-melons 80 ft. long and 15 ft. wide at bottom and 8 ft. wide on the top and 8 ft. high were given away during the day. Water-melons averaged 20 inches long and 8 to 10 inches in dia. Cantaloupes in plenty were also distributed.

8,000 to 10,000 people in attendance at Fair. Best time in trotting and pacing race. There was also 2 running races, a 5-mile cowboy race and bronco breaking contest. Rocky Ford is a town of 1,500 people. Melons are the principle plants grown. A little corn and oats with considerable alfalfa and fruit bearing trees are grown.

SEPT. 7–20: Pitched hay every day Received a letter from home on the 14th. One man sick with mountain fever.

SEPT. 21: I packed bed, received check of $15.25 and prepared to leave for Illinois. Paid 25-cents for shoes, $1.75 for a hat, 35-cents for a necktie, 10-cents for a shave and $31.50 for round trip ticket to Chicago, Illinois. Started at 9:30 a.m. Purchased paper, 5-cents fruit= 10-cents. Passed La Janta, Las Anninas, Garden City, Kingsley, Great Bend, Hutchinson and smaller towns. Country along the railroad is but in few places good. Most of Kansas has had extra good returns this year. Western Kansas is rolling evenly and large scale. Much grazing land. Forage plants with wheat = primary crops.

SEPT. 22: Passed through Eurporia, Topeka, to Kansas City at 7:10 a.m. Left KC at 8 a.m. and passed through northwest MO. Southeast Iowa and northwest Illinois and arrived in Chicago at 9 p.m. Paid 40-cents for supper and lodging. Corn along railroad section in MO. Not very good. Best corn on route to Ancona, Ill.

SEPT. 23: Clear and pleasant. 5-cents for street car fare. Spent day at Lincoln Park. A good copulation of annuals and plants. Paid 25-cents to ride on Ferris Wheel.[19] 265 ft. high gives a good view of city. Candy = 5-cents and 25-cents for Chicago map.

Sept. 24: Paid 10-cents for breakfast. Shave and a haircut – 20-cents. Purchased new clothes for $3.54. Purchased theater ticket for 30-cents. After took a stroll on lake front in eve.

Sept. 25: Stored parcels = 30-cents. $3.31 fare to Lexington. 25-cents for Art Museum entrance fee. Excellent cast of sculptures and fine paintings, ancient vases beads, mummies etc. 5-cents for fruit. Left Chicago. Corn along route good. Arrived in Lexington at 6:40 p.m. Stopped at Clawson's[20] and saw a few acquaintances.

Sept. 26: Will make Clawson's my stopping place until I secure work. Walked out north 4 or 5 miles. Good corn = well eared, stands well. Sent $10.00 for boxing and shipping my trunk to me from Phoenix, AZ.

Sept 27: Rain all day. 1 ½ inches mud on roads. Put $25 in State Bank of Lexington.

Sept. 28: Walked out west in a.m. Corn nearly as good but is tangled and down more than north of town. Remained at McColm's day and night.

Sept. 29: Came to town. Attended Abbot's sale. Went a few miles northwest in afternoon. Corn good but weedy. Attended a Democrat Rally in evening. Plenty of noise with fair speaking and good singing. Loaned a fellow boarder $2.00.

Sept. 30: Loafed around town Walked east and north. Clear and pleasant all day.

Oct. 1: Hired to shuck corn for P. Peck, receiving 2 ½- cents per bushel, board and washing and mitten made. Am to commence Monday next. Returned to Lexington in p.m. Got a job scooping corn for a day or so.

Oct. 2: Arose at 4:10, walked 3 miles in country and scooped corn for Josiah Biggs. Mr. Biggs is very low in health being unconscious.

Oct. 3: Remained at Biggs overnight and scooped corn until noon, then came to town. Went to Ino McColm, 8 miles in country southeast of town. Corn more or less down between here and Selma but will average a good crop. Paid 50-cents for a shirt. 90F

Oct. 4: Paid for board up to date, $3.50 and 40-cents for canton flannel. Will work for Hotsenpiller's tomorrow.

Oct. 5–6: Worked on corn crib. Worked for Hotsenpiller, received $2.25 for work for 2 days. Went to town in eve. Shave and washing = 18-cents. Attended Republican Rally.

Oct. 7: Remained in Lexington last night. Walked 4 miles north to P. Peck's place where I will husk corn. Warm and clear.

Oct. 8–13: Shucked corn all week. Paid 35-cents for husking-hook. No bad weather all week. Corn is good, 60 bushels per acre.

Oct. 14: Walked to Shaffer's in p.m. Saw N. B. Schaffer who just returned from Arizona with cattle-feeders. He shipped 30 head in one car with no loss. Was 8 days on road and drove 10 days to station. Three or four year old cattle costing him $27 per head here, not counting his own expenses.

Oct. 15–20: Shucked corn all week. Many days too warm for comfort. Went to Chenoa in eve of the 20th to Democrat Rally. Large crowd at rally, but I did not hear speakers. 25-cents for painkiller.

Oct. 21: Walked to Lexington in morning but was to late for mail. Got J. Peck's to bring it out to me tomorrow. Returned and rested. Cloudy and cool.

Oct. 22 – 25: Shucked corn all but 3 hours when rained out. 60 – 65 bu. per acre. Heard from home and Charles, who is now in Peoria, Illinois.

Oct. 26: Charles came here last night at 10 p.m. He and I went to Lexington and Chenoa, when he left for Peoria at 2:11p.m. Returned and husked corn in evening. Brother in better physical condition than when in Chicago.

Oct. 27–28: Shucked corn. Very warm

Oct. 29–Nov. 3: Cooler and more pleasant for working. Still shucking corn.

Nov. 4: Remained at Peck's all day.

Nov. 5: Finished shucking corn at Peck's. Filled south crib.

Nov. 6: Went to Lexington in morning. Paid 5-cents for tablet, 3-cents for tallow. Went to Chenoa in afternoon and tried to vote but my right to vote being challenged. So not being able to secure anyone to sign an affidavit with me, as to my period of residence, I was unable to cast a vote. I received pay for shucking 1,652 bushels corn and scooping off 7 loads of corn for Peck = $42.17. Paid 5-cents for smoke treat and 25-cents for mittens. Returned to Peck's in evening.

Nov. 7: I got a job of shucking corn at Charles Murdy's. Will receive 2 ½ - cents per bu. for shucking. Haul to Ballard until weather breaks up roads.

I give for a bushel the same number of pounds as taken for a bu. at the elevator. Took my clothes from Peck's and shucked a load of corn in p.m.

Nov. 8–10: Shucked corn. On 10th had to quit due to snow.

Nov. 11: Got mail in Lexington. Snowed last night. Purchased paper and breakfast.

Nov. 12–14: Shucked corn. Cold Ground frozen 3 inches deep in field. Shucked 79,78, and 86 bushels respectively in the three days.

Nov. 15: Snow last night. 1 ½" deep. Went to Chenoa in p.m. Mittens = 25-cents

Nov. 16: Shucked 57 bu. of corn from 11 rows. Sleet and rain at 2 p. which stopped work of husking. Storming in evening, sleet and rain freezing on all exposed surfaces.

Nov. 17: Corn to icy to husk in morning and ground to muddy in evening. Went to Chenoa. Many telegraph poles down from the weight of sleet on wires held by old poles.

Nov. 18–25: Rain and warmer. Shucked 32 bu. More rain. On 25th walked to Lexington. Snow 1" on ground. Washing = 8-cents

Nov. 26: There is no more corn to shuck for Murdy. Went to Chenoa and recv'd $22.49 for husking corn. Went out with Hen Bruffy for a few days to work. Put $15 in South Bank of Chenoa.

Nov. 27–29: Shucked corn for Bruffy at $1.50 per day.

Nov. 30: Husked 4 rows of corn in a.m. then went home as that ended his corn shucking. Received $5 for work. In evening I saw some farmer's who were not through but they wanted no more help. A little warmer today.

Dec. 1: Came to Lexington. Purchased clothes for $1.05, shave 10-cents, 35-cents for lunch and 70-cents for lodging and breakfast in the morning. I walked 5 miles northwest of Lexington looking for corn husking but found none. I got a job for next week at B. B. Stevens at 2½ -cents per bushel plus board.

Freezing at night and thawing in mid-day. Sent notice of A. E. Slagel and C. E. Slagel to pay note when due in one month.

Dec. 2: Paid 5-cents for paper. Sent letter home. Took old clothes and went north of town. Took dinner with Willis Shaffer and in evening went to the B. B. Steven's farms. Cold northwest wind.

Dec. 3–6: Shucked corn all days. Quite warm for hard work. Corn makes from 50-60 bushel per acre.

Dec. 7: Light rain in morning. Shucked 24 bu. of corn in afternoon.

Dec. 8–9: Shucked corn both days.

Dec. 10: Came to Lexington in morning. Paid 16-cents for washing, bought glycerin and apples for 20-cents. Then went back to Steven's place.

Dec. 11–15: Hauled corn for Steven's Very cold driving team.

Dec. 16: Measured corn and I shucked for Steven's which was 485 bu. Received a check for $12.12 for shucking and $3.75 for hauling corn. Came to town and put up at Clawson's.

Dec. 17: I put the Slagel notes in the hands of A. B. Davidson for collection when due. Charging 10% for collection. Paid $1 for information about trunk, $3.50 for 1 week's board from yesterday morning at Clawson's. Cashed check and put $20 in Bank of Lexington.

Dec. 18: Walked to Chenoa. Drew $65 from bank then walked and rode back to Lex. where I put $55 in S. B. Bank of Lexington. Apples = 10-cents

Dec. 19–21: Walked to Ino McColm's. Nice visit. Paid $1.25 for watch cleaning.

Dec. 22: Remained in Lexington till 10:15 then paid $3.31 and went to Chicago. Went to Union depot at 2 p. down to State Street. Went to A. M. Ward and Company store and paid $10 for suit of clothes, $8.75 for overcoat and $15.96 for underclothes, necktie, shirt collars, socks, handkerchiefs, muffler, valise gloves shoes and hat, in all $34.71. Took purchases to Queen Hotel and paid 75-cents for room. Retired with a severe headache.

Dec. 23: Feeling better this morning. Purchased $4.65 for ticket to Waterloo, Indiana. Went over to L.S. & M.S. depot and at 10:30 a.m. and started for home where I arrived at 3:25 p.m. Went home and remained there the rest of day. So good to see family.

Dec. 24 -26: Remained at home most of the time. Paid 25-cents for a shave on Christmas. Very pleasant days and weather.

Dec. 27: Remained at home with folks.

Dec. 28: Came to Wolf Lake. Paid $3.40 railroad fare for Ma and I. Relatives in usual health and spirits. Grandmas is frightfully bloated but active and cheerful.

Dec. 29–30: Visited among relatives. I have lost $10 somewhere.

Dec. 31: Went to Bear Lake in a.m. The county has ditched the low country hereabouts and reduced the area of various lakes about ½. Ate dinner with Uncle Thumma and family. Ate supper at Mel Richmond's.

Morning after Prescott, AZ. fire. On July 14, 1900, late evening the fire began, burning blocks of Prescott's business district.

Duplication of WBH's March 30th journal entry.
"Garden spot in Arizona"

Williams, Az. Mill and Box Factory advertised "as the best equipped mill in the southwest". On July 19th, Bert observes that this business was the main source of employment. *Postcard among SED possessions.*

Union Depot Pueblo, Co. 1900 trip west.
Postcard among WBH's possessions.

Steel Plant, Pueblo, Co. *Postcard among WBH's possessions.*

George Washington Gale Ferris, an engineer is known for creating the original Ferris wheel for the 1893 Chicago World's Columbian Exposition. Each car was 24 ft. wide and 10 ft. high; accommodating 60 riders.

1901

January 22, 1901 Britain's Queen Victoria dies at age 82. Theodore, "Teddy" Roosevelt on September 14, 1901 assumes the Presidency, due to the assassination of William McKinley. King Camp Gillette, a former bottle-cap salesman, began selling safety razor blades.

January 1, 1901: Remained at Grandma's. Paid 40-cents to attend Glee Club concert, which Aunt Ella and I attended in eve. Entertainment was fair for amateur girl singers.

Jan. 2: Came to Kimmel in a.m. and train being late we waited 'till 2:10 p.m. before leaving Kimmel. Went up to McCrory's for short time. Saw Lester Till in town where he has grocery. Came to Waterloo at 5:48 leaving Ma in Auburn. Gave Ma $2.

Jan .3: Remained at home. Gave Cora 2-cents. Cold and clear.

Jan. 4: Received draft for $50 from S.B. of Lexington, Ill. Much warmer.

Jan. 5: Paid 10-cents for shave. Went to Auburn Junction at 10:40 a.m., where I paid 10-cents for pie and $3.67 for fare to La Fayette for which place I started at 11:50 a.m. Arrived at LaFayette at 3:15 p.m. I paid 5-cents for apples, $1.75 for board and lodging till Monday morning. From 20 to 34 F.

Walked around the town in p.m. to the Purdue University[21] campus and back . Paid 18-cents railroad fare to Auburn Junction.

Jan. 6: Attended preaching at Trinity M.E. Church in a.m. Gave 5-cents to collection. Also, attended church in eve. Misting.

Jan. 7: Paid 5-cents for car fare. Went to U. S. Ex. Station and arranged for attendance at the University. Paid $10 for entrance fee. Aided by a Y.M.C.A. member, I secured a room and board at 21 University on the opposite side of the grounds. Will pay $3.00 per month for room and $2.75 per week for board. Sent for trunk. Paid 25-cents for stationery, supplies and 15-cents for postage supply. Paid 10-cents for shave and 5-cents for scratch book.

Jan. 8: Arose at 7a.m. Ate breakfast and got a start in work in Horticulture, Live stock husbandry, soils, crops, etc. In p.m. paid a visit to the laboratory in U. S. Exp. Sta. Paid 25-cents for note books, 5-cents for street car fare, 25-cents for initiation fee of the Agricultural Society, which I attended in eve.

Jan. 9: Attended iron work instruction at the east end of mechanical building in a.m. Then remained in room most of time 'till 4:30, when I attended lecture on plants by S.M. Coulter. Mist most of morning until 4 p.m. Ground was frozen in morn, but soon thawed.

Jan. 10: Attended classes in Horticulture, Live Stock, Husbandry and soil and crops. Paid 65-cents for text book. 10-cents for shave. Attended Lab. Work in soils and lecture at 4:30 p.m. Slightly cooler and cloudy all day.

JAN. 11: Attended classes in Horticulture, Vet. Hygiene, Soils and Crops in morning. Stock judging and lecture on poisonous plants in p.m. Paid $1.15 for tickets to lecture course, $3.50 for room rent for 1 month. Cooler with ½ inch of snow about 30F.

JAN. 12: Attended lecture on Plant structure by Coulter. Also saw two bitches spayed at infirmary. Went up town and paid 50-cents for a jacket, 15-cents for collar, 20-cents for collar buttons and 10-cents for rule, 25-cents for shoe polish and 5-cents for stamps. Remained in room most of the afternoon. Paid $2.20 for board up to and including this evening.

JAN. 13: Attended west side M.E. Church in a.m. and eve. Jaunita Glee Club gave sacred concert in evening. Very good singers. Gave 5-cents to church.

JAN. 14: Attended work shop in iron in a.m. Also a lecture on poultry at 11:30 a.m. Attended stock judging in afternoon. Paid 32-cents for fruit, 25-cents for quinine tablets. Received delayed Christmas present from Cora. A neck tie and pretty scarf-pin.
Felt very sick today. Severe headache and that "tired feeling" in limbs. Took sweat bath in evening.

JAN. 15: Feeling better this morning. Attended regular classes. Paid 10-cents for shave. Spring-time today.

JAN. 16: Quite well today, save for slight cold. Attended all my classes. Thawed some during noon hours. Clear.

JAN. 17: Attended classes. Cold south west wind with a slight sprinkle of snow.

Jan. 18: Paid 10-cents shave. Attended classes. Went to LaFayette in p.m. to judge Percheron stallions at LaFayette Importing Co. Stables.

Jan. 19: Saw a bitch spayed and colt treated for ring-bone, in a.m. In afternoon went to stock farm and read. Paid 5-cents for apples and 26-cents for stamped envelopes.

Jan. 20: Remained in room all day, except for meals. Went to church in evening. Warm partly clear.

Jan. 21: Attended classes. Paid 10-cents for shave and $2.75 for last week's board.

Jan. 22: Attended classes. Paid 15-cents for paper for Soil Lab. notes. Warm Attended meeting of Purdue Agriculture Agency Sec'y in evening.

Jan. 23: Followed usual work. Warmer. Clear, light freeze nights, thawing day time. Attended orchestra at Grand Opera House, uptown in evening.

Jan. 24: Attended classes today. Paid 18-cents for washing. Cloudy and could with snow flurries.

Jan. 25: Followed school work.

Jan. 26: Attended Vet lecture in morning. Went to freight offices, but trunk is not here. Read "Press". Paid $2.75 for this week's board. 2 ½ inches of snow fell today. About 30F.

Jan. 27: Read during the day. Attended Westside M.E. Church in evening. Text-"None other name given under heaven or among men whereby we must be saved, (if at all)." Gave 5-cents to collection.

Jan. 28: Attended regular classes. Clear 20-35F

Jan. 29: Ditto

Jan. 30: Usual work. Paid for scratch books and 5-cents for lemons.

Jan. 31: Same routine. Purchased notebook for 5-cents.

Feb. 1: Attended 2 classes and lecture in a.m. Farmers Institute in afternoon. Cool, stiff southwest wind.

Feb. 2: Attended Vet lecture and Farmers Institute in a.m. Went to town at noon. Paid $1.13 for freight on trunk and 30-cents for storage. Attended Farmer's Ins. in p.m. Snowed all p.m. 3½ inches deep. Have hard headache from cold.

Feb. 3: Feeling better. Sprinkle in a.m. Freeze in evening.

Feb. 4: Routine. Colder very icy walking. Snow flurries.

Feb. 5: Routine. Paid 5-cents for apples and 31-cents for washing. Cold and ice in morning, then clear and some thawing.

Feb. 6: Paid $1.30 for book on "Feed and Feeding" by Prof Henry, also 5-cents for apples. Attended regular classes.

Feb. 7: Purchased book on "Study of Breeds" for $1.05. Mostly cold and clear.

Feb. 8: Routine. 1 inch of snow, though rain and sleet in p.m.

Feb. 9: Attended lecture on tuberculosis in morning. Went to barn in p.m., where they were conducting tuberculin test. First they inject tuberculin, then take temperature, every 2 hours in day time for 2 days. If temperature rises it shows they have tuberculosis. Paid $2.75 for board in evening.

Feb. 10: Attended Trinity M.E. in morning and evening. Lincoln memorial service in evening. Gave 10-cents for collection.

Feb .11: Attended usual classes. 1 inch of snow.

Feb. 12: Routine. Cold and clear.

Feb. 13: Forge work and lecture in a.m. Went to Fred Dorver's in northeast LaFayette in p.m. to his greenhouses of carnations. Very fine. Large number and varieties. Greatest carnation grower in the United States. Paid 5-cents for car fare.

Feb. 14: Usual work. Melting and clear.

Feb. 15: Ditto yesterday. Concert in evening. Freeze tonight. Clear

Feb. 16: Attended Vet lecture and clinic in morning. Cashed draft. Paid 31-cents for washing and $2.75 for board.

Feb. 17: Attended Trinity M.E. Church in morning and Westside M.E. Church in evening. Gave 5-cents for collection. Warm and very sloppy. Clear

Feb. 18: Usual classes in morning. Paid 20-cents for a ride to Cason's farm, 3 miles northwest of college, where we judged cattle of short horn breed.

Feb. 19: Routine. Paid $1.05 for Professor Craig's book on stock judging. Cold, cloudy with cutting northwest wind. Some snow spitting.

Feb. 20: Ordinary classes. Cold and clear.

Feb. 21: Classes as usual with Friday lecture on horses. Mostly clear. Very cold in morning with light wind. Sprinkle of snow in evening. Paid 15-cents for fruit and candy.

Feb. 22: Holiday. Nursed headache all day. Paid 25-cents for Purdue Band Concert held at Baptist Chapel which I attended in evening. Very good.

Feb. 23: Attended Vet. lecture and clinic. Then walked around town until noon. Paid 25- cents for quinine tablets, $2.75 for board and 20-cents for washing. Saw the City Reservoir at Columbia Park. It is about 50 ft. high x 300 x 200 feet. Is 80 feet deep from top or surface. Throws water over all the highest buildings of town. Water is pumped from wells in Wabash River. The reservoir is cemented. Interesting to observe.

Feb. 24: Remained in room all day. Attended church in evening. Heard Gilbert, a young Yale engaged in the Volunteer movement for the evangelization of the world in this generation. A very good and earnest speaker. Gave 5-cents for church.

Feb. 25: Attended regular classes. Snowing, ¾ inch in morning, but warmer and melting by p.m.

Feb. 26: Usual work. Clear and cool.

Feb. 27: Attended lecture by L. Taft in evening. Excellent.
Feb 28 Routine. Mostly clear.

March 1: Usual classes in a.m. Went 2 miles east of here to Crouch and Son's[22] importing stables and judged some German Coach horses. Warmer and cloudy.

March 2: Attended Vet Lecture and farmers institute in a.m. and p.m. Paid $2.75 for board. Warm and sloppy.

March 3: Attended Trinity M.E. in morning and evening. Evening sermon on Judas Iscariot. Warm and windy.

March 4: Classes as usual except special lecture in afternoon. Paid 8-cents for ribbons.

March 5: Attended usual classes in morning. Paid $1.65 for fare to Fort Wayne, Indiana. Started at 3 p.m. and arrived in Fort Wayne at 6:45, when we went to Wayne Hotel, paying 50-cents for room and 25-cents for supper. Very cold and blustery with a little snow.

March 6: Ate 15-cent breakfast at 6 a.m. At 8 a.m. started in hacks for Mandamin Dairy Farm, the creamery of which we visited last night. The creamery was a unique place being as much advanced in lines of sanitary milk and cream as any in country.

Feed silage at farm. The farm which we visited was 8 miles southwest of town. They have an excellent and conveniently arranged barn. Keeping mostly Jersey cows. All animals were in fine order. Some Galoways and Holsteins. They milk about 135 cows or more. Keep only Jersey bulls. From here went to J.C. Peter's short horn farm. He also feeds silage. Has a very complete equipment. After lunch at Peter's we went to Bass Brookside Farm of Galloway cattle and Clydesdale horses. From there we went to the Home of Feeble Minded, an institution of 700 inmates. Ate supper there and then listened to entertainment by the most intelligent of the inmates. Many of them are as intelligent looking as any wholly sound minded person.

At 8:25 we took the Wabash R.R. for Wabash and put up there at 9:30 at Tremont House.

MARCH 7: Visited Wolf and Talbert's Belgian stable in a.m., then went west to Lagro, 6 miles out on railroad from where we went to White River Cattle Company, 5 miles out of Lagro. Saw only one excellent Hereford cow. Returned to Wabash in carriages and took Big Four at 11:30 for Indianapolis. We arrived at 3 p.m. Put up at Oneida Hotel. Then took street car for Greenwood to Polk's Dairy Farm, 10 miles out. The dairy farm consists of 160 cows, giving milk. They are fed wholly on ensilage, the residue from canning factory, i.e. pea vines and corn shucks. He has the largest silo in the world. Holds 1800 tons. He has also a large outdoor silo. Returned to city at 6:00 p.m. Ate supper and attended Park Theater to a comedy farce. $1.00 lodging and breakfast, 10-cents for lunch, $1.90 fare to Indianapolis, and 30-cents for return trip from Greenwood, 25-cents for supper, 45-cents for hair cut and shave and 30-cents for the show.

MARCH 8: Went to stock yards in morning and saw yards and stock etc. Then went to Kingan and Company packing house, a very large concern. After dinner went through State House and to Soldiers and Sailor's monument. Then back to hotel after which we went on Big Four to Greensburg about 40 miles southeast of Indianapolis. Put up at DeArmond House. Walked around town in evening. Went to Passion play. Play better than fair. Went through Elk's Hall in eve. Paid 25-cents breakfast, 10-cents street car fare, 15-cents for a collar, 50-cents room rent, 15-cents for dinner, 5-cents for apples: 70-cents fare to Greensburg and 30-cents for show.

MARCH 9: At 7 a.m. started in carriages for Robbin's Shorthorn Farm about 6 miles away from Greensburg. Visited farms of Ino and Will

Robbins. They have about 150 head in all, containing some very famous ones. Ate dinner at Granddad Robbins after which we visited the Jersey dairy of another Robbin's who has about 100 Jersey's. He too has some celebrated animals. All have many imported animals. Ate supper as guest of Robbins, at DeArmond Hotel. At 6:05 left for Indianapolis where we arrived at 7:45. Went to English Theater, where "My Lady Davity" was playing. Good acting but poor play. At 1 a.m. we started for LaFayette. Paid 10-cents for shine, 50-cents for play and $1.75 fare to LaFayette.

March 10: Arrived at LaFayette in rain at 3:45 a.m. Retired at 4:15 and slept till noon. Remained in room until supper time. Attended church in the evening.

March 11: Attended classes. Paid 11-cents for envelopes and 25-cents for washing

March 12: Routine. Misting and spitting snow part of the day.

March 13: Classes as common. Misting most of day. Attended concert in evening which was poor.

March 14: Ditto yesterday.

March 15: Attended usual classes. In afternoon saw an exhibition working of a sheep shearing machine, which runs on same plan as horse clippers. Does very nice work and less cutting skin than with shears. Turning from warm to freezing.

March 16: Fine warm and clear day. Walked to gravel pit, U.S. farm and over to town in a.m. Paid 3-cents for paper. Remained in room in p.m. Paid $3.80 for board to date.

March 17: Attended Trinity M.E. in morning and evening. Good sermons. Walked out to Soldiers Home, 4 miles north of town. This is a state institution, the counties having a small building each, with larger buildings for commissary, old men's home. Old people's home, a chapel and assembly room, etc. It is situated among elegant scenery for this State. It passes the old Tecumaseh trail and 5 or 6 miles north is the old battleground of Tippecanoe. Paid 10-cents for street car fare and 5-cents for cakes. Gave 5-cents to church collection.

March 18: Usual work in class. Heard Mrs. Ballington Booth in eve speak on Lights and Shadows of Prison Life – a very entertaining and forceful talker. Warm and windy.

March 19: Class work as commonly. Windy, cloudy and intermittent sprinkling. Attended meeting in eve after which faculty tendered us a reception.

March 20: Usual work in class. Paid 20-cents for two cold chisels which I had made. Radical change to cold with slight snow flurries and stiff southwest wind.

March 21: Attended usual classes. Paid $5.15 for room rent to Friday eve and paid 27-cents for washing and 25-cents for basketball game. Game in evening between Purdue and Butler, with the former winning 42-12. End of time here for now. Will look forward to returning next year. Time well spent.

March 22: Attended classes in morning. Paid $2.20 for board, 5-cents for street carfare, 5-cents for lead pencil, $3.18 for fare to Chenoa, Ill. Left at 1:45 and arrived at Sheldon at 3 p.m. Left there at 4:25 and arrived in Chenoa at 6 p.m. Purchased gum 2-cents, 5-cents for postal cards and 24-cents for fare to Lexington. Put up at Clawson's.

March 23: Loafed around town. Paid 25-cents for trunk delivery. Rain from 4 p.m. on till 10 or later.

March 24: Sunday Cloudy and rain in p.m. Remained indoors most of day.

March 25: Starting day with rain and I then went north of town to Shaffer's and farther. Returned to town in evening.

March 26: Remained at boarding place. Some mist and cool.

March 27: Paid 10 cents for shave, 5-cents sandwich. Went to McColm's and Mrs. Beasly's sale.

March 28: Went north of town to old man Bound's and hired to him at $21 per month and washing. Will commence Monday next.

March 29: Went to tile and brick factory in morning. Paid $2.50 for shoes and shirts. Board paid through Sunday eve of $4.25. Sent baggage out to Bowen's by the old man himself.

March 30: Loafed at boarding house. Snow last night. Received from Frank E. Brown $2.61 for shoveling corn last fall. 10-cents = shave

March 31: Cloudy, spitting snow. Attended church in a.m. and in p.m. I walked 4 miles north and 1 mile west of Lexington where I will work for Thos. H. Bounds at $21 per month and washing, until corn shucking when I will if all goes well shuck by the bushel.

April 1: Commenced work this morning. Transferred corn into cribs today. Cool

April 2: Rain and snow flakes fell all day so I simply loafed.

April 3: Shucked 14 shocks of corn today, averaged 2½ bu. Fodder very dry in p.m.

April 4: Shucked shock corn in a.m. and hauled it into crib in p.m. Mostly clear.

April 5: Cut up old brush and wood in a.m. Trimmed hedges for an hour or more in afternoon. Rain

April 6: Trimmed hedge. Set up all night with Henry Bound's sick mare.

April 7: Slept in morning and lounged around the place in afternoon. It was sunny, so ground drying fast.

April 8:Trimmed and piled hedge today, completing the trimming for this Spring.

April 9: Shucked shock corn in morning and disked corn ground for oats in afternoon.

April 10–13: Disked ground which was sowed in oats. Also hauled a load of hay in morning of the 13th Weather stiff wind blowing first two days and cool. Warmer last 2 days, with mist and sprinkle slightly. Some sun on the 12th. Worked at home place in after of the 13th. Received word from home and letter from Charles.

April 14–20: Disked oats ground, then harrowed same fields Plowed oat stubble also bringing in remaining shock corn. Finished west field. Mostly clear, pleasant

Apr 21: Remained at place in a.m. and went to Shaffer's in p.m, where I got my telescope.

Apr 22–May 3: Hauled hay, plowed oat stubble at H. Bound's. Much trash on ground causes poor job of plowing as it collects under plow beam and throws plow out of ground. Finished cutting stalks. Plowed on south 80. Dry and cool forepart of week.

May 4: Harrowed 20 acres and more on H.B.'s place. Drove to town in evening. Paid $1 for Orange Judd Farmer magazine for 1 year and 25-cents for haircut, 77-cents for postage supplies, 51-cents of which I sent for a present for Professor Keep, Paid 35-cents for a hat, 5-cents for fruit, 10-cents – shoe polish and 12-cents for laundry. Returned at 11 p.m.

May 5: Clear east wind. Remain here all day. Pleasant day.

May 6: Harrowed 35 acres of H.B.'s ground.

May 7–9: Started to harrowed on south 80, Rain continued to stop progress. I planted ground on 8th . Warmer

May 10–11: Helped take cattle to pasture. Disked on home 80, harrowed on S 80 acres. Rain last night making most of the ground too wet to work.

May 12: Clear and cold. Remained place all day.

May 13: Disc and harrowed ground in west field in a.m. and planted corn in afternoon.

May 14: Planted corn all day and finished planting making in all for the old gent about 63 acres in corn.

May 15: Reset and repaired fence in feed lot. Clear and warm.

May 16: Worked on lot fence all day.

May 17: Scooped corn at Henthorn's old place until 3 p.m , after which I ground feed. Mostly clear. Hot 85F

May 18: Harrowed corn ground on S 80.

May 19: Walked to Meadow's in p.m. to find out the time of trains.

May 20: Scooped corn at Strickland's and Traver's and hoed potatoes in eve. Very dusty place to scoop corn at Strickland's.

May 21: Harrowed corn ground on S80 a 'till 9 a.m., when rain stopped me for the day.

May 22: Finished harrowing on S80 and harrowed home place in eve. Hauled manure.

May 23: Finished harrowing corn ground in morning then hauled manure and tore down fence remainder of the day.

May 24–25: Reset fence on south side of barn yard and cleaned up generally around lots. Hot Friday morning turning cooler and misting in late afternoon. Cold Saturday and cloudy.

May 26: Went to Meadows in morning and paid $1 for fare to Peoria and return. Arrived in Peoria at 9:25 a.m. Walked about town 'till 10:30. Met brother, Charles and went to First M.E. Church, as Mina Hall was leader of Ex. League in evening. I remained and attended that and preaching.

She is a very sensible appearing woman of about 27 or more, but not handsome face. Went to Lake View Park in p.m. I saw a ballgame. Paid 1-cent for street car fare, 5-cents for a paper, 25-cents for the ballgame, 35-cents = grub and 5-cents for church collection. Left Peoria at 11:30 p.m.

May 27: Arrived in Meadows at 2 a.m. and walked out to Bound's where I arrived at 3 a.m. Arose at 4:30 a.m. and repaired orchard pasture fence in p.m. I cut old posts into wood lengths. Cool and cloudy.

May 28: Repaired orchard pasture fence in a.m. and worked on Alex White's fence in p.m. 'till 5:30, when we put wire on past fence. Warmer and clear.

May 29: Set posts on A. White's fence in a.m. and set posts on S80 on Bound's.

May 30: Put wire on A. White's fence in morning after which I set posts on Bound's S80 acre. Walked to town in p.m. where I heard Cannon talk and brushed clothes with several of my acquaintances. Received bid to brother's wedding. Paid 30-cents for supper and treat. 5-cents for peanuts and 12-cents for laundry.

May 31: Finished setting posts on S80a today. Clear and pleasant.

June 1: Put wires on posts in a.m. and repaired fence along road on home place.

June 2: Walked to Meadows after dinner to mail regrets to my intended sister-in-law, Mina's Aunt in Peoria for not attending brother's wedding on Tuesday. Paid 5-cents for candy.

June 3: Came to Lexington in morning and withdrew $24.50 from Bank, all I have there. Paid 5-cents for peanuts. Paid 88-cents for return fare to Bloomington, 15-cents for dinner, $18 for present to brother, Charles – a cut glass pitcher, ½ doz. tumblers and a heavy glass tray. Paid $1.50 for a alpaca coat, 5-cents for fruit and 25-cents for supper. Went at 11:57 a.m. returned at 5 p.m. Bloomington has built up fine since the fire and is still at it. Mostly clear and very warm.

June 4: Hoed vines in S80a, also in west 20a in evening. Very dusty.

June 5: Hoed vines and plowed corn in West 20a. Corn very small. Pleasant

June 6: Rain last night. Hauled away 'most of an old cob pile' and plowed corn. Too wet.

June 7–12: Plowed corn. Trash interferes greatly. Finished west 20 acres at noon on 8th. Plowed in S80a in afternoon. Visited at Shaffer's on the 9th. Cool and partly cloudy early in the week and hot and mostly clear weather by the 12th.

June 13: Plowed corn in a.m., when we finished for the first time. Cut vines and helped H. Bound's put hay in mound. Hot and mostly clear. Some heavy cumulus clouds with thunder in west and north west in late evening. Game in left foot but better in eve.

June 14: Plowed corn for H.B. until 3 p.m. when an approaching rain stopped us. Rain for ¾ hour, very, very heavy with slight amount of hail. Stiff east wind, unroofing a corn crib.

June 15: Mowed weeds in a.m. and cleaned up yard, hauled out cobs and set posts in pasture fence. Hot mostly clear. Paid 25-cents for pain-killer.

June 16: Cloudy Remained at place all day.

June 17–18: Plowed corn on home place. Changeable to clouds.

June 19: Plowed corn here in morning, which field I completed for 2nd time at noon. Plowed corn in S80a until 3:30, when rain stopped us. Very warm.

June 20: Picked cherries today

June 21: Plowed corn until 8:30 a.m. when again stopped by rain. A large amount of water fell. Cut vines in late afternoon.

June 22: Cut vines in morning. Worked most of my poll tax in p.m. Hot very. Rain at night. Heard from Charles and home.

June 23: Very warm. Remained at home all day.

June 24–25: Plowed corn in S80a. Hot

June 26: Plowed corn 'till 10:00 a.m. when rains came. Picked cherries in late afternoon.

June 27: Hoed sweet corn in a.m. and plowed corn until 5 p.m., when NW rain storm stopped work. Cool after rain.

June 28: Mowed weeds in S80a and trimmed up a big willow tree for road tax in p.m.

June 29: Trimmed hedges and plowed corn. Warm and clear.

June 30: Remained at home.

July 1: Plowed corn in S80a. Rained after which I shelled and ground corn. I was poisoned Saturday from ivy on hedge fence.

July 2: Tried corn plowing in morning but being too wet, I dug post holes the rest of the day for H. B. Hottest of season. Poison worse.

July 3: Went to Lexington in a.m. Paid 35-cents for haircut and shave and $1 for antidote for poison, 5-cents for sponge and 25-cents for lemon essence. Mowed weeds in afternoon. Poison apparently same.

July 4: After doctoring for poison, I went to Lexington. Heard Sherman of Illinois H of R. Good talker. Paid 25-cents for dinner, 25-cents for supper, 15-cents for refreshments, 15-cents for soap. Saw exhibition Cake Walk[23] by Bloomington negro couples and later saw fire works, which were extensive and fine. Caught a ride most of way out. Poison troubling considerably in evening. Very hot and clear. Right leg swelled some.

July 5: Plowed corn in a.m. and my right leg swelling badly so I laid off in p.m.

July 6: Plowed corn all day. Poison about same as yesterday, commenced using night-shade and cream on poison.

July 7: Cool Remained at place all day. Poison slightly better.

July 8: Plowed corn all day. Rode while working, Poison finally better.

July 9: Mowed weeds and plowed corn. Poison still better

July 10: Hoed potatoes 'till 3 p.m. Then mowed weeds and hoed sweet corn.

July 11: Hoed potatoes and put up hay in S80a. Poison nearly well. Nightshade and cream being the chief agents of cure. Pound juice out of former and mix with cream.

July 12–13: Hoed vines and potatoes and put up hay. Also mowed some in yard at house.

July 14: Visited at P. Peck's and attended Sunday School in p.m. Gave 5-cents to SS. I think poison is gone.

July 15: Put up hay at H.B.'s in a.m. and shocked oats for Henthorn in p.m.

July 16–17: Hauled manure to meadow. Hot.

July 18: Shocked oats for P. Jenkins all day. On Davis farm.

July 19–20: Hauled manure to meadow and shocked oats. Oats are too green.

July 21: Loafed about place. Hottest of season. 107F

July 22: Picked blackberries in morning and shocked oats remainder of the day. Light breeze, but very hot.

July 23: Shocked oats. Continues hot.

July 24: Shocked oats on home place 'till 4:40 p.m. after which I shocked oats on S80a. Slightly cooler with some clouds in eve.

July 25: Shocked oats 'till 9:30, when we finished. Put binders away until noon. Hauled manure in afternoon.

July 26: Hauled manure –3/4 of the day. Was sick at stomach, vomiting through the eve. All day cooler.

July 27: Feeling much better. Strong south west breeze with numerous cumulus clouds. Gave a lad 5-cents for helping work yesterday.

July 28: Similar weather to yest only more clouds. Remained at place all day. Light sprinkle.

July 29: Hauled manure after 8 a.m. before which it rained.

July 30: Hauled manure, most of the day. Quit work at 6:30 p.m. The old man finding fault because I quit so early, I quit him. Packed any goods in late evening.

July 31: Bound's brought me to town in morning and I put up at Karbaugh's Hotel. Settled with Bound's receiving $76.36 I had lost 4 ¼ days and to avoid trouble, I let him count out holidays. Also paid $1 per month for washing which I had understood was to be done as part of my pay. All in all it was the very worst place I have worked at in the State. I am glad I quit as soon as I did . Paid 10-cents for shave and put $65 in S.B. of Lexington.

Aug. 1: Loafed about town all day. Will go to work Monday morning next for Joe Humphrey at $20 per month until corn cutting, if I get along all right. During corn cutting and shucking time will get all of that I can to do. Paid 5-cents for nuts. Some clouds but mostly clear. Pleasant temperature. 75F in the shade.

Aug. 2: Remained about town. Cool south breeze. Purchased magazine for 10-cents.

Aug. 3: Loafed about town in a.m. Helped B. B. Steven's thresh in p.m. for 3 hours for which rec'd 50-cents.

Aug. 4: Loafed about town. Paid 5-cents for paper. Went to Joe Humphrey's in evening where I will work for a time at $20 per month, board and washing. Paid $2.25 for board.

Aug. 5: Raised wires on east pasture fence in a.m. and painted crib roof and some on barn in p.m.

Aug. 6: Took old bins apart and mowed weeds in a.m.. Helped B.B. Steven's thresh oats in p.m. Clear and quite warm with cool nights.

Aug. 7: Helped Steven's thresh. Mowed weeds in afternoon. Hot.

Aug. 8: Painted barn and porch roof. Paid 16-cents for washing.

Aug. 9: Painted porch roofs and chimneys, then trimmed hedge.

Aug. 10: Painted slats for barn in a.m. , then trimmed hedge and cut thistles in p.m. Rested an hour or more after 2 p.m. Paid 10-cents for shave and 5-cents for peanuts.

Aug. 11: Remained about place.

Aug. 12: Nailed strips on barn. Picked some manure loose north of barn. J. Peck commenced hauling manure this morning.

Aug. 13–17: Cleaned up around the barn and feed lot. Very warm in day time all week. Received letter dated the 14th, announcing the death of Uncle Andrew Hartshorne and his burial on the morrow. Pa and Ma went to funeral at Batavia, New York.

Aug. 18: Cloud and cool. Remained at place all day.

Aug. 19: Hauled old lumber from bridge, 3 ½ miles south west of Lexington. Paid $10 as present to home, which I drew from S.B. of Lex. Paid 11-cents for envelope and money order.

Aug. 20: Hauled away barn yard cleanings. Warm and cloudy.

Aug. 21: Hauled manure to garden, dug potatoes, etc. Some rain, clouds and clear. Hot.
I am 25 years old today

Aug. 22: Made manure pen in a.m. and scattered manure in garden in p.m. Hot, very.

Aug. 23: Hauled a load of gravel from Harness' pit and 3 from Van Dolah's

Aug. 24: Hauled 5 loads of gravel from Van Dolah's pit. Cooler than yesterday, but still very warm. Paid 10-cents for a shave and 50-cents for shirt.

Aug. 25: Remained at place all day.

Aug. 26–29: Hauled 5 loads gravel each day. Hot all the time. A cave-in on Wed. covered up a man to his neck and broke horse's shoulder. Horse was killed and man only sore.

Aug. 30: Owing to belly-ache, I did not work today. Cooler in eve though hot in day.

Aug. 31: Leveled feed-lot in a.m. Tore bins apart, cut wood, etc. in p.m. Paid 10-cents for shave, 50-cents for shirt, 15-cents for socks and $3.00 for shoes, and 5-cents for peanuts.

Sept. 1: Visited at Shaffer's north of town. Hot late in day, with some clouds.

Sept. 2: Hauled 5 loads of gravel. Cool.

Sept. 3–5: Hauled 6 loads of gravel each day.

Sept. 6: President McKinley[24] was shot twice this p.m. by anarchist. Probably fatally wounded. One shot in breast, not harmful but one shot went through stomach is very dangerous. This assassination attempt is most appalling. Striking down our great and good and Christian President. It occurred at Buffalo, N.Y. while shaking hands with the people at the Temple of Music.

Sept. 7: President McKinley better. Hauled 5 loads of gravel. Paid 30-cents for corn cutters, 10-cents for shave and 5-cents for peanuts.

Sept. 8: Went to cemetery today. Paid 5-cents for paper.

Sept. 9: As Humphrey is sick, I did not go to hunt a corn cutting job, but hauled 5 loads of gravel. Cloudy, cool, light sprinkle in morning.

Sept. 10: Hauled 5 loads of gravel. President is better, hope for recovery.

SEPT .11–12: Hauled 2 loads of gravel on 11th. 6 loads on 12th.

SEPT .13: President McKinley is worse. Hauled 6 loads of gravel.

SEPT .14: McKinley died at 2:15 a.m. So passes one of our great President's, a martyr to his faith in all people and his friendliness in meeting them.

SEPT. 15: Remained at place all day. Paid 5-cents for paper.

SEPT. 16–18: Hauled 16 loads of gravel in 3 days. Cold

SEPT. 19: This is our President McKinley's burial day at Canton, Ohio. Today one of our greatest President's and best men is laid away. Great in life, most noble in death, a Christian all the time. A.W. Stewgol of Chicago Illinois spoke at school house auditorium on McKinley's life and death. Hauled gravel in a.m. – 3 loads Hauled 1 load of hay in p.m. Paid 5-cents for lost wager.

SEPT. 20: Hauled 1 load of clover hay and 2 loads of shock-fodder. Warmer mostly cloudy.

SEPT. 21: Hauled 3 loads of millet hay from near Selma. Paid 35-cents for haircut and shave, Received $30.75 for work of Humphrey. I am through at Humphrey's. Deposited $25 in S.B. Lexington.

SEPT. 22: Walked east and north of town in a.m. Some good corn and some very small and poor. Paid 5-cents for paper, 20-cents for dinner, 15-cents for supper and 25-cents for lodging.

SEPT. 23: Walked east of town for corn shucking job but not getting my price. I returned to Lex, then walked southwest of town, 2 miles and then north a few miles. Paid 25-cents for breakfast, 15-cents for fruit and nuts, 15-cents for supper, 25-cents for lodging, $3 for transcripting Lien. Saw Sq. Davidson and he has done nothing towards collecting notes from A. E. Slagel and Carrie Slagel. I have had to take a judgement on Slagel's former residence property as soon as he can.

Sept. 25: Breakfast=25-cents and 20-cents for dinner. Took clothes and went 5 miles northwest of Lexington for corn cutting job but failed to get it. Returned at 6:30 p.m. and stayed all night with Elza Bennet on N. Franklin's place.

Sept. 26: Came to Lexington in morning and hired to L. Siren till corn shucking at $20 per month. Commenced work in p.m. Jerked corn in p.m.

Sept. 27–28: Hauled manure

Sept. 29: Remained at place. Cloudy except in early morning. Light mist. Cool

Sept. 30–Oct 2: Hauled manure. Paid 10-cents for shave

Oct. 3–5: Hauled gravel, manure and gathered corn. Cold and Cloudy

Oct. 6: Remained at place all day.

Oct. 7–13: Hauled manure and gathered corn. Went to Lex. in eve of 10/11 and paid 10-cents for shave, 10-cents for salve, 25-cents pain-killer, $1 for mittens, 5-cents for treat, 5-cents for horse care. Cool

Oct. 14–19: Shucked corn. Average 40 bushel per acre.

Oct. 20: Remained at place. Quite warm and mostly clear. Paid 10-cents for treat yesterday.

Oct. 21–26: Shucked corn. Uncomfortably warm weather. Corn averaging 35 bushels.

Oct. 27: Remained at place day. Fine weather.

Oct. 28–Nov 2: Shucked corn. Avg. 30 bushel. Went to Lexington. Nov. 2 paid 50- cents for mittens, 50-cents for shirt, 10-cent shave and 20-cents =grub. Rec'd $2.00 from L D. Siren.

Nov. 3: Rain in a.m. Wind circled from south of west to north by east.

Nov. 4–17: Shucked corn Corn making 35 bushels per acre

Nov. 18: Finished shucking corn at L.D. Sirens. Quite cold.

Nov. 19?: Measured and counted corn = 1,879 bus., which I husked off of 54 acres, at 2 ¾- cents = $51.67. Work previous to husking = $11.12, Total = $62.79. Had received $2, received $60.79. Came to Lex. in p.m. and was paid in full. Pd. 10-cents for shave, 25-cents mittens, and 3-cents for pins.

Heard of a job south of town which I will investigate tomorrow. Deposited $55 in S.B. Bank of Lexington

Nov. 20: Paid 50-cents for lodging and breakfast. Walked 3 or 4 miles southwest of town and got a shucking job of Peter Lutge at 2½ cents. Shucked corn in p.m. Wagon box measure.

Nov. 21: Shucked corn.

Nov. 22: Rain all day. Shucked but 14 bushels

Nov. 23: Shucked corn. Dance at place tonight. Nice evening.

Nov. 24: Remained at place all day.

Nov. 25–30: Shucked corn all week. 21 rows each day but one and 20½ on Saturday.

Dec. 1: Came to Lexington and paid 34-cents for washing. 10-cents for shave, 50-cents dinner for two, 10-cents candy and 5-cents for paper. Returned in p.m.

Dec. 2 –3: Shucked corn, Completed my husking for the season. Cold.

Dec. 4: Received pay for 807 bus. corn = $20.20. Paid 25-cents for mittens. Went to L.D. Siren and prepared my goods for shipment to home. Came to town in p.m. and paid 35-cents = hair cut and shave, 25-cents for supper.

Dec. 5: Paid 50-cents for lodging and breakfast, 10-cents=washing. $3.31 fare to Chicago, 50-cents for baggage delivery. Drew $50 from S.B. Lexington. Started to Chicago at 9:52 a.m. Arrived at 1 p.m. Walked down to Acme Hotel where I paid 15- cents for room and left valise. Walked around town remainder of evening. 15-cents for lodging, 15-cents for dinner, 10-cents for supper and 5-cents for nuts. 20-cents = show = bum

Dec. 6: Paid 15-cents for lodging, 10-cents breakfast, 1-cent paper, 5-cents for street car fare, 25-cents for entrance fee to stock show. 15-cents =lunch, 5-cents street car fare, 10- cents supper, 15-cents sweets, 5-cents cough drops, 5-cents paper and picture of scenery and 30-cents for a show. Went to stock yards at 9:30 a.m. and passed through all buildings of Expo. Where was exhibited the best of all prominent breeds of stock. Horses were Percheron, Clydesdale, Shire and Belgian. Cattle = Shorthorn, Hereford, Galloway, Aberdeen-Angus, Polled Durham, Red-Polls and Devon. Sheep and Swine of all principal breeds. A great show of its kind. Returned to town in evening and went to Hopkin's Theater. Have caught severe cold.

Dec. 7: Weather turned warmer in the night and misting in morning. Have severe headache from cold. Remained in town all day, mostly in hotel. Dreary day. Paid $10.00 for suit, $1 for shirt, 25-cents for collars, 25-cents handkerchiefs, $2.98 for hat, $1.38 underclothes, 99-cents for watch, 25-cents for headache powders, 10-cents for dinner, 5-cent=fruit, 15-cents for dinner.

Dec. 8: Arose late. Paid 8-cents for breakfast, 25-cent storage charge on trunk, 5-cents for newspaper, 10-cents for sweets, $4.65 fare to Waterloo. Left Chicago at 10:30 a.m. and arrived in Waterloo, Indiana at 2:55 p.m.

Dec. 9: Remained at home most of day. Paid 25-cents baggage, 30-cents for meat. Cooler and cloudy.

Dec. 10: Received 2-cents for stamp. Cloudy most of the day.

Dec .11: Gave Pa $1 for covering freight charges on box containing books and clothes.

Dec. 12: A quiet day.

Dec. 13: Paid 25-cents for meat. Rainy all day. Considerable amount of H2O fell. As usual remained at home.

Dec. 14: Colder this morning with 2 inches of snow. Snowed more or less all day. Wind from the north. Paid 10-cents for shave.

Dec. 15: Zero in a.m. Went to telegraph office in evening.

Dec. 16: Below zero this morn. Clear most of the day. At home.

Dec. 17–18: At home

Dec. 19: Left home at 10 a.m. Paid $1.25 for overshoes. Left for Auburn Junction at 10:35 a.m. Paid $1.35 for fare to Kimmel and return. Paid 25-cents for a ride to Wolf Lake.

Dec. 20: Visited at relatives. H.A. Shambaugh left in early morning for Plymouth.

Dec. 21: Paid 42-cents for meat and lard, 25-cents = pail, 5-cents for box and a 10-cent shave. J.M.R. 40 acre farm sold for ditch tax of $475. Brought only $100. $100 is also an encumberance on it.

Dec. 22: Warmer, clear with mostly an east wind.

Dec. 23: Came to Kimmel in a.m. and left at 11:30. Stopped at Garrett and called on M. Thumma. Paid 10-cents for fare to Auburn Junction, where I arrived at 2:35. Walked to McCrory's. Also called on L.J. Till, who is doing a good grocery business. Paid 25-cents for return ticket to Waterloo. Purchased meat =25-cents, a book for Carter Richmond =25-cents, 25-cents for dinner. Quite warm with some snow.

Dec. 24: Came to Auburn in morning. Paid 50-cents for neck tie and cuffs. Ate dinner at Wm. McCrory's . Paid $7.40 for excursion to Barberton,

Ohio. Left Auburn Junction at 2:33 p.m. Arrived at Chi. JC at 6:30 p.m., made a direct connection for Barberton, where I arrived at 9 p.m. Paid 25-cents for hack fare.

Dec. 25: Went to CC Company in morning with Charles. Roast turkey for dinner. Received 2 handkerchief's from Mina and Charles. Cloudy and warm with light snow.

Dec. 26: Paid 10-cents for shave. Remained at house in morning except a walk down town. Went to Sterling Boiler Company and Soda Ash in p.m. Cora left this morning for Portland, Indiana.

Dec. 27: Left Barberton at 9:14 a.m. Cloudy. Made direct connection at Chicago Junction and arrived in Auburn at 2:30 p.m. Paid 15-cents for lunch. Walked to McCrory's then to L.S. & M.S. Depot. Paid 15-cents for ticket to Waterloo. I received a pair of slippers from H.A. Shambaugh family.

Dec. 28: Remained at home. Sent check for $75 to S.B. Lexington. Trimmed some limbs and cut wood 2 or 3 hours. Warm and light frost.

Dec. 29: Remain at home. Weather similar to yesterday. Light sprinkle of snow.

Dec. 30: At home. Pleasant relaxing with family.

Dec. 31: At home. Rec'd draft for $15 from S.B. of Lexington, Ill. 30F – 40F

Fountain at Purdue University, Lafayette, Indiana and is still in existence and in working order. John Purdue is buried close to this fountain and University Hall. John Purdue lived 1802 to 1876 and was the University's primary benefactor, *Postcard among WBH's possessions.*

The Indiana State Soldiers and Sailors Monument was designed by Bruno Schmitz and built on Monument Circle, a circular, brick-paved street that intersects Meridian and Market Streets, in the center of downtown Indianapolis, Indiana. It was dedicated in 1902 at a cost of $598,318. *Postcard in SED's possession*

Indianapolis State Capital was built in 1878
Postcard among SED's possessions.

Maud Ballington Booth was the co-founder of the Volunteers of America. She shared vivid accounts of life in prisons and called for their reform. She later toured with the Chautauqua circuit.

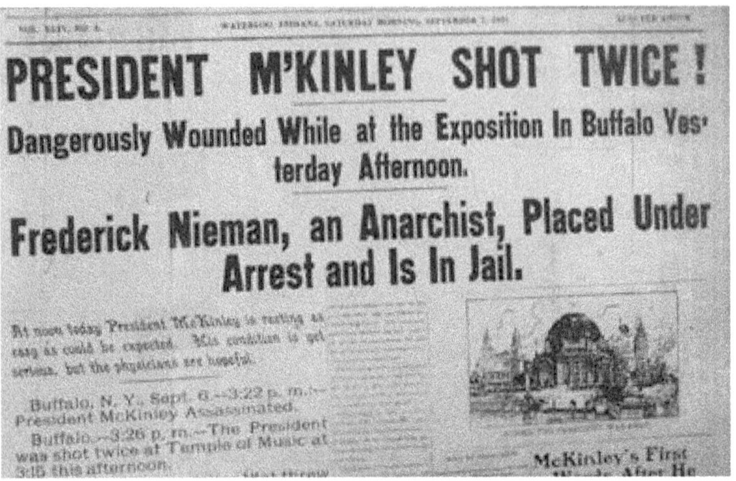

PRESIDENT M'KINLEY SHOT TWICE!

Dangerously Wounded While at the Exposition In Buffalo Yesterday Afternoon.

Frederick Nieman, an Anarchist, Placed Under Arrest and Is In Jail.

At noon today President McKinley is resting as easy as could be expected. His condition is yet serious, but the physicians are hopeful.

Buffalo, N. Y., Sept. 6.--3:22 p. m.--President McKinley Assassinated.

Buffalo.--3:26 p. m.--The President was shot twice at Temple of Music at 3:15 this afternoon.

McKinley's First

Waterloo Press Newspaper headline read Mc'Kinley Shot Twice, dated Saturday morning, September 7, 1901

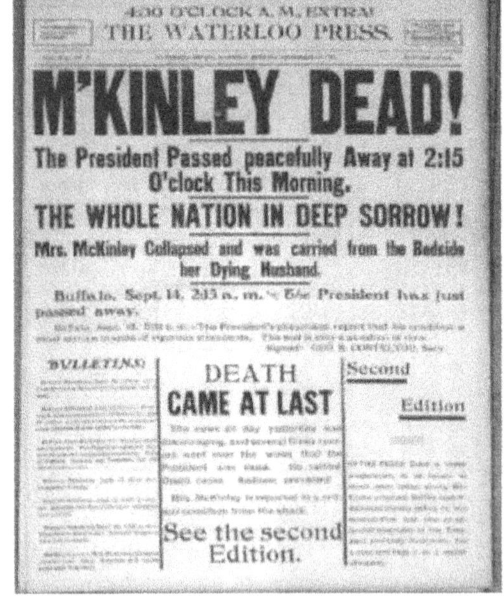

4:30 O'CLOCK A. M. EXTRA!

THE WATERLOO PRESS.

M'KINLEY DEAD!

The President Passed peacefully Away at 2:15 O'clock This Morning.

THE WHOLE NATION IN DEEP SORROW!

Mrs. McKinley Collapsed and was carried from the Bedside her Dying Husband.

Buffalo, Sept. 14, 2:15 a. m.--The President has just passed away.

BULLETINS:

DEATH CAME AT LAST

See the second Edition.

Second Edition

Waterloo Press Extra edition headline reads Mc'Kinley Dead! September 14, 1901

1902

Dr. Walter Reed published his results on yellow fever in 1902. He concluded that: the spread of yellow fever could be controlled by elimination of the mosquito. The Reclamation Act of 1902, is the U. S. federal law that funded irrigation projects for the arid lands of the West, which led to the eventual damming of nearly every major western river.

January 1, 1902: At home. Warm

Jan. 2–3: Good to be home.

Jan. 4: Walked to L.D.P. home office in a.m. Packed trunk in p.m. Cashed draft for $75. Gave Pa $5 and 5-cents for provisions. Cloudy 20F average.

Jan. 5: Mostly clear. At home until 2 pm. when I walked to Auburn. Stopped at Will McCrog then came on to Auburn JC. Paid $2.48 to Logansport. Left at about 6 p.m. Arrive at Logansport at 8:45. Stopped at Tucker House. Paid 50-cents for lodging.

Jan. 6: Arose at 6 a.m. Paid 20-cents for breakfast, 25-cents for transfer baggage. $1.11 for fare to LaFayette. Arrived at LaFayette at 10:45. Went to Exp. Station, after which I matriculated. Paid 5-cents for street car fare, $10 for tuition, 20-cents for dinner, and 50-cents for baggage transfer. Was helped to this by YMCA. I engaged room and board at 202 Chauncey Ave. Pay $3 per month for room and $3 per week for board. Bright and warm. Commenced board this evening for supper.

JAN. 7: Went over to town in morning and paid 10-cents for soap, 25-cents for shaving brush, 10-cents for tablet and 50-cents for overalls.

JAN. 8: Class in Rural Law, Ag. Chemistry, Dairy in a.m. Went to town and paid $1 for suit of overclothes. Paid $3.00 as my share of room rent for 1 month from Jan 6th to Feb 6th.

JAN. 9: Woodwork in a.m. Dairy work on farm in p.m. Warm and clear.

JAN. 10: Attended Ag. Chem and dairy classes, also lecture on poultry "T. E. Orr of Pittsburgh". Lecture by Prof. Arthur on vegetable parasites in p.m.

JAN. 11: Attended Rural Law in morning. Attended YMCA lecture by Dr. Hale in p.m. Paid 5-cents for a lamp shade. Cold.

JAN. 12: Attended church in City in a.m. YMCA lecture in p.m. and M.E. Church in eve. Gave 5-cents to church collection.

JAN. 13: R. Law and Dairying in morning and blank in p.m. Clear and warmer. Paid $3 for board.

JAN. 14: Classes in woodwork and dairying Lost 20-cents in bet.

JAN. 15: Usual classes and special dairy in p.m. Pleasant

Jan. 16: Routine. Continued fair weather.

Jan. 17: Attended usual classes and Farmer's Institute in afternoon. Borrowed 60-cents from Randolph to pay washing bill and vaccination fee. I was vaccinated on account of a case of small-pox in the University.

Jan. 18: Attended Farmers Institute all day. I owe 14-cents for washing.

Jan. 19: Attended YMCA Bible class and church on east side in a.m. and YMCA meeting and church on the Westside in p.m. Promised to give 5-cents per week for 9 weeks to Helm fund in Japan and China. Took a 2 mile walk in evening.

Jan. 20: Captain A.A. Rice having died Sunday morning[25] our Rural Law class had no lecture but passed resolutions of respect to his memory and arranged for attending his funeral tomorrow, at 2:30. We will furnish a simple floral offering. Repaid Randolph 60-cents.

Jan. 21: Attended woodwork in a.m. and also a lecture on swine. In afternoon, I attended funeral of Capt. A.A. Rice in East LaFayette in First Pres. Church at 2:30. A very well remembered, generous, moral, Christian man.

Attended Coulter's lecture in eve. and the P. Ag. S in later eve. 2½ inches snow last night and 1 inch or more this morning. Colder. Paid 5-cents for street car fare.

Jan. 22: Attended usual classes Paid 15-cents for flowers for Capt. A.A.Rice. 28F

Jan. 23: Warmer and melting. Paid 14-cents for washing of a week ago. Attended classes.

Jan. 24: Usual classes. Melted but little, colder. Attended live stock judging in p.m. at annex. My vaccinated arm is getting a little sore.

Jan. 25: Arm now quite sore underneath or at arm pit. Paid 14-cents for washing. Remained at home most of the day. Warmer, slightly.

Jan. 26: I attended YMCA Bible class in morning. Trinity M.E. preaching and U.M.E. in eve. Cold and snowing in eve.

Jan. 27: Usual classes except R. Law, which has no instructor. Cold with 2 or more inches of snow last night.

Jan. 28: Routine. Attended Agr. Scq in eve and talked on agricultural resources of Illinois. Paid 15-cents for cakes and fruit. Feeling better. Arm fevered and swollen some.

Jan. 29: Usual classes except R.Law and Agr. Chem. instructors being absent. Heard A.C. Harris of Indianapolis, ex-minister to Austria speak on industrial conditions of Austria. Good talk. Paid 15-cents for washing. Feeling about well.

Jan. 30: Usual classes. Warmer, not melting.

Jan. 31: Usual classes. Arm nearly well. Paid 5-cents for coconut. Went calling in the evening.

Feb. 1: Drew $10 from LaFayette Savings Bank. Paid 26-cents for stamped envelopes.

Feb. 2: Attended Bible classes at 8:30 a.m. and church in eve. Heard Judge Baldwin at Chapel at 5:45 p.m. on "Keys the Unlock" the Bible's meaning.

Instructive talk meant. A good one. Gave 4-cents to church collection. Very cold. More snow.

Feb. 3: Usual classes, Rural Law class having an instructor, a Mr. Bright of LaFayette. A young lawyer, good-natured and frank. Paid $3.00 for board, 90-cents for book, "Milk and It's Products" 11 degrees this morning at 7 a.m. at Drug Store.

Feb. 4: Usual work. Colder than yesterday.

Feb. 5: Usual classes, several below zero this morning. West wind strong.

Feb. 6: Routine. Paid $3 for room rent and loaned Gordon $3.

Feb. 7: Routine. Paid 25-cents for entrance to Basketball Game between Purdue and ISN. The score PU 39 – ISN 17. Purchased 5-cents worth of paper from Professor Johnson. Couldn't make change so owe him the 5-cents.

Feb.8: About zero in morning. Remained in room in a.m. Drew $10 from LaFayette Savings Bank in afternoon. Rec'd from A.N. Gordon, $3 as repayment of loan of 2/05/02.

Feb. 9: Attended YMCA and church today. Quite cold.

Feb.10: Usual classes. Paid $3 for board.

Feb. 11–13: Routine.

Feb. 14: Usual classes. Rec'd a book "Christians Secret of a Happy Life" which Ma had sent to me. Also a notification from Atty. A.B. Davidson, of Lexington, Illinois, that the Slagel money had been paid in. I notified him to take his collecting commission and put the remainder to my credit in State Bank of Lexington. This will amount to $100.00, probably.

Feb. 15: Attended Vet lecture in a.m. and went over to town. Paid 25-cents for shave and a hair cut, 25-cents for entrance fee to "King Dodo" a light opera matinee at Grand Opera House. Good show.[26]

Feb. 16: Attended 2 sermons and YMCA talk by Dr. Coulter
on everyday life. Gave 5-cents to church. Everyday life is the kind, most of us will lead. It is for its guidance that the Proverbs of Soloman were quoted concerning sins and their effects. 1. unchastity, 2. interferance, 3. slothfulness, 4. unbridled tongue, etc.
The dominant thought is that sin exists and that its trend is destructive, that we are not living up to our possibilities when we sin. Sin and foolishness are one.
Weather being fair. Snow melts slightly.

Feb. 17: Usual classes. Paid 5-cents for paper from Johnson.

Feb. 18: Routine. Paid $3 for board. Warmer

Feb. 19: Routine. Rec'd draft for $117 from A.B. Davidson, in full for Slagel account. The remaining of the $150 or more dollars going for costs, collection charges, court charges, etc. This is a better settlement than I had expected. Paid 10-cents for washing.

Feb. 20–21: Routine. Usual classes

Feb. 22: Remained in room all day. Went to town in eve. Paid 5-cent for shoe strings. Pleasant and clear.

Feb. 23: Attended YMCA and preaching. Gave 5-cents to church collection. Light rain in p.m.

Feb. 24: Routine. Attended lecture on "Backbone" by Thomas Dixon, Jr. of New York, at St. Paul's M.E. in evening. Good talker and entertainer.[27] Paid 25-cents for admission.

Feb. 25: Routine Paid $3 for board

Feb. 26: No Ag. Chem. class or special lecture. Paid 21-cents for washing.

Feb. 27–March 1: Usual work, read and studied and exercised.

March 2: Attended YMCA and church in eve. Also attended E.L. of M.E. Gave 5-cents to church collection.

March 3–5: Routine $3 for board. In p.m. on 5th went 2 miles north of town to dairy barn of Mr. Gove. Paid 10-cents for street car fare. Class picture taken.

March 6–7: Usual work. Chilly air. Paid 12-cents for washing, 40-cents for picture of dairy class (see photo), and 25-cents for basketball game.

March 8: Drew $10 from Sav. Bank. Paid $1.50 for room rent.

March 9: Attended YMCA. Gave 50-cents to Helm Fund. Paid 5-cents for street care fare. Went to Soldier's Home in p.m.

March 10–13: Attended usual classes. Heard from home.

March 14: Paid 5-cents for post card view of University buildings. Usual classes. Paid 1-cent for sheet paper.

March 15: Cloudy and misting. Paid 7-cents for postal cards and stamps, $1 to subscription to Breeders Gazette. Paid the money to Caswell through C. L. Disher.

March 16: Attended YMCA twice and church twice. Going to Catholic in a.m., the first time ever in a Catholic Church. Church is decorated with pictures and statues of Christ and Mary and the apostles and angels. Candles on alter burning. Fair sermon in English.

March 17: Usual classes. Paid 5-cents for more pictures of University grounds and buildings. Cold with light snow.

March 18: Routine. Attended farewell meeting of Ag. Science in eve. Fine time. Paid for board to Friday noon $1.55. Heard H. C. Taylor of China in eve.

March 19: Routine. Paid $1 for clock and 20-cents for rope.

March 20: Paid $1 for shirt and overalls. Drew $30 = remainder of account from savings bank. Paid 25-cents for show in evening. Found time at Purdue a very good experience.

March 21: Paid 20-cents for dinner and 5-cents st. car fare, paid $3.17 for fare to Chenoa, Ill. Left at 1:42 p.m., arrived at Sheldon at 2:55. Left at 3:55, arrived at Chenoa at 6 p.m. Left at 6:12 arrived at Lexington at 6:25p. Paid 24-cents fare Chenoa to Lexington and 20-cents for supper. Got lodging for night at Dr. Paine's. Retired at 8:30p.

March 22: Paid 50-cents for last night's lodging. Breakfast =15-cents, 15-cents for dinner, $2.00 for shoes, 10-cent shave. Went to N B. Shaffer's in morning, then returned to Lexington. Put $130 in State Bank of Lexington. This makes me $140 at S.B. of Lex. Baptist Church damaged by fire in p.m.

Was hired by F. James Hinthorn at $22 per month and washing. Went to his place in p.m. Took baggage with me.

March 23: Cooler and clear. Loafed.

March 24–27: Trimmed trees in orchard. Tinkered indoors. Spade oat ground Spader does much better work than disk but does not cut stalks as well. Very warm and clear.

March 28: Husked shock corn, cleaned shed and old house, etc. Plowed bog and planted potatoes. Tore down a fence by berry patch, etc. etc. etc.

March 29: Hauled old fence material, mowed briars in a.m. and spade oat ground in p.m.
A little wet. Rec'd first installment of Breeders Gazette, paper from home and also a letter from home.

March 30: Loafed all day. Cold west wind. ¾ inch of snow last night, disappearing during the day.

March 31: Hauled manure. Cold and cloudy.

April 1: Hauled manure from shed, where calves are fed. Hauled straw to grape patch and also trimmed apple trees. Very cold.

April 2: Partly filled old well, etc. and sowed oats in a.m. Spade with four horse spader in p.m. Some snow.

April 3: Chored in early morn. Spade remainder of day. Frozen 1" last night.

April 4–7: Finished spading oats ground. Harrowed oats ground. Plowed in west oat stubble. Hauled manure from north shed in a.m. Cold, stormy with some snow.

April 9–14: Plowed and harrowed oat ground Plowed finishing oat stubble west at 4:00, after which I plowed east of house on 10th Received report of my last school work. Studied hard proved to be useful. Harrowed corn stalks and east field, also plowed after 4 p.m. on 14th.

April 15: Plowed in east field and by house in a.m. Plowed in north end of east field.

April 16–19: Plowed every day.

April 20: Read, etc. Brother Charles has a son!

April 21-24: Plowed every day. Warmer but still cool and breezy.

April 25: Rainy and windy. Cut wood and shelled seed corn. Got Ream's spray pump in evening for use in orchard.

April 26–29 Plowed and cut fallen willows, sprayed orchard. Used Bordeaux mixture.

April 30: Set fence posts along west side of pasture. Rain last night

May 1: Plowed until 4 p.m.when rain stopped us. Tinkered with spray pump frame.

May 2: Went to Lexington in morning. Hauled hay and plowed in afternoon. Sent $40 draft home, paid $1 for subscription to Orange Judd Farmer. 35-cents for hat, 35-cents for hair cut and shave, 60-cents for razor hone, 32-cents for stamped envelopes, 3-cents for money order, 5-cents for writing tablet and 5-cents for candy. Hot.

May 3: Disked in a.m. and plowed in p.m. Hottest day of season. Plowing or breaking finished for season. Worked a mare in a.m. and she had a colt in evening.

May 4: Warm, clear in morning then hazy. Remained at place. Ed Dolan's barn burned by lighting in p.m. Heavy rain and some hail.

May 5: Set posts along west side of pasture 'till 4 p.m. Then harrowed until eve. Cool and mostly cloudy.

May 6: Disked in a.m. and set post in p.m. Rain from 12:30 to 2:30. Warm.

May 7–10: Set posts and harrowed and disked. Received last Wednesday a picture of the Smith children of St. Mary's, Ohio. A good picture and gladly received.

May 11: Remained at place. Cool and clear.

May 12–14: Harrowed. Disked. Worked a colt. Weather warm

May 15–16: Harrowed. Got 1050 # of hay in p.m. from A.H. Scrogin. Planted corn. This ends corn planting here for this time.

May 17: Sprayed 2/3 of orchard in a.m. and cultivated potatoes and planted pop-corn in p.m. Hot and mostly clear.

May 18: Tomorrow is Cora's birthday. 27 years old. Warm.

May 19: Cora's Birthday 27th. Cultivated corn ground in west field all day.

May 20: Patched barn roof and harrowed corn ground.

May 21: Harrowed all day. Completed harrowing for this Spring.

May 22: Set a few posts on west side of pasture and hauled 1 load of corn for Strickland Isom in a.m. Plowed corn in p.m.

May 23: Rain in early morning. Set posts and dug post holes. Plowed corn in afternoon.

May 24: Relaid left floor in barn and piled lumber in a.m. Plowed corn in p.m. Boss/Hinthorn went to Normal.

May 25: Remained at place all day. Was informed that Hinthorn had worked my poll tax for me last Tuesday, which will amount to $1.50 or 1 day off. First strawberries today.

May 26: Cultivated corn. Pleasant and cool

May 27–28: Cultivated corn competing the first cultivation of the corn of E 80a or 40 acres of corn.

May 29: Cultivated corn in west field. Ground cloddy and corn small.

May 30: Cultivated corn on vines territory in a.m. The boss going ahead and hoeing vines from corn hills. Went to Lexington in p.m. and saw the parade and heard William Murdock of Streator, make a good and patriotic speech. Paid 10-cents for candy.

May 31: Cultivated corn in west field all day.

June 1: Visited at Willis Shaffer's in p.m. on account of rain as I had started to Sunday School.

June 2: Hoed vines in west field in a.m. and cultivated corn in p.m. Warm.

June 3: Repaired orchard fence and hoed vines in a.m. and cultivated corn.

June 4–7: Cultivated corn. Finished first cultivation in p.m. on the 4th. and commenced crossing in east field. Hot but cool breeze.

June 8: Mostly clear and cool. Attended SS at Olivet at 2:30. Gave 5-cents.

June 9–10: Cultivated corn. Cool and some wind.

June 11: Hard storm and rain last night. A box-elder in yard broken off 12 ft. from ground. Wind-mill fan bent also wheel fan. Relaid rail fence, got an old wagon from C.J.W. McNeman's and cleared away fallen tree and limbs. Many trees broken in timber and much damage done throughout the county.

June 12: Trimmed limbs and grubbed box-elder bushes and hoed in garden in a.m. Worked on wind mill and picked strawberries in p.m. Hot and mostly clear.

June 13: Rain again. Set 25 posts along north end of west side of E 80a in a.m. I finished setting posts and picked cherries in p.m. Very hot.

June 14: Another less severe storm last eve. Lightning breaking the telephone wires in many places. Put wire along southside of pasture and picked cherries and sawed posts in a.m. Hoed vines in p.m.

June 15: Very hot and clear. Remained at place all day.

June 16–19: Cultivated corn. Clear Deliver Hinthorn horse - $140

June 20: Cultivated corn. Rain more than ½ of p.m. Whitewashed stable.

June 21: Whitewashed stable and hoed corn in a.m. and commenced laying corn in p.m. Cool and many shifting clouds. Longest day of the year.

June 22: Mostly clear and cool. Attended Sunday School in p.m. Only 15 or 20 present. Gave 5-cents for collection.

June 23: Finished crossing corn and cultivated garden and commenced on north side of southeast field to lay by corn in a.m. Cultivated corn in southeast field in p.m. Heavy dew last night. Have bad cold and sore throat.

June 24: Rain in morning after which I cultivated corn in north sod field, remainder of day.

June 25: Rain last night. Worked on west pasture fence. Helped build a platform for binder. My cold is getting looser.

June 26: Went 7 miles southwest for load of wood and posts in morning. Cultivated corn in west sod field in p.m.

June 27: Cultivated corn in morning. Ground sickle, repaired shed and barn, then mowed weeds.

June 28: An almost steady day of rain. Set a few posts in a.m. and swept some cob-webs in barn. Quite cool.

June 29: Rain last night. Remained at place all day.

June 30: Sawed and chopped wood. Some mist and rain. Comfortable as to heat.

July 1: Re-boarded west pasture fence. 3 more hours of light rain.

July 2: Ditto yesterday. Light rain here but heavy rain to north, with disastrous hail.

July 3: Put wires on west pasture fence and picked raspberries in a.m. Hauled in old posts and boards and made ice cream in p.m. Hot!

July 4: Went to Lexington and spent the day there. A man by the name of Settles, took my hat at the barber shop and left his, making me $2 out, unless I can find him. Paid 25-cents for hair cut, 25-cents for dinner, 25-cents for ball game, 15-cents for show, a 5-cent lemonade, 15-cents for oranges, and 5-cents for peanuts. Excellent ball game.[28] Score Lexington 5, Odell 0. A Vandeville show in the evening, which was quite good.

July 5: After trying to plow corn and stopping on account of wet ground. I mowed weeds remainder of the day, all around all the corn fields. Hot and mostly clear. Good southwest wind.

July 6: Cloudy. Hot with a cool breeze. Remained at place all day.

July 7–8: Cultivated corn in west field. Chored. Quite hot.

July 9: Put wire on west pasture fence. Also worked up some wood and broke old boards for wood. Some rain in afternoon.

July 10: Mowed in orchard and picked cherries in a.m. Picked cherries and repaired barn lot fence in p.m. Clear most of the day.

July 11: Picked cherries and made hay.

July 12: Hauled 1 load of corn for Bound's and set a few posts in a.m. Hauled 1 load of corn for Berg and mowed weeds in p.m. Drew $5 from S.B. of Lexington.

July 13: Mostly clear and hot. Rode a few miles around country in afternoon.

July 14: Hauled corn for Berg in a.m. and broke boards in p.m. Hot

July 15: Hauled 1 load of gravel and 1 load of old posts in a.m. Helped put up hay carrier etc. in p.m. Mostly clear.

July 16: Sawed posts in a.m. and split wood and mowed weeds in p.m. Considerable rain.

July 17: Put up hay 'till late. Pa died at 6 p.m.[29]

July 18: At 8 a.m. received message of Father's death, yesterday. Came to Lexington and left for Chicago at 10:15, arriving in Chicago about 1:45p.m.. Left Chicago for home at 8:30 p.m. where I arrived at 1:30 a.m. Pa's death was very sudden. He having walked around not more than 15 minutes before he died. A very acute pain in stomach, doubtless affecting his heart, caused his death though he had been weak since Saturday night, last when he had an attack of indigestion. He had drank too much water in the p.m. of his death or yesterday. As it was an extremely warm day and he had been plowing corn in p.m. Slowly but tiring to him. Drew $75 from S.B. of Lex. Paid $1 for message to Shaffer, $1.50 to Post Office message, $3.31 for fare to Chicago, 50-cents for answer to telegram, 50-cents for hack fare, $4.65 =fare to Waterloo, 1-cent for paper, 20-cents for shave, 20-cents for dinner, $4 = shirts, collars, cuffs, etc. Rainy all day.

July 19: Slept a few hours in morning, then helped a little to prepare for funeral. Pa has kept very well and looks quite good. Will have a lock of his hair kept. William Ettinger arranged everything, for funeral which was at 2 p.m., at home. Evan. Minister, Rev. Walmer, assisted by Butler and Cocking held services.

Many old friends attended the funeral. Uncle Will and Issac North, Albert and wife, Mel and Jennie, Will McCrory and Lovina, Mamma Thumma, wife, daughter, and Mrs. Wiley, Sister Dell Wolcott, Charles, Mina, Cora, Ma and myself present.

July 20: Remained at home all day. Visited with Albert and Jen, Charles and Mina, Sister Dell and Cora and Ma. Paid $1 for meat and bread.

July 21: Went to phone office in morning with Cora. Placed flowers on Pa's grave. Pa had long ago said I should have his tools. So I will care for them. Paid $1.20 for mill feed, $22.55 grocery account in full. $1.50 for subscription to Press until July 1, 1903, 10-cents for bread.

July 22: Went to phone office with Cora. Remained about home most of the day.

July 23: Remained at home, most of the day. Dell left in p.m. Cora returned $40, that I had given her for Ma.

July 24: Saw Eli Williamson about Pa's tools and I will put them away Saturday next. Paid 50-cents for oil, $75 for Ettinger's undertakers bill, 30-cents for return to Auburn Junction, $1.35 return to Kimmel. Went to Wolf Lake today. Got $10 of Charles and paid Ettinger in full. After waiting at Kimmel for 2 hours, I rode out to Wolf Lake with Jonah Mayfield at 2:30p.m. Grandma is so far as I can see in usual health though awfully bloated. Remained with relatives. The burned district of Wolf Lake is being rebuilt. Spent afternoon visiting. Mostly hot.

July 25: Visited in morning, then left for Kimmel at 10:30 a.m. Paid $1 for rig, 10-cents for shave, and 5-cents cigar treat. Left Kimmel at 11:30 a.m. Went to McCroy's and remained most of the p.m. Came home to Waterloo at 6 p.m. Gave Harry 10-cents.

July 26: Worked around home and brought Pa's tools over and stored them in wood house. Will give Eli Williamson a nail set to remember him by. Somewhat lonesome.

Ma came back from W. Lake at 1p.m. Paid 25-cents for hauling tool chest to house.

July 27: Placed flowers on Pa's grave and visited Cora. At 4 p.m. Ma, Cora and I came to depot. Ma and I left for Chicago at 4:30. Paid $4.65=fare to Chicago, 86-cents for Ma to Chicago, 5-cents for paper, 1-cent weighing. We arrived in Chicago at 9 p.m. At 10 p.m. Mr. Hall, Mina's father came and remained until 11:15, when Ma took the Rock Island R.R. for Peoria. I then went with Mr. Hall to his office and slept on cot until 5 a.m.

July 28: Arose at 5 a.m. and remained with Mr. Hall until 6:45 when I left. Paid 15-cents for breakfast, 10-cents for fruit, $3.31 fare to Lexington. Left at 9 a.m. and got to Lexington about 12:30. Sent letter to Cora and walked out to F.J . Hinthorn. Helped shock a few oats. Hot.

July 29: Went with Hinthorn to Lexington this morning. He owed me for work $82.47 of which he paid $80. I deposited $80 in S.B. of Lex. Saw H. Hague, who was supplied with laborer at present. Then hired to Frank Condor for 1 month at $23. Hinthorn having no further use of a man at present. Paid 5-cents for treat for Hinthorn. Hot

July 30: Commenced work for Frank Condor in morning. Hauled manure.

July 31–Aug. 2: Hauled manure. Good news from Ma that she needs no operation.

Aug 3: Arose early and walked to Meadows, where I paid 15-cents for lunch, $1 for excursion to Peoria, for which place, I started at 7:50 a.m. Arrived there about 9:30 a.m. Paid 10-cents for a shine, 14-cents for lunch, 5-cents for a paper, 10-cents for street car fare. Went to see Ma and Mina and the babe and all the remainder of the folks. Pleasant time. Nice people and folks are fairly well. Left Peoria at 6:45 p.m. and arrived in Meadows about 8:30 and got to Condor's at 10.

Aug. 4: Hauled manure and harrowed yard and trimmed hedges. Comfortable weather

Aug. 5: Trimmed hedge in a.m. and went to Lex in p.m. Paid $2 for pair of shoes, 25-cents = ballgame, 5-cents = peanuts and 1-cent for a card. Dwight shut out Lexington in game. Hot and mostly clear.

Aug. 6-9: Trimmed hedge. Poisoned by poison oak. Heard from Ma and Cora.

Aug. 10: Remained at place most of the day.

Aug. 11: Mowed weeds.

Aug. 12: Helped thresh at Frank Mahon's. Oats threshed well. 60 acres today. 35-40 bu. per acre. Rain at dark.

Aug 13: Heavy rain last night and this morning. Split some wood in a.m. and loafed remainder of the day. Warm.

Aug. 14–16: Went to Lexington on 16th and paid 50-cents for a shirt, 25-cents for soap,10- cents for lemons and peanuts, and 10-cents for shave. Did but little work as there is but little to do. Poison about well. Have a headache.

Aug. 17: Remained at place. Still have headache.

Aug. 18-20: Worked but little as it is too wet to thresh.

Aug. 21–23: Threshed oats at Barnard's. Oats badly spoiled – growing and wet. Slow work. Avg. 35 bu.

Aug. 24: Sundayed with Jas. Huithorn. Pleasant day.

Aug. 25–29: Threshed oats at Wisner's, Lehrnan's, Condor's, Paines and Huithorn's Huithorn's were best oats of any around. 50 bushels per acre. Good quality. Threshed 1,825 bushels in p.m. for Hinthorn.

Aug. 30: Threshed for Travis. Quite warm.

Aug 31: Remained at place most of the day. Paid 25-cents for washing.

Sept. 1: Threshed at Strickland's. Fair weather. Oats average 32 bushels.

Sep.t 2: Threshed at H. Box's. Oats averaged less than 40 bushels per acre.

Sept. 3: Hauled manure from D. Condor's in a.m. and from home place in p.m. Settled with F. Condor in eve, receiving $27.40 in full of account.

Sept. 4: Drove to O. Ogden's to look for corn cutting job but found nothing. Went to Lexington in afternoon and saw S. Ogden who could tell nothing until Saturday. Put $25 in bank. Paid 8-cents for laundry, 25-cents for ice cream and nuts, $1 for watch. Returned to Condor's in eve.

Sept. 5: Saw Huithorn about work but he wants none before the first of next week. Came to town and paid 15-cents for lunch, 25-cents for supper, 35-cents for hair cut and shave. Paid 25-cents for show and 5-cents for nuts.

Sept. 6: Remained in town. Paid 50-cents for lodging, $1.00 for eating, and 5-cents for nuts. Mostly clear, sprinkle last night.

Sept. 7: Went to Noel Shaffer's in morning. Remained most of day. Will cut corn for him at 8-cents per shock, commencing tomorrow. Walked to Hinthorn's and Condor's places and got some clothes, then returned to Shaffer's. Paid 50-cents for washing.

Sept. 8–13: Cut about 165 shocks of corn. Worked steady except ¼ of Thursday p.m. when rain prevented. Went to Lexington on the eve of

13th and paid 75-cents for overalls, 10-cents for shave 10-cents=salve and 5-cents for peanuts. Returned at 9:30 o'clock.

SEPT. 14: Remained at place. Pleasant.

SEPT. 15–20: Cut corn most of time. Went to Chenoa the eve of the 15th to take Shaffer to the train. Warm for part of week cooler during latter. Cut and tied about 160 shocks. Went to Lexington in eve and paid 10-cents for shave and 5-cents for peanuts.

SEPT. 21: Remained at place most of the day. Paid 25-cents for washing.

SEPT. 22–27: Cut corn. Much rain. Cool.

SEPT. 28: Visited at Birlingmair's in p.m.

SEPT. 29–OCT 4: Cut corn part of the time. About completing the corn cutting here. I have cut and tied 370 shocks here and 89 on the Demp place- 459 in all amounting to $36.72. Went horseback to Chenoa, Saturday evening and drove rig home in which Shaffer and family rode in to town going to Pontiac. Much rain and mist.

OCT. 5: Remained at place all day. Cloudy some light rain

OCT. 6: Cut a little corn making 374 shocks here and 89 on Kemp's or 463 shocks in all, which at 8-cents per shock= $37.04. Hauled manure in p.m.

OCT. 7–11: Hauled manure. Went to Lexington on Saturday evening. 10-cents =shave

Oct. 12: Remained at place in a.m. and got my grip at Frank Condor's in p.m.

Oct. 13–16: Hauled manure.Went to Lexington in eve of 16th. Heard from Cora in Peoria. Paid 5-cents for peanuts. Purchased mittens and overalls for 74-cents. Hauled load of coal from Chenoa on the 15th.

Oct. 17: Hauled manure. Cloudy and cool, southeast wind.

Oct. 18: Walked to Lexington in morning and paid 10-cents for a shave, and drew $20 from S.B. of Lex. Went to Chenoa at 10 a.m. and remained there until 2:16 when I left for Peoria. Paid $1.95 for ticket to Peoria. Arrived at Peoria at 4:15. Walked through town to see decoration then rode out to Mrs. Baker's. Went to corn carnival buildings in evening. A large exhibit of corn and a highly decorated corn building about 150 ft sq. Paid 35-cents = street fare, 30-cents – entrance fee to corn palace, 5-cents for trinket.[30] Paid 10-cents for a shine.

Oct. 19: Took a walk to Glen Oak Park in a.m. At 12:20 came to Union Depot in time to miss the train by a block. Paid 5-cents for street car fare and gave Cora 50-cents for a present for Ella. Paid 1-cent for paper. Paid 25-cents for football game, 15-cents for lunch. Left for Chenoa at 6:45 p.m. Arrived at Chenoa at 8:30 p.m. Paid 15-cents for lunch, then waited until 12:25 for train to Lexington. Came to Shaffer's at 1:15 a.m. and retired in barn under blankets and hay.

Oct. 20–22: Hauled manure. Mostly cool and breezy.

Oct. 23–25: Shucked corn. Am to receive 2½ -cents for corn on home place and 2¾ for that on Kemp's. Went to Lexington on evening of the 25th and paid 5-cents for cards, 10 cents for a shave, 50-cents=shirt and

5-cents = rubberbands. Warm and clear except on 25th when light rain and clouds.

Oct. 26: Remained at place.

Oct. 27–Nov. 1: Shucked corn on Kemp place. Light rain.

Nov. 2: Remained at place.

Nov. 3–8: Shucked corn. Mostly weather fit to allow work. Went to town in eve of 8th and paid 75-cents for 1 doz. pair of mittens, 10-cents for salve, 5-cents peanuts and 19-cents = chance on a horse.

Nov. 9: Got my trunk at Huithorn's in morning and remained at place in p.m. Clear

Nov. 10–15: Shucked corn except mornings of 11th and 14th, when rain prevented.

Nov. 16: Remained at place most of day. Paid 45-cents for washing.

Nov. 17–22: Shucked corn most of time. Went to Lexington on 20th and had Dr. Wm'son take dirt from my eye which was highly inflamed.

Nov. 23: Remained at place in a.m. and visited Willis Shaffer's home in p.m.

Nov. 24–25: Shucked corn. Finished on the Kemp place. Will have about 1,000 bu. and will take elevator weight for it. Mostly cloudy, cool with northerly winds.

Nov. 26: Shucked corn until 2 p.m., when snow prevented work. Light snow in p.m.

Nov. 27: Thanksgiving. Remained at place all day. Went to Lexington in the evening and paid 65-cents for pocket knife, 35-cents for mitts and 10-cents for salve. Cold and 1 inch or more of snow.

Nov. 28–29: Shucked corn part of time. Rain to snow in a.m. of 29th after which it cleared. Went to Lex. in a.m. of 29th and paid 2-cents for postal cards.

Nov. 30: Clear and pleasant.

Dec. 1–5: Shucked corn most of time. Finished shucking for N.B. Shaffer on the 5th, having shucked 1,400 bu. in one crib and 321 bu. in another, besides 3 rail pens on Kemp's place for which, I will take elevator measure. Part of time quite warm. Went to Chas Rosseau in evening of the 5th and will shuck for him at 2½ -cents per bushel and board.

Dec. 6: Went to Rosseau in morning and shucked 30 bushel of corn when owing to balky team and snow, I quit for the day. 2 inches of snow after 10 a.m. This corn above, I put into crib with his. Went to Lexington in p.m. and paid 75-cents for 1 doz. pro-husking mitts and 72-cents for laundry, came out to Shaffer's and remain over Sunday.

Dec. 7: Spent the day at Shaffer's. Went to Rosseau's in evening. Cold.

Dec. 8: Loafed

Dec. 9–16: Hauled corn for Shaffer and at Rosseau's shelling Shucked corn a part of the time. Rough weather.

Dec. 17–19: Shucked corn and hauled corn for Rosseau at Shaffer's shelling.

Dec. 20: Loafed owing to rain. Went to Lexington in p.m.

Dec. 21: Passed day at Shaffer's.

Dec. 22: Shucked corn part of the time. Some snow. Wed. and Thurs. on account of snow, I did not shuck. Cold strong wind.

Dec. 23: Paid $1 for handkerchiefs for Aunt Dell. $1.60 for mufflers for Carter and Dewey. 10-cents for shave and 13-cents for postage.

Dec. 24–27: *GAP – When reading Bert's "Cash Paid Itemized Ledger" there are entries of train tickets purchased to his mother's home in Waterloo, Indiana. A trip to Kimmel and Wolf Lake, Indiana. Also books that were purchased for presents.*

Dec. 28: Remained at place

Dec. 29–31: Shucked corn. Warmer

Class in Dairying at Purdue, West Lafayette, Indiana.
Used with permission by Daniel Horn

Evangelical Church, Waterloo, Ind.

Evangelical Church attended by WBH's family

Corn Carnival charm was purchased at the Peoria Corn Carnival in 1902 by WBH.

Picture of Elijah Hill, used with permission by Karen Hill Mail

WATERLOO, INDIAN

ELIJAH HILL PASSED AWAY

EXPIRES VERY SUDDENLY FROM HEART FAILURE

WAS AN EXCELLENT SOLDIER

And Had Many Friends His Life's Career Has Been an Honorable One

The sudden death of Elijah Hill, which occurred last Thursday evening, was a shock to the community as no one knew that his health was critical. In fact he was only taken sick Saturday with his army complaints, and had so far recovered, that on Thursday evening, he took his scythe to cut some grass and weeds for his chickens, and suddenly collapsed with heart failure, expiring soon after he reached his house. The deceased had a good record as a soldier, was a number one mechanic, an expert mill wright, and a citizen who had few or no enemies. He was somewhat reserved in his habits, but was always genial and honest with those whom he became acquainted. He was an honorable citizen and his death takes from our midst one of the old time residents, who will be missed by all who knew him.

Elijah Hill

Elijah Hill's partial obituary
from the *Waterloo Press* 1902

1903

Take me out to the ballgame . . . Making peace, the American and National Baseball Leagues produce the outline of a deal in which each league would maintain independence but coordinate schedules. Henry Louis Gehrig was born on June 19th and the First World Series was played in August.

January 1, 1903: Shucked corn. Warm with some clouds

Jan. 2: Rainy. Loafed and went to Lexington. Colder

Jan. 3: Shucked corn. Finishing up the job.

Jan. 4: Remained at place.

Jan. 5: Settled with Rosseau, receiving 50-cents for hauling corn, $15 for 600 bushels, at 2½ -cents and $17.32=630 bushels, at 2¾ cents or $32.82 in all. Also settled with Shaffer in p.m., receiving check for $23.30 and note for $100. Deposited $35 in S.B. of Lexington. Paid 25-cents for treat, 11-cents for shave and card for 1-cent. 32-cents for washing.

Jan. 6: Went to Lexington in a.m. and drew $55 from bank also cashed check for $23.30. Packed trunk and took to Lexington in p.m. Paid $1.20 express on trunk to Chicago. After loading hogs and waiting until 9:30 p.m., I took freight caboose for Chicago.

Jan. 7: Arrived at Brighton Park at 4:30 a.m. Took the street car for Chicago. Left valise at L.S. & S.S. Depot and got breakfast and made some purchases at Fair store. Paid 5-cents for street car fare, 10-cents eating, $4 for pants, $1.35 for sweaters, $1.50 oversuit, $1.25 handkerchiefs, 20-cents for parcel checks, hair cut and shave = 35-cents and $4.65 for the fare home. After looking up trunk, I caught train for home at 2 p.m. and arrived in Waterloo at 6:04 p.m. Cold and stormy, snow.

Jan. 8: Paid 10-cents for bread. Remained at home, most of time.

Jan. 9–13: Remained at home, except for occasional town trips. Very cold and snow.

Jan. 14: Paid 25-cents for treat. Got another affidavit of Wm. Ettinger in furtherance and of Ma's pension claim.

Jan. 15: Butchered, etc. Warmer.

Jan. 20: Remained at home. Avg. 30F

Jan. 21–31: A simple daily routine of eating, sleeping, reading with a little work for exercise. Melting to warm, to colder on 30th 20-cents for sundries.

Feb. 1–8: An exercised passing of time. Paid 32-cents for sundries, 75-cents for money order for Mrs. Careton of Michigan. Loan to Cora = $6 Mostly warm for season. 6 inches of snow on the night of 7th.

FEB. 9–15: Snow mostly gone on 15th. Ordered $3.55 worth of goods from A.M. Ward and Co. Cora assuming payment. Order was sent on 12th.

FEB. 16–17: Very cold with 4" snow on night of 15th and morning of 17th. Paid $1.75 for freight and butter. Freight being for Cora's bedroom suit.

FEB. 18–19: Continued cold. Routine of loafing.

FEB. 20: Beginning to warm. Paid 15-cents for varnish.

FEB. 21–23: Melting just a little. Pd 29-cents freight, on goods from A.M. Ward and Co.

FEB. 24–28: Trimmed trees etc. Paid 40-cents for butter.

MARCH 1–10: Cleaned up trash and brush. Trimmed trees, dug cellar drain, etc. Mostly warm. Paid 5-cents for chalk.

MARCH 11–14: Went to Auburn to visit McCrory's on the 13th. Saw Lester Till, who is doing well. He built a nice dwelling the past summer. Paid 25-cents for haircut, 10-cents for postal cards, 25-cents for railroad fare. Paid 40-cents for butter and received 50-cents.

MARCH 15: Passed time by reading.

MARCH 16: Bid goodbye to family. Went to Chicago at 10:30 a.m. Arrived at 3:45 p.m. Paid 65-cents = fare to Chicago and $3.75 to Bloomington.

MARCH 17: Arrived in Bloomington at 3:25 a.m. Remained there until 8 a.m., when I came to Shirley from where I rode and walked to L. H. Kerrick's place, 5 miles south of Shirley. I will work for $22 per month. He is an extensive breeder of Angus cattle and has about 2,000 acres of land. It is to learn the operation of a large place that I came here, as the wages are meager and while the surroundings are pleasant, being unacquainted, it is not as pleasant to be here as where I am better acquainted. There are about 300 hundred pure bred angus and 150 or more grades. About 700 acres will be put to corn and 250 acres to oats, the remainder being pasture and grass and rented land. Paid 15-cents for telephoning. While at Bloomington, I paid $3.75=boots, $1.50 = shirt, overalls and galluses, $1 =clock, 10-cents for breakfast, 17-cents for railroad fare to Shirley. Drove into Shirley in p.m. and got my trunk. Warm and mostly clear.

March 18: Commenced work this morning. Hauling husked corn from field to crib. Strong south wind with some sunshine.

March 19: Hauled corn in a.m. and all sorts of work in p.m. Short heavy rain in evening.

March 20–31: Made fence, fed cattle, harrowed stalks, etc. Some cold weather mingled with the warmer- but little rain.
Attended basket supper, 5½ miles east of here on the evening of the 28th. Paid 25-cents for ice cream.

March 22: Fed cattle = $1.25

March 29: Fed cattle = .50

April 1: Tested a drain drill, which would not work. Disked in p.m. Warm.

April 2: Disked in a.m. dilled oats in p.m. The disk drill worked very well in dry disked ground.

April 3: Rain. Choring

April 4–18: Hauled lumber, On 5th Sundayed i.e. chored, read, shaved, and rested. Dilled oats finishing on the 9th, repair work, hauled hay and straw, built fences.

April 19–25: Hauled manure and plowed during most of the time. Received 20-cents for 2 cakes of shaving soap and paid $1 for washing. Cool most of the time.

April 26: Loafed. A very pleasant day- sunshine and warm.

April 27 – May 2 Plowed most of the week. Received 10-cents for stamps sold. Ground too wet. Plow pulls heavily. Ground is being plowed very shallow.

May 3: Passed Sunday as usual, reading, etc.

May 4–9: Rubbed ground most of the time. Ground in cloddy condition and hard to work into shape.

May 10: Warm pleasant, clear day.

May 11–16: Rubbed or dragged ground about all week. Dry and warm.

May 17: Attended Sunday School this a.m. Put 5-cents in collection. S.S. commenced last Sunday. 29 were present.

May 18–24: Rubbed or dragged ground, planted corn. Cleaned up around place and on 23rd went to Bloomington. Paid 45-cents for hair cut, shave and shine. Paid 20-cents for dinner, 10-cents for Malena salve, 25-cents for Bay Rum, 5-cents =soda, 2-cents for paper, $1 shirt, 10-cents =shoe polish, 25-cents for head ache tablets, 35-cents for straw hat. Loaned Ed Peltz a V of which he returned $3

May 25–30: Rain most of the time. Worked at various jobs and remained at place.

May 31: Sundayed in usual way.

June 1–7: Worked at various jobs. Quite wet.

June 8–13: Cultivated corn and on 13th in p.m. ground feed. Loaned J. Price 50-cents and E. Oeltz, 50-cents. Price returning 35-cents and Oeltz returning 40-cents.

June 14: Attended S.S. in morning. Read and went to Funk's Grove in eve.

June 15: Received box of rosebuds from Cora, but all were dried having been on the road over 3 days.

June 16–29: Cultivated corn except on the 18th when I went to Bloomington to get lumber dressed. Loaned Disher $3.25, paid 53-cents for stamped envelopes, and 35-cents for hair cut and shave. On 19th received of Price 15-cents in full and also $3.35 in full from Oeltz.

June 21: Paid 5-cents to Sunday School collection. Attended township Sunday School convention in p.m. at M.E. Ilvain. Paid $1 for washing.

June 22–27: Mowed weeds and made hay in Sec 4.

June 28: Attended S.S. 5-cents to collection. Warm

June 29: Went to Bloomington in morning to see Ringling Bros. Show. Paid 40-cents = railroad fare, 5-cents=fans, 40-cents eating, 10-cent=magazine. Returned in eve. Hot. Good show! Found 5-cents,

June 30–July 3: Made hay, ground feed and mowed meadow. Dishler repaid loan. Mostly hot.

July 4: Went to Lexington in morning. Paid $1.10 for railroad fare, 25-cents for dinner, 10-cents for malena salve, 25-cents for the ball game, and 35-cents for lodging. Ball game pretty good. Bloomington Pastures winning 7-2. Took supper at Ino McColm's. A very good moving picture show given in evening. Mostly of fire department of Peoria and their work. McKinley's last acts, etc. These pictures were thrown on an elevated screen in the street.
Hot in a.m. and rainy and hot in p.m.

July 5: Visited Shaffer's today. Paid 25-cents for breakfast. Hot and clear. Came to Kerrick's farm in eve. Good working experience here but miss the gang.

July 6–18: Worked in hay. Mostly cool weather considerable rain during latter part of the week. Grandma is failing rapidly Her leg has broken and gangrene set in, though she may live for months yet.

July 19: Drove to Shirley in a.m. and a few miles east in p.m. Pleasant day. Paid $1 for last month's washing.

July 20: Made hay i.e. mowed and raked.

July 2–25: Worked in hay and oats. Took bull to Heyworth on 24 and brought back a load of coal. Paid 10-cents for bananas.

July 26: Grandma is better. Remained at home, reading. Very hot and clear.

July 27–29: Worked in hay mowing weeds, etc. Finished putting up hay crop on morning of the 29th. Good rain today.

July 30–Aug. 1: Worked at various jobs.

Aug 2: Spent day at place.

Aug 3–9: Hauled manure most of the time.

Aug. 10–15: Hauled manure, threshed oats. Oats avg. 30-35 bushels per acre. On 11th I received $25 on account with Kerrick by Disher.

Aug. 16: At place all day. Paid $1 for last month's washing.

Aug. 17–22: Hauled manure and sowed rye in p.m. of 22nd. Went to Heyworth in eve of 18th. Paid 35-cents for shave and hair-cut and 20-cents =ice cream. I was 27 years old on the 21st.

Aug 23–29: Hauled manure. I hauled from 8 to 10 loads per day. The distance is from ½ mile to – length of haul. Very HOT!

Aug. 30: Sundayed as usual.

Aug. 31–Sept. 1: Hauled manure.

Sept. 2: Went to Bloomington with oats and returned with oil cake. Loaned Harris $4. Paid for Kerrick $2.35. Paid $3.50 for shoes and 10-cents for pencil.

Sept. 3–5: Busy at work.

Sept. 6: Sundayed

Sept. 7–12: Worked on seed house, most of time.

Sept. 13: Sundayed

Sept. 14–19: Various kinds of work. Loaned Disler 75-cents which I had received from Ed in repayment in full of loan. $3.10 is now due me from Kerrick, for money advanced to him.

Sept. 20: Sunday as usual.

Sept. 21–26: Hauled corn to Funk's Grove elevator from Kerrick's farm.

Sept. 27: Sundayed as usual.

Sept. 28–30: Hauled corn. Finished hauling corn from Kerrick's place.

Oct. 1–2: Went to Springfield on 1st and returned on the 2nd. Rec'd $10 from Disher for Kerrick and $10 from Harris as repayment of $4, which he owed me, leaving me owing him $6. Paid $1.50 for fare to Springfield and return. $1 =Fair entrance, 75-cents for eating, 75-cents for lodging and $1 for nick-nacks.

Oct. 3-10: Cut corn. Worked in seed house and hauled and baled hay.

Oct. 11: Passed Sunday as usual.

Oct. 12: Hauled baled hay and piled old hay in p.m. Learning experience here but need to move on.

Oct. 13: Came to Shirley in a.m. and took train to Bloomington. Saw Kerrick and rec'd $113.50 in full of account. Rec'd $5 from Ed Peltz and $1 from Harris in full for borrowed money this squaring me with all of the Kerrick people. Gave Ed Oeltz 25-cents for wash woman, paying her in full. Also gave him what clothes I had there. Sold cake of soap for 10-cents. Paid 17-cents for fare to Bloomington, 10-cents=rubber cement, 35-cents for grub, 49-cents for fare to Lexington, 75-cents for lodging, 5-cents for peanuts and 5-cents for paper. Stopped at night at Clawson's.

Oct. 14: Walked 3 miles north of town and back in a.m. Corn is green and some very weedy. In p.m. went to Hinthorn's to put up over night. Some rain.

Oct. 15: Hired to Hinthorn at $1 per day until corn husking then 2¾ cents per bushel. Brought belongings here in eve.

Oct. 16: Picked apples and dug potatoes. Cloudy and cool.

Oct. 17: Dug potatoes and hauled one load of gravel. Very cool.

Oct. 18: Passed Sunday at place.

Oct. 19–22: Hauled manure and gather pop-corn. Pd. 50-cents for mittens.

Oct. 23: Helped thresh mullet.

Oct. 24: Hauled dirt and manure. Went to Lexington in p.m. Paid $2.50 for underclothes and shirt, 50-cents for Vaseline, tablet, soap and rubber bands.

Oct. 25: Remained at place all day.

Oct. 26–31: Husked corn in the west field all week. Paid 55-cents for washing and mittens.

Nov. 1: Sundayed as usual.

Nov. 2–7: Husked corn most of the time. Rainy for part of week. Corn molding slightly owing to warm weather and green corn. Did not husk corn in p.m. of 6th on account of spoiling corn.

Nov. 8: Quiet and restful day passed.. A fine day.

Nov. 9–14: Husked corn in west field about all week. On 13th, I paid 75-cents for mittens and 25-cents for washing, 1½ days work in east field. On the 14th, I went to Lexington and paid 25-cents bay rum and malena salve.

Nov. 15: Read and rested.

Nov. 16–21: Husked corn in east field. Crib getting nearly full.

Nov. 22: Pleasant day. Remained at place.

Nov. 23–28: Husked corn most of time. Husked but ½ as much on 26th on account of sore finger. Thanksgiving as usual. Went to Lexington in p.m. of 28th after ½ inches of snow in morning. Hair cut and surged 50-cents, washing,=53-cents.

Nov. 29: Cloudy cold and snowy. Remained at place.

Nov. 30–Dec. 5: Shucked corn during favorable weather which was all week. Monday-99 bushels + Tuesday-94 bushels+Wed.-96 bushels + Thurs. 101+ Friday 99+ Sat. 90+.

Dec. 6: Remained at place.

Dec. 7–8: Shucked corn for Hinthorn. Warmer
Finished at Hinthorn's on 8th. Which with 7½ days worked at $1 per day and old acct of $2.47= $100.58 due me from Hinthorn. Will settle when I got through shucking.

Dec. 9: Shucked corn at Frank Condor's. 90 bushels.

Dec. 10: Storming so did not shuck.

Dec. 11: Shuck corn at Condor's - 90 bushels.

Dec. 12: Rain in a.m. turning to snow in p.m. and strong north wind. Thermometer dropping to 16F

Dec. 13: Remained at Condor's

Dec. 14: Shucked 45 bushels today. 4-6 inches of snow on ground. Work slow and somewhat disagreeable. Rec'd check for $6.75 from Condor for work shucking – in full of account.

Dec. 15: Returned Hinthorn team and wagon which I'd been using at Condor's and in p.m. went to Lexington. Cashed check given by Condor for $6.75. Sent "Evening Post" to Aunt Dell Averill for 1 year. Also received my subscription to same for 1 year. Both costing $2.50 plus 3-cents for sending by P.O. Money Order. Came out to N.B. Shaffer's in evening. Good visit.

DEC. 16–19: Shucked corn in p.m. of 16th and all 17th, 18th. Cold and snow on ground – quite deep.

DEC. 20: Spent today at Shaffer's.

DEC. 21–22: Finished shucking corn at Shaffer's shucking in p.m. of 22nd at Willis Shaffer's. Warmer.

DEC. 23: Settled with Shaffer having husked 29 bushels and rec'd therefore $8.88. He's paying me 88-cents with check , which I cashed in a.m. Paid 26-cents for washing, $1.75 for 5 handkerchiefs, 25-cents for pair of mittens for Wm. Shaffer Jr. Returned to Shaffer's home in the eve.

DEC. 24: Hauled straw most of the day. Rainy in morning, turning colder. Paid 50-cents for candy.

DEC. 25: Received treat and handkerchief from Shaffer's. Snowing and grown cold. Hard north wind driving snow -- a regular blizzard. 10 degrees at dark. In evening we played "Flinch"[31] until 12:30 a.m. Great fun!

DEC. 26–31: Got a load of coal. Made ready for shelling. Shoveled corn to sheller and transferred corn from rail pens to double crib. Some snow flurries.

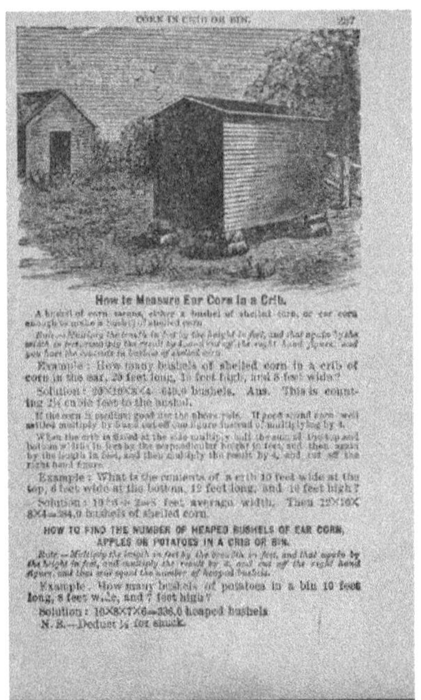

How to Measure Ear Corn in a Crib.

[illegible]

Example: How many bushels of shelled corn in a crib of corn in the ear, 20 feet long, 10 feet high, and 8 feet wide?

Solution: [illegible] bushels. Ans. This is counting 2½ cubic feet to the bushel.

[illegible]

Example: What is the contents of a crib 10 feet wide at the top, 6 feet wide at the bottom, 12 feet long, and 10 feet high?

Solution: [illegible] feet average width. Then 12×10×8×4=384,0 bushels of shelled corn.

HOW TO FIND THE NUMBER OF HEAPED BUSHELS OF EAR CORN, APPLES OR POTATOES IN A CRIB OR BIN.

[illegible]

Example. How many bushels of potatoes in a bin 10 feet long, 8 feet wide, and 7 feet high?

Solution: 10×8×7×6=336,0 heaped bushels

N.B.—Deduct ½ for shuck.

A page taken from WBH's book, *The Busy Man's Friend Book*, 1896. The book contains legal and business forms, warnings about swindling schemes, how to measure everything, including plowing, (distance traveled), measurement tables for corn and grain and even how to figure the height of a tree.

Ringling Brothers Circus attended by WBH in 1903 in Bloomington, Illinois. Courtesy from Bloomington, Illinois Historical Society

1904

J. M.. Barrie's Peter Pan's first stage performance premiered on December 27, 1904. The World's Exposition was hosted by St. Louis. The United States took over construction of the Panama Canal and on October 4th the NYC subway opened with 350,000 people riding the 9.1 mile track.

January 1 – 1904: Moved corn all day

Jan. 2: Snow and cold. Chored Paid 10-cents for shave, 10-cents for Malena, 3-cents postal cards, 28-cents for washing.

Jan. 3: At place. Not feeling well on account cold and grippe. Cold.

Jan. 4: Chored – preparing for butchering in a.m. and moved corn in p.m. Clear and a bit warmer.

Jan. 5: Helped butcher 6 hogs. Very cold with south wind. Took J. S. Amos to Lexington in evening. He is leaving for Ohio on account of his mother's illness. Loaned him $10.

Jan. 6: Helped finish the butchering today. Not feeling well.

Jan. 7: Feeling bum. Went to Lexington in p.m. Paid $1 for Peruna[32] and 15-cents for lemons. Still cold.

Jan. 8: Finished moving the corn and hauled cob the remainder of the day. Warmer and clear.

Jan. 9: Chored 10-cents for shave.

Jan. 10: At place all day.

Jan. 11–12: Chored.

Jan. 13: Attended sale at Schopp's, Ino. Stock sold. Well. Very cold.

Jan. 14: Helped Willis Shafer haul straw. Pleasant day. Noel Shaffer bought 31 pigs at Beasley's sale.

Jan. 15: Brought hogs home from Beasley's in a.m. and shoveled corn to sheller at Holsenpiller's in p.m. Cold.

Jan. 16: Shoveled corn 'till 3 p.m.

Jan. 17: At place in morning. Got clothes at Hinthorn's in p.m.

Jan. 18: Hauled hay to Wick at Lexington, owing to carrier not working did not get wagon unloaded. Received $2 from Holsenpiller.

Jan. 19: Went to Lexington and unloaded hay then brought wagons out. Paid 10-cents for a shave. Rained for 1 hour.

Jan. 20: Rain all day.

JAN. 21: Cloudy- very high water owning to amount which fell and ground being frozen; all rain off at once. Paid $1 for Peruna.

JAN. 22: Hauled hay to Lexington. Cold.

JAN. 23: Chored. Went to Lexington in p.m. Hinthorn claimed that I had made no allowance for poll tax. Re/worked for him. I paid him $1.50 by making that allowance. Believe however that I have paid it twice. Received $99 from Hinthorn full of account. Deposited $100 in State Bank of Lexington. Paid 31-cents for washing. Clear.

JAN. 24: At place

JAN. 25–27: Snowed Cold –9F Jan 26 -7F Chored.

JAN. 28: Hauled hay to Lexington. Clear and cold.

JAN. 29–30: Hauled corn for N.B. Shaffer, at Willis Shaffer's shelling in p.m. Went to Lexington on 30th . Received $10 from J. S. Amos= payment of loan. Withdrew $120 from S.B. of Lex. and put $100 in Home State Bank.

JAN. 31: At place all day.

FEB. 1: Went to Lexington in a.m. and paid 50-cents for barbering, 15-cents for malena and Vaseline. Also made arrangements to get ticket to Waterloo, Indiana. Packed clothes and took them to train in p.m. Paid $7.96 for ticket. Settled with Shaffer in eve, receiving $9 for work and $5 as 1 year's interest on note or up to Jan 2, 1904.

FEB. 2: Got up at 1:45 a.m. and after dressing, I walked to Lexington. Left for Chicago at 3:15 a.m. and arrived at 7:45. Paid 33-cents for breakfast and lunch. Paid $16.43 for goods from Ward's, 10-cents for a shave, 5-cents=paper and $1 for a hat. Left at 2 p.m. for Waterloo and arrived at 7:40 p.m. which was an hour late due largely to a wait west of LaPorte. Cold and stormy.

Feb. 3: Cold and partly cloudy

Feb. 4: A breath, breakfast and a sleep.

Feb. 5: Ditto yesterday. Warmer with some mist.

Feb. 6–8: A passing of time with Ma.

Feb. 9: Went to Wolf Lake today. Grandma continues to get bloated larger and naturally not to be as strong, as formerly. Paid 30-cents fare to Auburn Junction and return from Auburn. Paid $1.35 return fare to Kimmel from Auburn Junction and 25-cents hack fare.

Feb. 10: Visited. Good to see family.

Feb.11: Returned home. Paid 5-cents for railroad fare from Auburn Jct. to Auburn, 29-cents for freight on A.M Ward goods and $2.00 for subscription to daily Rec. Herald, for 6 months. Received as present from Grandma and my Aunt's, a watch fob.

Feb. 12–19: At home. –13F

Feb. 20–25: At home. Paid $1.81 for goods from Ward's.

Feb. 26–March 11: At home Cold to warm and springy.

March 12–22: At home. 8 inches of snow, then springy.

March 23: Came to Chicago on #157. Arrived at 3:20 p.m. went to Art Institute and around town. Paid $7.71 fare to Lexington, 50-cents =sasprilla, 50-cents barbering, 80-cents = lodging & grub. Received $160 from home.

March 24: Came to Lexington at 12:28 p.m. Put $100 in Home State Bank and $50 in S.B. of Lex. Went out to N.B. Shaffer's in eve. Heavy rain at night.

March 25: Went to Lex in a.m. Gave J.B. Clawson $10 to secure board bill until, I leave town.

March 26: Cold snow flurries. Paid 10-cents shave, 15-cents=collar, $2.55 clothes, 10-cents = malena. Hired to John Pils until August 1, at $25 per month. He having the privilege of keeping not longer or until corn husking commences at same wages, by giving me 2 weeks notice. Am not hired to him after corn husking commences. Am to begin work Monday, March 28th. Took my clothes and self to his place 3½ miles, north east of Lexington.

March 27: Remained at place all day choring reading. Etc. Cool.

March 28–29: Worked on bridge over stream in pasture.

March 30–31: Worked on hedge a short time when rain stopped my work. On 31st worked on wood pile. Warm with rain at night.

April 1: This being "Good Friday", a holiday among these Germans. I went to Lexington. Paid 25-cents for dinner, 10-cents for a shave, 1-cent for postal card. Cool and windy. Rec'd $8.75 from J.B. Clawson=balance due me.

April 2: Cut wood and cleaned yard. Cool strong west wind.

April 3: Easter. I remembered it with 4 eggs for breakfast. Fine clear crisp day. At place all day.

April 4: Sharpened disks in a.m. and piled hedge in p.m. Warm.

April 5: Drove colts and scattered and hauled manure.

April 6: Drove colts, hauled oats and disks to field and tore up old platform.

April 7: Drove colts, cleaned berry patch and hauled straw. Cool and windy.

April 8: Rained last night and more or less all day. Drove colts in and sorted potatoes in p.m.

April 9: Snowy and misty, most of the day. Sorted potatoes in a.m. and greased harness in p.m. Cold.

April 10: Remained at place all day. Pil's went to church – gone all day nearly.

April 11–12: Greased harness and disked with spading harrow. Ground very wet.

April 13: Disked. Warmer

April 14: Spaded. Finished 40 acre piece and commenced on 60 acres south piece. Hard freeze last night.

April 15: Spaded. Very cold and strong wind.

April 16: Hauled manure in a.m. and spaded in p.m. Clear but cool Ground frozen to hard last night to permit it's being worked in a.m. Went to Lexington in eve and paid 52-cents = laundry, and 10-cents for a shave.

April 17: Remained at place all day. Clear.

April 18: Finished spading in oats in morning. Harrowed stalks in p.m. Cool.

April 19: Harrowed and raked stalks today.

April 20: Put stacked hay into barn.

April 21: Hauled manure and plowed using a new I.D. gang. Runs as easy as any gang of the kind. Plows have no landside.

April 22: Plowed all day.

April 23: Raked stalks. Finished the stalk raking for the year at this farm. Warm and clear until 3p.m.

April 24: Rain last night. A heavy and considerable down pour. Pil's mother being sick the whole family went away last eve and Henry Pil's are batching today.

April 25: Hauled a few loads from old straw stack. Cold rain.

April 26: Rain all last night and until 8a.m. Hauled manure from old straw stack and from barn to pasture.

April 27: Cut seed potatoes and plowed.

April 28: Plowed sod meadow. Plows hard and to wet.

April 29: Plowed and hauled manure

April 30: Hauled manure in a.m. and plowed. Shave=10-cents, 10-cents for fruit, 10-cents=drugs and 50-cents for shirt.

May 1: Remained at place.

May 2–7: Plowed with gang breaking plow. Most of the soil is close and heavy breaking hard partly caused by being too wet. Went to Lexington, Saturday evening and paid $1 for sansaparilla, 39-cents for washing and 35-cents for barbering. Weather is warming up to the season.

May 8: Remained at place in a.m. Walked over to Shafer's in afternoon.

May 9–12: Plowed and harrowed. Low ground is very cloddy.

May 13–18: Disked and harrowed on South 80 acres. Ground works up well. Cold and cloudy with northwest wind.

May 19: Sister Cora's 29th birthday anniversary. Harrowed all day on 50 acre field. Finished planting corn today.

May 20: Reharrowed 50 acre field today. Warmer and clear.

May 21: Harrowed in south 80 acres in a.m. and went to Lexington in p.m. The boss giving us a half holiday. Drew $10 from Home State Bank. Got a shave=10-cents, 69-cents for laundry, 5-cents =nuts, 25 -cents soap, $2.00 for a stick pin for Aunt Dell, 50-cents for Sunday hat, 10-cents for lemons and 10-cents for malena. Returned to town in eve to band concert.

May 22: Very windy. Warm mostly clear. Sold a coat hanger for 5-cents.

May 23–24: Harrowed until 9 a.m. when I finished harrowing for this year. Also, cut stock in a.m. Helped grade roads in p.m. Very warm and clear.

May 25: Painted wagon and took farm machinery apart in a.m. and in p.m. put machinery away. Plowed and hoed potatoes in garden.

May 26–27: Hauled corn first for Frank Watson and on 27th for J. J. Pils. Corn mostly of poor quality.

May 28: Hauled corn in a.m. for Mr. Breese and replanted corn in west field in p.m.

May 29: Cloudy and light rain over ½ day time.

May 30: Ma's 52nd birthday anniversary. Replanted corn in west field. Field is badly infested with vines.

May 31: Replanted corn in same field as yesterday. Drying rapidly.

June 1–3: Cultivated corn. Using surface cultivators. Ground cloddy and weedy. Not a very good job being done in cultivating. Rain at 4 p.m. on 3rd.

June 4: Some rain in a.m. Cut willow poles for chicken roosts and hauled bedding a.m. and in p.m. Went to Lexington and paid 45-cents for washing and 15-cents for a shave.

June 5–11: Cultivated corn from 2½ acres to 10 acres per day according to conditions of ground and weeds. Finished getting over all of it the first time on the 11th. Twenty five acres are badly infested with vines and twenty five with grass. Went to Lexington the evening of the 11th. Paid 23-cents for washing and 10-cents for a shave. On the 8th, I paid 58-cents for a money order for one year's subscription of Union Gospel News and 2-cents for postage. A clear and pleasant week.

June 12: Remained at place. Clear and hot.

June 13–18: A steady week of corn cultivation. Have crossed all but 45 acres and plowed 25 acres for the third time. Mostly hot and very dusty the latter part of the week. Went to Lexington on the eve of the 18th and paid 15-cents for shave and 15-cents for washing. Also purchased a sansaprilla for $1.

June 19: Remained at place.

June 20–23: Cultivated corn. Dry and warm

June 24–25: Pulled smart weeds and morning glory vines except in p.m. of the 25th, when I went to Lexington. Washing=23-cents, 15-cents for a shave, 50-cents=drawers. Hot.

June 26: Spent most of the day at Shafer's.

June 27–28: Cultivated corn in 50 acre field and S 80a.

June 29: Pulled vines from corn hills. Rain an hour or more in the morning.

June 30–July 1: Cultivated corn. Ground works nicely, very fine and clear.

July 2: Finished "laying by" the 80a in a.m. and mowed weeds along road by 80a in p.m. Also weeded in strawberry bed. Went to Lexington in evening and paid 10-cents for shave. Cora and Ma will be in Peoria, a week from tomorrow. So I will go over to Peoria for a visit.

July 3: Remained at place all day. Quite hot and windy from southwest.

July 4: Spent the day in Lexington. Paid 35-cents for grub and 25-cents for ball game. Gambling was run wide open. I had a headache in late evening.

July 5–7: Cultivated corn and mowed weeds around yards. Hot.

July 9: Hauled manure and plowed corn. Went to Lexington and got a shave and haircut = 35-cents, lemons were 10-cents and 23-cents for my laundry.

July 10: Remained at place. Clear and hot.

July 11: Cultivated corn until 3:30 p.m. when rain prevailed further cultivation.

July 12: Stored cultivators and repaired bridge in morning, mowing grass in afternoon.

July 13: Cut grass and hauled hay for Rosseau.

July 14: Only chored in a.m. and turned hay in p.m. Rain.

July 15: Hauled manure and hay. We put in 9 "loads" in p.m. Headache in eve, due to heat.

July 16: Made hay. Took out 14 loads from the fields. Went to Lexington in evening and heard Chenoa band concert. 5-cents for peanuts. Very hot today, but a good breeze was going most of the time. Clear.

July 17: At place.

July 18: Mowed grass here and at Rosseau's. Hot and breezy.

July 19: Put up hay at Rosseau's. His meadow made less that ¾ per acre.

July 20: Pitched hay at home place. Quite hot.

July 21: Reraked meadow and hauled manure in a.m. Shocked oats in p.m. Oats are very green on the low ground.

July 22: Hauled corn for S. Hefner to Lexington. Pleasant.

July 23: Shocked oats. Pleasant temperature. Went to Lexington for shave 10-cents, $1 Sasaparilla and 31-cents for washing.

July 24: Remained at place.

July 25–27: Shocked oats.

July 28: Shocked oats 'till noon and cut oats at Henry Pils in p.m. Weather for the most part cool.

July 29: Cut and shocked oats today.

July 30: Hauled manure. Went to Lexington in evening. Received from John Pils $5.00. Purchased drawers for 50-cents and 75-cents for overalls.

July 31: Arose at 4 a.m. and after dressing, I rode to Chenoa through a rain which began at 4 a.m. and lasted until 8:30. Put horse in feed barn and at 7:46 left for Peoria on T.P.& W. Arrived in Peoria about 9:30 a. and took the car for Maywood Avenue, where I passed the day with Ma, Cora and Charles and family. William, Jr. is a 45 lb.er and a nice boy. Left Peoria at 6:55 p.m. Got rig and drove home, retiring at 10 p.m. Paid $1 for R.R. fare, 5-cents for street car and 50-cents for horse feed and care.

Aug 1: Hauled manure. Henry Pils left today and will work for Straw, south of Lexington.

Aug 2: Built a fence around hay stack and commenced threshing at Al Harmon's. I ran a rack-wagon. Oats are very heavy and good quality. Yielding 35-40 bushels per acre.

Aug 3–6: Threshed at Al Harmon's, Frank Watson's, Gus Shultz, H. Alper's and Robert Vaughn's.
Thus far but little delay has been experienced, the oats threshing out well and yielding from 30-50 bushels per acre.

Aug 7: Remained at place in the morning and visited Shaffer's in p.m. Temperate to warm.

Aug. 8–13: Threshed at Vaughn's, Williams, Caldwell's, Siren's, Bierman's, Marc's and Linden and Elders'. No stop except a 1 hour delay at Elders' caused by rain. Dry and cool until Saturday. Rain passed around us several times.

Aug. 14: Clear and hot.

Aug. 15–17: Threshed at Adreon's, Pil's and Bierman's. Hauled oats to town in a.m. of 16th and paid 35-cents for washing.

Aug. 18: Threshed at Bierman's finishing about 3 p.m. after which I hauled a load of corn for Berryman. Quite hot most of the time.

Aug. 19: Rain slowly. Fixed fence etc. during a part of the day.

Aug. 20: Hauled in bedding and pulled butter-privets in a.m. Went to Lexington in p.m. A sale of Montana horses commenced in p.m. but after disposing of a half-dozen, the sale was stopped owing to low prices realized. All were light horses and very few were broken. $61 was the top price of those sold. Paid 15-cents for a shave. Hot and clear.

Aug. 21: This is the 28th anniversary of my birth. Cloudy and warm. Remained at place all day.

Aug. 22: Cleaned around straw stacks today until 4 p.m. After which I trimmed hedge along road.

Aug. 23: Hauled manure and corn for William Lyider. Purchased postal cards for 5-cents.

Aug. 24: Hauled corn for Al Harmon in a.m. and for old man Harmon in p.m. I recv'd a sickening letter from a relative of Pils, indicating that she is "partially cracked in the attic". Wanted me to come to see her but I think I shall not, to put it more emphatically.

Aug. 25: Hauled manure in a.m. and helped Rosseau thresh oats in p.m.

Aug. 26: Scooped corn for Clinton Elder in a.m. and hauled 1 load of corn for Elder and two for M. March in p.m.

Aug. 27: Hauled corn for M. Marc –4 loads all day. Cool nights for a considerable time past and cool air all day. Street fair in progress in Chenoa this week.

Aug. 28: Clear

Aug. 29–30: Hauled manure.

Aug. 31: Plowed ditch through pasture in morning and scraped out dirt from ditch remainder of the day.

Sept. 1: Hauled manure and scraped out ditch. Very hot in sun.

Sept. 2: Scraped out ditch finishing it late in evening.

Sept. 3: Hauled manure all day. Went to Lexington in eve and paid 35-cents for barbering.

Sept. 4: Hazy. At place all day.

Sept. 5: Trimmed hedges.

Sept. 6: Hauled 2 loads of corn for Shultz. Trimmed hedge.

Sept. 7: Finished trimming hedge in morning, also repaired fence and mowed weeds. Cut butter privets in potato and corn ground. Cleaned ditch.

Sept. 8: J. Pils and I drove to Fairbury and back. Attended the fair. Good crowd but poor exhibits. Fair racing. 25-cents for dinner, 25-cents entrance fee, 15-cents for a show, 10-cents for seat in grand-stand, and a 5-cent sandwich. Brought a young mare of Pils back from Fairbury where she was being broken to drive. Foggy in morning.

Sept. 9: Hauled coal for Lexington. (2 loads) Hot sun

Sept. 10: Hauled coal in a.m. and played ball at H. Rowland's in p.m. The game was between our threshing gang and Prairie Hall. Our threshing gang won, in our favor 23-17.

Sept. 11: Cloudy and some rain

Sept. 12: Hauled load of lumber from J. J. Pils farm, west of Ballard to this place. Mowed weeds in p.m. Drove to Lexington at 11p.m. taking Pils and wife and several other German people to the depot. They are leaving on the 12:41, on the southbound train for St. Louis.

Sept. 13–16: I dismantled two old buildings besides doing chores as no one but me was here. A considerable frost on Tuesday, 13th night.

Sept. 17: Sent a check for $25 to S. B. of Lexington for which they send same amount in form of draft to Cora M. Hill, Waterloo, Indiana.

Worked on old building until noon. After hauling a load of corn and fodder, I drove to Lexington to get Pils and family who returned from St. Louis at 5 p.m. Paid $1 for watch and 15-cents for a shave.

Sept. 18: Remained at place all day. Rain last night and in morning. A large amount of water fell.

Sept. 19: Finished dismantling old building and removed nails from lumber. Cool air and hot sunshine.

Sept. 20: Hauled lumber from old building in north field to near barn where it will be used in a corn crib. Foggy and some rain. Got the gauge-plow, ready for use.

Sept. 21–23: Plowed in northwest oat stubble field. Ground plows well but is somewhat lumpy, moisture conditions are satisfactory. Turn about 4 acres of surface per day.

Sept. 24: Rain in a.m. Shucked corn in p.m. Corn will make 45-50 bushels per acre. First Republican Rally in Lexington in evening. Too muddy to attend.

Sept. 25: Cloudy with fog in morning. Walked to Shafer's in p.m. but found no one there.

Sept. 26–28: Worked on corn cribs. Some rain in the course of these days.

Sept. 29: Plowed in north west stubble field.

Sept. 30–Oct. 1: Cut corn in S 80a field. Corn is twisted and blown down making corn cutting very difficult. I cut and tied 28 shocks, 14 hills square. Unless prevented by some unforeseen event, I shall go to the World's Fair at St. Louis. week after next.

Oct. 2: Remained at place.

Oct. 3: Cut corn in a.m. and plowed in p.m.

Oct. 4–6: Plowed and hauled corn for Caldwell. Cold.

Oct. 7: Heavy frost last night. Plowed. Went to Lexington in evening, where a street fair is in progress. Usual shows and fakes. 30-cents washing.

Oct. 8: Husked corn and plowed. Received $40 from Pils for work. Will go to St. Louis tomorrow night or Monday morning.

Oct. 9: Went to Shaffer's and remained there until 8:30p.m. when I went to Lexington and remained there until 12:41a.m. of October 10th, when I left for St. Louis World's Fair. [33]

Oct. 10: Arrived in St. Louis about 7a.m. Got breakfast and went to the fair ground. I visited several state buildings, which are for the most part only places of rest and quiet. A few state buildings notably, Washington, has exhibits of products of all principal kinds. Visited the government building, and "mines and metallurgy". These exhibits are very complete and accurate and of great extent. The Gov't bldg. being especially instructive to me. I paid $4.85 for railway fare to St. Louis and return, 56-cents to eat, 60-cents for souvenirs, 15-cents =shows, 75-cents =lodging, 55=cents for entrance to the fair and street car fare. I retired early and had no difficulty in securing lodging.

Oct. 11: Visited the Gov't bldg, some more state buildings and the "Varied Industries". Went to Boer Var in p.m. Attended musical recital by Guilyant in Festival Hall. Excellent! Paid grub=96-cents, shows and entrance fee=$1.80, lodging 50-cents, and 15-cents spent on miscellaneous.

Oct. 12: Visited "Fisheries Manufacturing and Liberal Arts. Also visited Fine Arts. Expenses were grub 51-cents, shows=50-cents, 50-cents for fair entrance fee, 50-cent lodging, and 35-cents for miscellaneous.

Oct. 13: Enjoyed Agriculture and Horticulture, Brazil, etc. exhibits. Expenses: grub 70-cents, lodging 50-cents, shows=35-cents, fair entrance fee=50-cents, souvenirs=36-cents and miscellaneous of 50-cents spent.

Oct. 14: Visited Transportation, Education, Electricity, Machinery, Forestry, Philipines and Jerusalem. Expenses: grub=90-cents, lodging=50-cents, show=92-cents, souvenirs=$1.50, fair entrance fee=50-cents and miscellaneous=7-cents. There will be much to always remember of the great World's Fair!

Oct. 15: Went to Union Station in morning and left for Lexington at 12:02 p.m. and arrived in Lexington at 5:30 p.m., a half hour late. Walked out to Pils in evening.

Oct. 16: Spent the day at place.

Oct. 17–22: Plowed except in p.m. of 18th and 19th, when I harvested potatoes also in a.m. of 20th shucked corn. I paid $1 for a wedding present for Henry Bierman.

Oct. 23: Heavy frost last night. Pleasant. Remained at place.

Oct. 24: Plowed

Oct. 25: Hauled straw to barn and dug potatoes.

Oct. 26: Hauled straw to barn. Transferred seed corn and shucked corn in p.m. This ends my working by the month for Pils.

Oct. 27: Commenced shucking corn by the bushel for which I am to receive 3-cents per bushel. Corn is badly down and tangled. Very cool nights.

Oct. 28–29: Shucked corn. Corn is yielding about 50 bushels per acre. Went to Lexington in the evening of the 29th. Paid $2.15 for clothes, $1 for mittens, 15-cents for lemons, 10-cent shave, 5-cents for pins, $1 for sarsaparilla, 10-cents for malina.

Oct. 30: Remained at place.

Oct. 31–Nov. 5: Shuck corn. Shuck from 70 to 80 bushels per day. A few frosts. Paid 25-cents for a shucking hook and received 10-cents for the sale of soap.

Nov. 6: Clear and pleasant. Heavy frost last night.

Nov. 7–12: Shucked corn. In p.m. of 10th, I came to house and sent to bed after husking about two rows of corn. I was chilly and full of aches. Felt much better the next morning. Cold north wind. Paid 75-cents for mittens. Ma came to Peoria on Wednesday the 9th.

Nov. 13: Remained at place.

Nov. 14–19: Shucked corn. Hand improving slightly from boils. Filled one crib the morning of the 14th and began on another crib in the same building. Went to Lexington of 19th and bought mittens and a peg for for $1, and 5-cents for nuts and a 10-cent shave.

Nov. 20: Came to Chenoa in morning and took TP&W at 7:40 a.m. for Peoria. Paid $1 for fare to Peoria and return. Arrived at 9 a.m. and visited with Charles and family. William, Jr. is growing finely and rapidly, learning to talk. Arrived in Chenoa at 8:35 p.m. and after eating a 15-cent lunch and paying 50-cents for livery bill, I drove out to Pils. Quite cold.

Nov. 21–26: Shucked corn Shucked by weight.

Nov. 27: Walked to Shaffer's and back. Spent most of the day at home.

Nov. 28–Dec. 3: Shucked corn by weight. Quite cold.

Dec. 4: Remained at farm all day. Warmer and clear.

Dec. 5–6: Shucked corn by weight at Pils. I finished up his husking about 2:30 p.m. of the 6th. In eve, we measured cribs I filled, which measurements were as follows: Avg. 11ft 6¾ in length - 48 ft. and width 9 ft. Contents= 1,998 bushels. I had also shucked by weight, 785 3/5 bushels, making a total for Pils of 2,783 3/5 bushels in 35 working days. An average of 79.5 bushels per day. I will receive 3-cents per bu. which will be $83.50 for corn shucking here.

Dec. 7–8: Took Pils outfit and shucked corn for Charles Rosseau at 3½ cents per bu. Shucked 81 bushels on 7th and 73 bushels on the 8th.

Dec. 9: Shucked 40 bushels corn for Rosseau in a.m. and hauled corn for Pils at Bierman's in p.m.

Dec. 10: Hauled corn for Pils from Biermans.

Dec. 11: Spent part of the day at place and part at Shaffer's.

Dec. 12: Took load of corn to O. Dawson's at Lexington in a.m. I brought out a load of 50.1" X 1 12' white pine rough boards and covered the rail corn pens in afternoon.

Dec. 13: Helped bank houses and hauled corn for Pils from J. Breeze in p.m.

Dec. 14: Settled with Pils today, receiving $215.50 in full of account. Pils paid me for straight time although I lost a week at the World's Fair. I deposited $210 in the Home State Bank. Came out to Shaffer's in the evening.

Dec .15: Helped Shaffer butcher. Clear and cold.

Dec. 16: Remained at Shaffer's helping some with meat, etc.

Dec. 17: Went to Lexington for a shave 10-cents.

Dec. 18: At Shaffer's most of day. Went to Pils and got my mail in afternoon.

Dec. 19: Helped get machinery ready for sale.

Dec. 20–21: Scooped corn for Rosseau for a short time, then came back to Shaffer's.

Dec. 22: Shaffer's sale to day. Most of the property sold well, especially the horses. $158 being the highest for a 6 year old bay mare.

Dec. 23: Went to Lexington and paid $1 for overshoes, $1 for mittens, 30-cents for handkerchiefs and 11-cents for postage.

Dec. 24: Went to Lexington and paid $1.14 for handkerchiefs and 50-cents for candy, 10-cent shave. Took supper with and remained all night at Willis Shaffer's. Received a treat and necktie from him.

Dec. 25: Spent the day at Shaffer's and Birlingmair's. A cool but green Xmas.

Dec. 26: Packed household goods.

Dec. 27: Warm to cold and blizzardy. 0 degrees. I walked to Pils and got my mail. Received a handkerchief and necktie from Aunt Dell, a sack from Cora. I also heard from St. Mary's, Ohio.

Dec. 28: Helped S. W. Shaffer crate household goods.

Dec. 29: At N.B. Shaffer's.

Dec. 30: Got mail at Pils and received $8.50 of Rosseau, in full of account.

Dec. 31: Went to Lexington in a.m. and packed goods at S.W. Shaffer's, a part of the day. N.B. Shaffer paid the note against him of $105 and I bought him at 6% discount.

3 notes follow:
Amt. Maker Security
$47.00 W. H. Potts Miller Adreon
$33.50 Pat Kennedy J. Kennedy
$35.00 Ed Adreon Pat Kennedy.
I paid $107.57 for the above. All are for one year without interest.

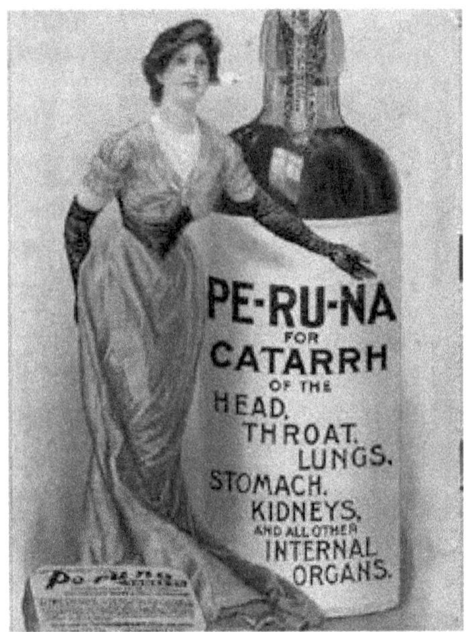

Peruna for Catarrh of the head, throat, lungs, etc. - all internal organs.

Bromo Quinine, a laxative, La Grippe and Colds

Malena in pill form, cost 25-cents in silver or stamps.

Perry Davis Pain Killer It is no wonder that a formula of vegetable extracts, camphor, ethyl alcohol, and opiates would make a sick person feel better.

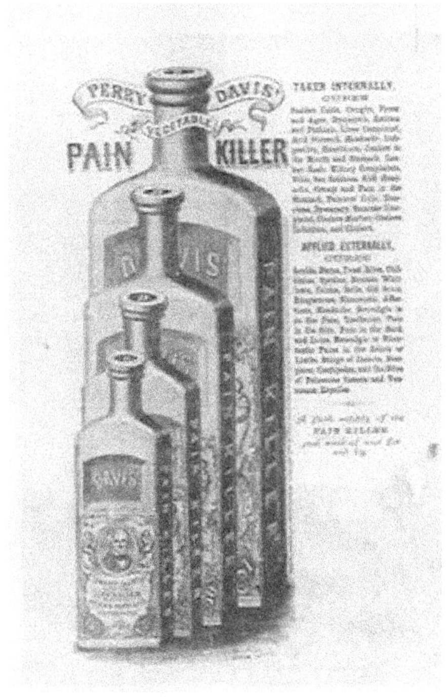

Busy People Fail

in general health—a bad taste in the mouth, foul, sick stomach, torpid liver, constipation, drowsiness, dizziness, stupor and headache—any one or all of these symptoms indicate the downward fall. Stop long enough to take one or two **Ma-Le-Na Stomach-Liver Pills**, the best Tonic-Laxative, every night for a week or two, and you will be surprised at the beneficial results. Take them at once as delay is dangerous and may prove disastrous.

NO RISK

as they are purely vegetable, absolutely safe, the best nerve, stomach and liver tonic and gentle laxative, and guaranteed to cure constipation, sick headache, foul stomach, torpid liver, lazy kidneys, dyspepsia, piles, and to invigorate and build up the whole system, and to clear and beautify the complexion, or money refunded. Being a tonic as well as a laxative, they are double strength and do double work. If you wish to look well, be well and keep well, take

Ma-Le-Na Stomach-Liver Pills.

Don't be Fooled into buying worthless substitutes and imitations. Those that substitute and imitate to rob us will substitute and adulterate to cheat you. Take only Ma-Le-Na Stomach-Liver Pills.

Try Them To-Day. Sold by Druggists and Dealers, or a box will be sent by mail, postage paid, on receipt of the price, 25 cents, in silver or postage stamps.

MALENA COMPANY, Manufacturers.
Warriorsmark, Pa., U. S. A.

Ma-Le-Na will cure everything! Stomach, liver, lazy kidneys and beautify your complexion. "Avoid the downward fall" it warns!

Sarsaparilla cures Catarrh, boils, carbuncles, even rheumatism

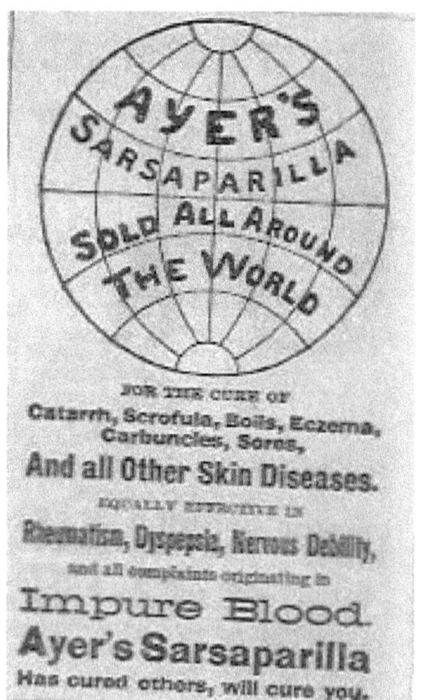

1904 St. Louis Exposition *postcard among WBH's possessions*

Souvenir St. Louis World's Fair, Porcelain Cup
among WBH's possessions.

1904 Indian Head penny souvenir. "A pot full of money".
among WBH's possessions.

1905

The U.S. Forest Service was formed in 1905. President Teddy Roosevelt lobbied Congress to create this agency and appointed Gifford Pinchot to manage the Forestry Service. Ty Cobb made his Major League debut, playing for the Detroit Tigers, hitting a double in his first at bat in the game.

January 1, 1905: I passed the day here and at Willis Shaffer's. Cloudy with some mist.

Jan. 2: Packed goods at N.B. Shaffer's. I bought of J. Willis Shaffer for $118.44 a note for $126, given by J. Kennedy and Pat Kennedy as security due, December 22, 1905, without interest. I paid him with check on Home S.B. for above amount.

Jan. 3: Packed goods.

Jan. 4–5: Packed goods and took temperature of cattle in town. Cold and stormy. Shaffer began loading car today.

Jan. 6: Helped load car today. Paid 40-cents for barbering and 25-cents for eating.

Jan. 7: Completed loading car. Very cold and in a.m. quite a storm. Retired about midnight after seeing the Shaffer boys starting to Washington. Paid 50-cents for lodging and breakfast.

Jan. 8: Walked to J. Pils in a.m. and remained at the place all day. Cold west wind.

Jan. 9: Packed goods in trunk and putting "grip" wearing apparel for the winter months. Light fall of snow.

Jan. 10: Walked to Lexington in morning, Drew $25 from S.B. of Lexington. Paid 24-cents for railroad fare to Chenoa. Left Chenoa for Peoria at 12:55 p.m., at which I visited Charles and Mina. Paid 20-cents for lunch, 10-cents shave, 50-cents for a cap and $1.44 for railroad fare, also 10-cents for a shine and 5-cents for street car fare.

Jan. 11: Spent the day at Charles home, playing with Wm. Jr. Snow and rain most of the day.

Jan. 12: Left Peoria for Waterloo at 8:30 over C.R.I.&P. and L.S.&M.S. changing at Englewood. Gave Wm. Jr. 25-cents, 25-cents for storage of grip, 5-cents for street fare, 5-cents for paper and $8.40 for railroad fare to Waterloo. A moderate winter day.

Jan. 13 –15: At home. Passed time reading. Cold to warmer.

Jan. 16–21: Reading, shelling beans. Warm fine winter weather. Pleasant to see family.

Jan. 22: Bright, warm.

JAN. 23–29: Snow on 23. Cold north wind and drifting.

JAN. 30–FEB. 4: Loafed. Very cold on Thursday and Friday. Went to Wolf Lake. Folks there are in usual health except for colds. Grandma appears about as she has for several years past except an added grayness of hair. She has had a severe cold for several days that does not give way readily to treatment. Her appetite is quite poor as a result. Pd. $1.65 for R.R. fare, 10-cents for lunch, 10-cents = stage, 25-cents = hair cut and shave.

FEB. 5–7: Clear and cold. Visited Grandma's and Uncle John Thumma's. Pd. 10-cents for shave.

FEB. 8: Came to Waterloo. B&O No. 16 was 4 ½ hours late. Stormy day with 3 inches fall of snow. Pd. 20-cents for lunch, 50-cents = drawers, 10-cents for garter, 10-cents = stage. R.R. fare 5-cents.

FEB. 9: Snow 2-3 inches fell. For paper and insurance paid $2.25.

FEB. 10: Cold and for the most part clear. Charles is 32 years old today.

FEB. 11: At home. Cold continues.

FEB. 12: Same routine –Reading, eating, sleeping. Lincoln's birth anniversary.

FEB. 13–18: My physical idleness continues, as does the coldness of the atmosphere. Pd. 50-cents for meat. Loaned Cora 50-cents.

FEB 19: As are the other days passed so also is this.

Feb. 20–25: Made two thresholds, repaired another and repaired the fittings of several doors; trimmed the grape vines and some of the trees. Ma went to Wolf Lake on the 25th. Snow melting fast.

Feb. 26: Pleasant crisp day.

Feb. 27–March 4: Cooked, trimmed trees, etc. Quiet pleasant weather most of the time. Ma returned.

March 5–March 9: Did a few odd jobs. Snow about gone. Pd. $1.75 for wood.

March 10: Came to Chicago on #157. Walked about town until evening where after supper. I went to S. A. Jack's Show and then retired. Pd. $6.91 = R.R. fare, 5-cents = writing paper, 25-cents = show, 25-cents for lodging. Rec'vd $25 as payment of loan from Cora.

March 11: Arose at 6 a.m. and after breakfast, went to depot and by 9 a.m. started for Lexington. Arriving at 12:15 p.m. Pd 25-cents for dinner, $2.73 = clothes, $1.50 = shoes, 2-cents = papers and 10-cents for storage on property. Rode out to Pils in evening.

March 12: Remained at place all day. Arranged my outfit in a convenient way read, etc.

March 13: Did but little work except chores today. Cool.

March 14–18: Hauled corn for H. Bierman, hauled fodder and hauled corn for Ed Adreon. Husked corn and hauled manure. Tested seed corn. Weather cold and snow.

MARCH 19: Cloudy. Northeast wind. At place all day.

MARCH 20–25: Cut down big hedge, drove colts and chored. Warm Spring weather. Went to Lexington on Saturday and paid 56-cents for laundry and 53-cents for stamped envelopes.

MARCH 26: Cool clear day.

MARCH 27–APRIL 1: Sowing oats, spading, harrowing, etc. Rain. Shucked corn, put wire on S. fence of pasture. The spader does poor work owing to clogging by corn stalks. Weather for most part warm as May.

APRIL 2: Rode to Lexington in a.m. Hazy Grass is green and growing.

APRIL 3–8: Disked, harrowed, raked corn stalks, also repaired fence. Saturday I sent for and rec'd part of order for 6 bottles of Peruna and 25-cents bottle of Perry Davis pain killer. In all $5.25. Rec'd but 4 bottles of Peruna but will get the other two soon. Been feeling rather tough – sore throat, pain in left knee.

APRIL 9: Clear, pleasant Spring day.

APRIL 10–15: Harrowed and raked cornstalks and plowed ground with 2 gang breaking plow. Hauled corn – 1 load for Aderon and 3 loads for Siron Fry. Saturday was the 3rd birthday anniversary of nephew – Wm. Hill. Left knee has been lame all week.

APRIL 16: Cold clear morning. Knee feeling better today.

APRIL 21: Good Friday A holiday with the German Lutherans

April 23: Easter Took a little walk for exercise in a.m.

April 30: A beautiful clear day. Remained at place. Gathered wild flowers and read.

May 28: Rode to Chenoa and went to Peoria. Visited Charles until 6 p. Cora was there for a visit. Went to First Baptist Church in morning. Text "For God hath sealed us and given us an earnest of the spirit in our hearts." Good sermon. Church collection 10-cents. Horse care = 50-cents

June 5: Cultivated corn. Got over all of the corn once.

June 6–9: Commenced crossing corn.

June 10: Heard from Cora –she got home OK from Peoria.

June 11–12: Picked cherries. Worked in garden.

July 1: Worked in garden and went to Lexington in p.m. Attended Steven's Livery Supply Sale. Horses, carriages and harness's sold well for the most part.

July 4: Went to Lexington and on to Bloomington at 9:45 a.m. returning to Lexington by early afternoon. Attended a fair ballgame between Bloomington Pastures and McLean: the former winning 12-8. Witnessed a balloon ascension and also a few aerial stunts. Paid 70-cents for R.R. fare, 50-cents for grub, 50-cents for horse care, 25-cents for ball game.

July 5: Put up hay. Hay will make 1 ½ tons per acre. Long hot days.

July 8: Mowed grass and weeds with scythe and mower.

July 25: Repaired hay rack. Helped thresh at Al Harmon's. Pulley wheel running fan was broken and caused a 3 hr. delay.

July 26: Oats will make from 40-55 bushels per acre. Oats look as well or better then expected.

Aug. 7–12: Clouds but hot all day. Threshed at J. Pils, E. M. Adreon, G. C. Elder, Wm. Linden and M. Marc having 30 acre at latter place yet to be threshed on eve of the 12th. The avg. yield of oats was as follows: 43, 53, 44, 39. Oat straw is below the usual length for this time of year.

Aug. 13: Not feeling well – stomach –better toward eve.

Aug. 14: Hauled straw from straw stacks. HOT sun. Caught a cold so feeling slightly tough.

Aug. 15–18: Threshed at M. Marc's, Berryman's, Steven's and Caldwell's. 41 bu. average. Oats quite damp.

Aug. 20: Went to Bloomington to the Chautauqua.[34] Pleasant day. Fair sized crowd, good speakers and music. J. H. Sutherland preached in morning and George H. Thompson of Indianapolis made an address in evening. 25-cents for admission to grounds.

Aug. 21: Today, I am 29 years old. Threshed oats at Caldwell's, Williams, and Vaughn's.

Aug. 22–25: Threshed oats at Vaughn's, Shultz, Harmon's and Watson's. Average 46 bu per acre.

Aug. 29: Plowed with sulky in a.m. Ground plows hard and dry. Attended ball game between Prairie Hall and our own threshing gang at Vaughn's pasture. Good time had by all.

Sept. 3: Cool last night and today. Visited at Al Edwards in p.m. Nellie Adreon the oldest child and only daughter of Ed Adreon and wife has been sick nearly two weeks with a complication of diseases, fever etc. promises to recover.[35]

Sept. 6: Nellie Adreon is much worse today. I was up to Adreon's until midnight.

Sept. 7: Nellie died at 12:20 a.m. Nellie was only 15 years old. Went to Adreon's in evening and sat up all night.

Sept. 8: Slept an hour in morning, then attended funeral held at Chenoa Catholic Church at 9 a.m. There was no service preached simply a mass being said over the dead. I could understand but very little as it consisted mostly of signs and movements and a low mumbling of some ritual. Afterwards went to the Catholic cemetery. A very solemn day.

Sept. 9: Pils and I ate dinner in Chenoa and then went through the canning factory. About 125 hands are employed and about 1/3 being girls and women. There were about 36 huskers, 24 sorters and 20 in the canning room, 10 people in the cooking room. On last Wednesday 94,000 cans were put up between 7 a.m. and 9 p.m. There are 1,500 acres in sweet corn, $18 per ton being the present price paid. About 26 teams are used to gather the corn.

Sept. 11: Drove team of horses to Chenoa taking Pils.
He is absence through 18th.

Sept. 17: Drove to Chenoa and took train to Peoria. Visited Charles and family and went to Glen Oak Park, where an Indian band from J.T. played. Stork will visit Mina in a month or 6 weeks.

Sept. 21–23: Plowed in S 80a using 6 horses on gang plow.

Oct. 1: Spent the evening at Al Edwards.

Oct. 2: Hauled load of coal from Lex. and cleaned chicken coop.

Oct. 4: Dug and picked up potatoes = 25 bushels. Went to Lexington at 11 p.m. and took passage for Springfield at 12;41 a.m.

Oct. 5: Arrived in Springfield at 3:45 a.m. Went to fair grounds and at 7 a.m. viewed the machinery exhibit and horse barns etc. and attended the races in afternoon. Large crowd fine day. Home at 11:59 p.m.

Oct. 6–15: Plowed potato batches, gathered stray potatoes, husked popcorn. Went to Lexington in eve of 14th and heard LaFollette[36] lecture on civic problems, the Railroad's control, in particular urging the curbing of corporate power by means of rate control through an Interstate Commerce Commission with power to order as well as recommend. He strongly advocated the Austrailian ballot for effecting nominations, giving every man a voice in the selection of candidates as well as in their election. The R.R.'s being the arteries of the body of the State their control would control the corporate bodies in which power is now so strongly centered – a forceful interesting, thoughtful speaker .

Oct. 16: Put straw in barn and brought a load of coal from town for Pil's father. Fine day.

Oct. 17: Repaired throw-boards and had my teeth repaired. Set fence posts and cleaned ditches in p.m. Paid $2.00 for filling two teeth. Dr. King doing the work.

Oct. 23–28: Shucked corn. I husked 90 bushels. In p.m. of 28th Wm. Le Ducgot of north Chenoa shot and killed Charles Nicol and Hugh Jones and wounded others at the State Bank of Chenoa. As yet no cause is known though he was a boozer. He got in the safe vault and proped it open with a book and kept all away until some time during Saturday night when he surrendered.[37]

Oct. 29: Le Duc in Bloomington jail.

Oct. 30–Nov. 4: Shucked corn in S. 60 acres. Filled crib of about 1,000 bus. on the 3rd. After which I will weigh the corn and shuck. Threshed on Nov. 4th.

Nov. 5 –11: Shucked corn Weather cold and wet. Avg. over 100 bushels per day. Went to Lexington o the 11th and paid for barbering. Paid 50-cents for mittens which I will give to William Jr. when I go to Peoria tomorrow.

Nov. 12: Drove horse to Chenoa and went to Peoria. Spent day with brother. The new kid is a boy, Horace Leslie and 3 weeks old, born October 20th-1905. All are well.

Nov. 13–24: Finished shucking for J. Pils. We figured out how much I shucked. I filled a crib holding 1,016 bus. in the first 10 ½ days and then shucked 1,763 bu. in 17 ½ days. An average of 99 ¼ bushel's per day.

Nov. 25–28: Scooped corn for C. G. Elder, all day or rather fed the conveyors as the corn rolled out of crib. Shucked corn for Rosseau.

Nov. 29: A Press notice says that Mrs. Simon Shaffer was dead and would be shipped to Lexington for burial.

Nov. 30: Thanksgiving day a bright and pleasant day. Shucked 18 rows of corn approx. 80 bushels.

Dec. 1–6: Shucked corn off and on due to blustery cold weather. Snow and sleet. Visited Rosseau and got pair of overshoes.

Dec. 9: Settled with Rosseau, receiving check for $19.25. Paid $1 for overshoes. Went to Pils and got mail and in afternoon we went to where I saw Simon and Ino Shaffer who came here last Monday with the body of Mrs. Shaffer who died the previous Wed. of blood poison, induced by erysipelas.

Paid 65-cent for socks and mitts, 10-cents Malena, $2.53 P.M.O. for Evening Post for self and Aunt Dell. Cashed check and left $10 on deposit at S. B. of Lexington. The cashier Keller said they would collect my notes for me without charge and gave consent.

Dec. 11: In a.m. I started to walk to Anchor where a neighbor told me there was much corn yet to be shucked. I walked 6 miles east and 3 ½ miles to Colfax, then walked back to Anchor. In p.m. walked 6 miles to a Mr. Hart's where I remained all night. Very tired as I was not used to walking. Pleasant December day.

Dec. 12: Walked 3 miles southeast to three different farms but all were supplied with shuckers so returned to Hart's and stayed.

Dec. 13: Rode to Anchor with Hart and at 12:36 left on I.C. for Bloomington where I stayed all night. Pd. 77-cents for R. R. Junc. 1-cent for gum, 30-cents for grub, 35-cents for lodging.

Dec. 14: After breakfast I left Bloomington for Funks Grove. I then walked, 4 miles southeast past Kerrick's place, then north past Shirley. Walked and rode to Bloomington where I arrived at 12:50 p.m. Went to Union Station and took interurban for Towanda. After dinner walked to Lexington where I remained all night. Cough drops = 5-cents, grub 30-cents lodging and breakfast 75-cents.

Dec. 15: Went to Ocoya at 8:05 a. and walked back through country to Ballard and thence to Pils. Cold.

Dec. 16–17: I took load of corn to Ballard for Pils in morn and settled account with Elder receiving $3.50 for 2 days corn shucking and $1.75 for 1 day shelling corn.

Dec. 18: Passed the day at Al Edwards. Quite cold.

Dec. 19–21: Remained at Edwards on the 19th. Load of hogs to Chenoa for J. J. Pils. Purchased socks = 25-cents. Returned to Edwards. I have quite a severe cold. Much rain making roads 2" deep mud. Received a silk muffler from Peoria (Charles and family) for Christmas.

Dec. 23: Went to Lex. in a.m. with Al Harmon and got a few Christmas gifts. Handerchiefs for Ma, Cora, Grandma, Ella and Jennie. Gifts for Harry McCrory, and nephews Wm. and Horace Hill. Christmas cards = 30-cents, postage = 10-cents, bread and oranges = 50-cents, smokes for Al Harmon = 10-cents Returned to Edwards in p.m. There is a small pox scare in town, a few supposed cases having been found and quarantined. Some snow.

Dec. 24: At Edwards all day. In eve Al, Whit and I went to German Church for an hour or more to the Christmas tree and exercises. Exercises at church were similar to those in English churches except language.

Dec. 25: Christmas Day at Edwards. Fine weather and day.

Dec. 26: Came to J. Bierman to stay while Mrs. B. is in the hospital at Chicago, where she went today for an operation for gall stones.

Dec. 27: At Bierman's all day. Mrs. B. had 16 small stones removed. Reports she is OK.

Dec. 28: Same old stand.

Dec. 29: Went to Lex. for barbering. Expected John B. home but he did not come.

Dec. 30–31: Went to Lexington and came back with John and Mrs. B. She is getting along well. Spent 31st with the B's. Fine weather.

Political cartoon of La Follette in 1911. As Governor, note the depiction of his breaking the railroad trust in Wisconsin. *Chicago Tribune* 1911

1906

On April 18, 1906, at 5:12 a.m., the San Francisco 8.2 earthquake hit. In 1906, Albert Einstein introduces his Theory of Relativity. The first phonograph (record player) is manufactured.

January 1, 1906: *Mr. Hill leaves detailed notes in the back of every daybook. January 1, 1906 he noted. Present Worth: Cash in H. S, Bank of Lexington $256.56, Cash in S. B. of Lexington $351.50, Cash in pocket $12.10, Due from Pils $272.75 = $892.91 (Purchasing power in 2024 would be $31,281.71).*

Passed day in Green Street neighborhood.

Jan. 2–6: Took J. Birlingmair to Lexington depot on the 3rd. He is going to Chicago, on to Denver. On the 6th got driving team reshod in Lexington.

Jan. 7: At. B's all day. Rosseau's and R. Ellis families here.

Jan. 8–12: Hauled corn. On 10th settled with J. Pils for last year's work receiving check for $272.75. Went to Lexington and left on deposit of S.

B. of Lex. the above check. I now have a total of $880.81 on deposit. Cold to warm. 11th and 12th shrug-like days.

Jan. 13–22: At Birlingmair's. Mr. and Mrs. B. came back from Chicago on 18th. Mrs. B. doing well though this was the first day she sat up since operation, 3 weeks before. Took Mrs. Hart to Cooksville on 20th. Sleeted a heavy coating of ice covering all exposed things. Many telephone wires and poles down on 19th.

Jan. 23: Heard from Cora. Grandma was operated on the morning of the 20th at Fort Wayne Lutheran Hospital. A 3½ lb. tumor was removed from ovary. Diseased ovary was also removed. She stood operation remarkability well and is getting along nicely.

Jan. 24–25: Went to Bloomington in a.m. Paid 75-cents for flowers for Grandma. Sent 1 dozen carnations.

Jan. 26–Feb. 2: Worked on P. H. Telephone lines, straightening poles and therefore received $1.

Feb. 3: Went to Lexington and paid $3.00 for sundries. Drew $60 from bank. Tried to get ¾ of 1 fare rate for round trip to Granada, Colorado but could not do so at Lex., so will go to Peoria on Monday and try there.

Feb. 4: At Pils, packed trunk, etc. Time to explore.

Feb. 5: Walked to Ballard and failed to get car to Chenoa so I walked. Left Chenoa at 2:50 p.m. Got Homeseekers ticket to Alva, Okla. Sent flowers to Grandma. Supper then bed.

Feb. 6: Arose at 5 a.m. had breakfast and walked to depot and at 6 a.m. left for Kansas City, Kansas. Arrived at 5:20 p.m.

Feb. 7: Slept fairly late. Got to Wellington Kay at 9:10 a.m. when I changed for Attica. Arrived there at 1:30 p. and took train to Medicine Lodge – a 21 miles ride. Talked with real estate men of land values, crops, climate conditions etc. Paid 63-cents for fare, Med. Lodge $1 Hotel bill, 5-cents magazine, 10-cents lunch.

Feb. 8: Rode out in country 4-5 miles down the Medicine area to look at land. Corn growing seems to have made around 25-30 bushels per acre. Last years wheat does not show much having been pastured closely. Most of land is rough except some fields in river bottom that are flat and within 3 ft. of water. This "lowland is salty alkali and not much good. The land along river ranges in price from $10 - $25 per acre, with nothing on and up to $100 if set in alfalfa. Practically all of the farmers include both rough and flat land – the former kind much in excess. Water in many places is alkali. Country did not impress me favorably. Came back to Lodge remained overnight. $1.00

Feb. 9: Met a rancher from 25 miles northeast of Med. Lodge and rode across country with him and in eve after dinner he took me to Coats on Englewood branch of St. Fe Railroad in Pratt Co. Remained there overnite.

This man – E. Shore owns 2000 acres and wants for 1 section $25: for another without improvements except some wheat land $12 -½ per acre. This looked to me to be a more reasonable price than at Medicine Lodge. Wheat avg. last year 12-13 bus. per acre and 15 bu. is about the yearly average. The cost of sowing and harvesting a crop of wheat is from $5-$6 per acre. Coates country quite like Illinois.

Feb. 10: Left Coats and came to Rago then on to Harper. Left for Alva getting there about midnight. Retired at Hotel = $1. Harper is valued from $15 to $50 per acre according to location and improvements – a good wheat country but an avg. corn crop is about 30 bu. Corn is quite uncertain owing to liability of drought.

Feb. 11: Remain at Alva. Town of about 2,000 or more. County seat is Woods Co. Northwest Normal School located there – a $120,000 building. No mail.

Feb. 12: Left Alva at 8:30 a.m. and walked east to Ingersoll, 15 miles. The most of this country is a level laying one-a red soil. Wheat looks fine. Wheat is the principle crop with some oats alfalfa and corn. Oats yield an avg. 40 bu. Farms are rented for ½ of crop. Land in vicinity of Ingersol and Ashley sells for $7,000 - $10,000 for 160 acres. Shave = 15-cents, $1.25 for hotel. Some rain.

Feb. 13–14: Remain in Ingersol 'til 12:10 p.m. when I left for Alva where I will stay a few days. Commenced getting colder. 75-cents = Hotel

Feb. 15: Remained indoors most of the day. Cloudy and cold

Feb. 16: At Alva all day left and stopped at Wellington from 4 p. to 7:30p

Feb. 17: Arrived in Kansas City at 6:30 a.m. After breakfasting, I walked around city for a few hours and passed remaining time at depot until 9:35, when I left for Peoria over the C & A. Kansas City is a large city of good buildings. The Railway grounds being 60' below the town.

Feb. 18: Arrived in San Jose at 8:30 a.m. and as I couldn't get a train for Peoria 'till tomorrow, I walked to Pekin – 18.2 miles and then took Street Car for Peoria and went to Charles home. Very tired but soon rested.

Feb. 19–20: Remained at Charles place – playing with kids who are in fine shape. Well and fat.

Feb. 21: Left Peoria at 12:20 for Chenoa and then came to Ballard and walked to J. Pils in eve and remaining overnight.

Feb. 22: As Pil's does not care to hire a man for as short a time I wish to work here. I will not work for him this season. Walked to Lexington in morning and bought (3) notes for $780.00, leaving them at the S. B. Bank for collection. Notes are as follows:

Amt.	Date due	Maker	Surety
$225	Nov. 21st	O. E. Stinson	John Pils
$320	Nov. 21st	E. F. Mitchell	J. A Spiegel
$230	Dec. 21st	Ino Jonty	S. J. Hefner

All bear 6% interest. I paid for these with check on S. B. of Lex. for $550. And with check on Home S. B. of Lex.

I cashed an individual deposit cert. at S. B. of Lexington for $10, leaving me $4.25 at bank and $26.56 at Home S. B. of Lexington.

In eve I walked to J. Bierman's remaining the night. Saw H. Ellis about work but he had his help. 25-cents for dinner.

Feb. 23: Day being cloudy and remained at Bierman's.

Feb. 24: Went to Lexington and hired to Charles Rosseau at $25 plus washing for month or 'till corn is laid by commencing the 15th of March.

Feb. 25: This is Grandma's 75th anniversary. She continues to improve as rapidly as could be expected.

Feb. 26–March 7: At Bierman's He left for Anchor. Went to Lexington on 2/28, 3/3/and 3/6 Barbering 20-cents. Visited friends. Much snow.

March 8–11: Went and brought Bierman home from Anchor. Boots $3.50. Loafed at place.

March 12–18: Worked for Rosseau commencing on 12th. 6" snow fell this week. Cold 0 degrees. Got mail from home.

March 19–25: Tested seed corn and built shed on south side of barn.

March 26–31: Set telephone poles, cleaned up barn lot, manured garden etc. Ground drying rapidly. 6 degrees, cold wind.

April 1: A clear, still, pleasant day.

April 2–7: Drove colts to Lexington. Set up spade and disk, spaded oat ground. Picked seed corn, built fence around garden and plowed garden on 5th and 6th. Ground works well.

Saw by Lexington paper of Charles F. McColm's death on the 2nd and burial on 5th. Charles had been having rheumatism but had improved some – then his back was affected and his constitution being weak he died at noon. Charles was as close a friend as I had in this county – was a good man, very accommodating and good heart. Very sorry not to have heard of death in time to attend funeral. He was 49 years old and unmarried.[38]

April. 8–14: Built fence by garden. Disked and spaded oats ground, examined seed corn, etc.

April 15–21: Harrowed oat ground and harrowed stalks on corn ground. Rosseau lost 2 colts – one from general weakness due to poor milk supply and the other was found dead on morning of 22nd.

April 22: Cold north wind. Helped mare in foaling in eve.

April 23–28: Plowed corn ground. Using gang plow with Rosseau's boy on sulky plow behind me.

April 29: Took a stroll east in p.m. Hazy day.

April 30–May 5: Plowed 2 ½ days, Harrowed and disked plowing for 2 ½ days. Fall plowed ground works up well – is quite weedy.

May 6: Another colt foaled last night; is strong and of good size.

May 7–12: Disked and prepared corn seed for planting. Planted corn all week, 110 acres.

May 13–19: Cora's 31st birthday anniversary on the 19th. Plowed, harrowed, hauled corn.

May 20: Took 5 mile walk in p.m.

May 21–June 2: Cultivating corn every day. Ground in fair shape but many stalks are bothersome. Moved granary. Wednesday was Decoration Day and Ma's 54th birthday anniversary.

June 3–7: About 12 acres left to cultivate. Paid 60-cents for money order to Union Gospel News for 1 year subscription and Bible studies.

June 8–9: Worked at summer kitchen most of the time.

June 10–13: Cross cultivated corn. I was using a two-row shovel cultivator which does fair work but plows out considerable corn that is out of line.

June 14–30: Picked cherries at J. J. Pils. Plowed 15 acres per day. Mowed weeds.

July 1–3: Finished cultivating. Received in full of acct. from Rosseau $93.28. Paid 25-cent = cigar treat. Left $50 at S. B. of Lexington.

July 4: Walked to Lexington and went to Bloomington. After dinner took Limited for St. Louis. Remained here all night. Lodging 50-cents Left County with $61.88.

July 5: Remained in St. Louis looking at town till 9 p.m. when I left for Larned, Kansas via K.C. I went with a bunch of others, costing me $8.50 railroad fare. Looked for Della Ulmer in directory but none there – only an Anna Ulmer, a clerk at the May Co.

July 6: Rode all night to Kansas City, then on east to Larned, Kansas. Corn in Kansas = best I've seen out of McLean County and that north of Lexington. Very short below Springfield, Ill. Corn in east Kansas is very patchy. Saw a few fields of excellent wheat a few miles before we arrived in K. City. Arrived at Larned at 8 p.m. There being a large number of idle men here, and now poor time to get out among farmers.

July 7: Walked about town and loafed till 3:45 p.m. when left for Kingman, Kansas. Arrived at 6:30 p. Kingman town of good buildings of 2,000 people and county seat. Pd. 25-cents for supper and 50-cents for lodging.

July 8: Stayed here until 7 p. where I went south 7 miles with a threshing outfit. Slept overnight in a barn. Pd. 65-cents = grub.

July 9: Rain last night till 10 a.m. This will postpone threshing 2 or 3 days at least. Not wanting to remain here, I left for the S&E, walking as far as within a few miles of Harper, where I and another fellow stayed over night. Walked about 16 miles today. Pd. 15-cents for grub.

July 10: Walked to Harper in morning about 4 miles. 15-cents for a shave. I left town about 10 a. walking east. Quite hot. Walked to Danville and remained all day. Pd. Lodging and grub = 80-cents.

Work will commence when wheat is dry – about one day yet. As I desire to work here for a time will remain. Wheat looks good, corn also. The bulk of the land in this locality is put to wheat.

July 11: This is a burg of perhaps 50 people. Walked to Argonia in afternoon.

July 12: In town in a.m. Afternoon walked to country and helped stack wheat but rain prevented.

July 13–14: Stacking wheat at $2.00 per day. Very HOT weather.

July 15: Came to town and pd. 50-cents for sundries. Heard from home.

July 16–17: Stacked wheat on 16th. 17th came to town to cash check for wages = $6.00.

July 18: I walked southwest from town, 5 ½ miles and got a job threshing at $2 per day plus board. Pd. $1.00 for comforter or quilt.
Worked in p.m., pitching at machine.

July 19: Pitched at machine and scooped wheat in a.m. Rain in p.m.

July 20: Went to a farm equipment sale. Machinery went at a fair price and horses sold a trifle under prevailing price at private sale. Loafed.

July 21: Threshed in p.m. 972 bushels of sacked oats, of good quality in about 5 hours. Oats were very dark but of fair weight.

July 22–29: Much rain of sufficient frequency thereafter to prevent threshing. Was in Freeport on 25th. Went to Argonia on 28th and purchased postal supplies – pd. 10-cents. On 29th loafed about shack.

July 30–31: Threshed for 1½ days. Very HOT.

Aug. 1: Stacked wheat for Duncan. Rec'd $2.00 check

Aug. 2: Helped stack wheat in morning and thresh in afternoon.

Aug. 3–4: Hard rain on 3rd. Went to Freeport and paid 10-cents for shave and 5-cents socks.

Aug. 5: Went to Sunday School in p.m., attired in working clothes. Put 2-cents in collection.

Aug. 6: Loafed about shack as ground is too wet to haul grain over or operate thresher.

Aug. 7–9: Threshed at Duncan's and Buggard's.

Aug. 10: Worked ¾ of day when rain delayed the threshing.

Aug. 11: Went to Argonia, Kansas in morn. Rec'd $2.00 from Hostetler and pd. 50-cents for shave and refreshments.

Aug. 12: Loafed at shack.

Aug. 13–18: Threshed wheat, working full time. Heavy dews for part of the week.

Aug. 19: Went to town and pd. 40-cents barber bill, 25-cents dinner, 25-cents hat.

Aug. 20: Finished threshing late in the eve. Finally a cool breeze.

Aug. 21: I am 30 years old today. Went to Argonia. Pd. 25-cents for soap and 25-cents for salve for poison, 50-cents = picture of threshing crew. Rec'd check for $26 from Hostettler in full. Cashed check and left $25 in F. & M. Bank of Argonia.

Aug. 22: Threshed all day. Headed grain is harder to handle than bundle grain. Stacks of headed wheat are put up same as haystacks. Cool in evening.

Aug. 23: Worked in a.m. when rain prevented further threshing.

Aug. 24: Threshed all day. Rain this eve.

Aug. 25: Went to Argonia in a.m. and got 10-cent shave. Hot sun. Rec'd $4 from Hostetler in full of account.

Aug. 26: Loafed at shack

Aug. 27–Sept. 2: No work except on Thurs. morning for ½ day, too wet. Attended sale Wed. Paid 25-cents for lunch. One 4 yr. 1200 lb. well broken mule brought $197.50. Spent Sat. in town, pd. 45-cents for grub, shave etc. Heavy 4 inches of rain fell.

Sept. 3–16: Cut corn at Hostetler's So much rain, wheat is poor condition.

Sept. 17–18: Rain in morn. Remained at shack camp. Cool

Sept. 19: Settled with Hostetler, sold bed for 25-cents rode to Argonia and in p.m. left for Wellington. Remained in Wellington over night. Pd. 70-cents for grub and treat, 62-cents for railroad fare, 25-cents for lodging. The town is not growing much.

Sept. 20: Remained in Wellington until 4 p.m., when I left for Enid, where I spent the night, railroad fare $2.03. Enid is town of 15,000, a large amt. of buildings going up – Court House, Pres. Church, several stone buildings and warehouses. Country to Enid same as south Kansas.

Sept. 21: Remained at Enid 'til 10:30 a.m. when I left for Lawton, OK. Have to go via Perry owing to bridge out at Dover. Arrived at Chickasha at 9 p.m. and remained overnight. 60-cents for grub – 25-cents for lodging. Chickasha is a growing town in fair to good locality.

Sept. 22: Left Chickasha and arrived at Lawton at 1 p.m. Lawton is town of 10,000 people, a moderate amount of buildings. Pd. $1.00 for lodging – 1 week.

Sept. 23–27: Loafed about town. Pd. 75-cents for overalls, 10-cents = baseball game, 10-cents postage, 55-cents per day for grub.

Sept. 28: Came to Chattanooga, OK. in afternoon and went 9 miles northwest with a W. C. Miller, to pick cotton for sometime, waiting for President Roosevelt's proclamation giving regulations concerning disposal of Indian Pasture lands is made public .[39] Pd. 65-cents for railroad fare, 15-cents for lunch, 90-cents for canvas for cotton sack and 50-cents for shirt.

Sept. 29–Oct. 6: Picked cotton except on 30th and 5th. Picked from 115 lbs. to 126 lbs at 85-cents per 100 lbs. per day.

Oct. 7: Went to Chattanooga and spent day as there was a farm product exhibit and excursion from Ok. City.

Oct. 8–9: Spent time in "Indian Pasture" Some fine laying land, good short grass and but very little long grass in the western part of Pasture. Pd. $3.00 for locator's services.

Oct. 10–12: Picked cotton at Miller's Nice weather. 141, 148, 145 lbs.

Oct. 13–21: Picked cotton at Shorn's a few days. Have lost $30 in bills from watch pocket where they were saved, maybe the thread breaking and bills dropping out.

Oct. 22–27: Picked cotton at Shorn's Cold weather.

Oct. 28: Settled with Shorn, receiving $12.17 having picked 1217 lbs. of cotton. Took 16 mile drive northeast with Miller.

Oct. 29: Shucked corn for Miller for a $1.00.

Oct. 30: Fingers being sore so did not work. Helped Shorn in afternoon thresh. Wheat = 4 bu. per acre, Oats = 20 bu. per acre

Oct. 31: Helped Miller thresh. Settled up with him = $12.15

Nov. 1: Drove team to Chatawa in morning. Purchased supplies =$1.75. I left Chattanooga at 2p. walking east to the first mile stone, east of township line between 13 and 14 then walked south 4 miles. Found corners ok except last two in long grass on bottomlands.

Nov. 2: After breakfast went S-E, 10 miles, located enough corners to know the ground. Camped at dusk.

Nov. 3: Started East to line of pasture. Went E. to Temple and at 11 p.m. took train to Waurika, from where at 1:15, I left for Chickasha. 45-cents to Waurika and $7.90 R.R. fare to Chickasha.

Nov. 4: Arrived at 4 a.m. and went to bed sleeping 'til after noon. Remained in town all day. 35-cents grub, 75-cents=lodging

Nov. 5: Went east from town to Alex. Where I went out with a farmer, Vaughan to husk corn at 3-cents per bu. Pd. 55-cents for gloves and mittens, 25-cents for breakfast, 15-cents for lunch and envelopes. Pleasant day. There is some corn in the valley that will yield 70 bus per acre and most of it will equal 50 bu. This is good corn country.

Nov. 6–7: Husked corn, about 45 bu. Poor and weedy

Nov. 8–10: Husked corn.

Nov. 11: Went to Alex in a.m. and pd. $3.10 for clothing. Cool wind.

Nov. 12–17: Husked corn. Warm most of the week, turning cold on Saturday.

Nov. 18: Rec'd $15.00 from Vaughn. At house all day. Some mist, sleet and snow.

Nov. 19: No work. Weather miserable.

Nov. 20: Chopped wood in afternoon. Rec'd draft from S. Bank of Lexington for $150.00.

Nov. 21: Chopped and hauled wood all day. Cut two loads all day.

Nov. 22–23: Snapped corn about 80 bus. per day.

Nov. 24: Hauled and cut for Jeffrey's all day.

Nov. 25: Spent day working on Pasture bids

Nov. 26: Went to Chickasha and deposited $200.00 in Citizens National Bank and drew a check for that amt. certified by bank payable to "The Sec. of Interior" for bids on pasture lands. Will not use check until next week. Made affidavit before Notary Public of qualifications to make bids or to homestead land. Paid 25-cents for Notary fee, 25-cents for dinner. Sent money order home = $5.05, 10-cents for magazine. Came back with Vaughn in eve.

Nov. 27: Gathered 72 bus. corn for Ed Vaughan.

Nov. 28: Cut and hauled wood from 8:30 a. to 3 p. Rain

Nov. 29: Rain and misty No work.

Nov. 30: Cut wood at Jeffrey's.

Dec. 1: Sent my bids for pasture lands – 24 different tracts and a certified check on the Citizens National Bank of Chickasha for $200, to be applied so much as needed to first payment of 1/5 of whole amt, if any bid accepted.

Dec. 2: Passed day at Vaughan's. Weather clear.

Dec. 3–4: Gathered corn for Ed Vaughan.

Dec. 5: Cut and hauled wood in a.m. Gathered corn in afternoon.

Dec. 6–8: Corn dry and stems brittle, breaking easily . Continue to gather corn for Vaughan.

Dec. 9: Windy and misty all day.

Dec. 10–16: Finishing up gathering corn.

Dec. 17: Cut wood by cord. Received from B. J. Vaughan $6.15 in full of his corn gathering account.

Dec. 18: Cut wood. Quit job in eve. Settled up with all the Vaughan's receiving $27.65 and $2.50.

Dec. 19: Vaughan, Sr. made me an offer of $1.25 per running cord for wood cutting and hauling which I accepted. Cut wood.

Dec. 20–22: Cut and hauled corded wood. Fine clear weather. Pd. 5-cents for soap

Dec. 23: Went to Alex. in morning.to purchased handkerchiefs, stamped envelopes and a writing tablet = 80-cents.

Dec. 24: Continue to cut wood.

Dec. 25: Christmas Day Remained at place and in afternoon went to Alex.

Dec. 26–31: Cut wood. Loafed and read on 30th Cool brisk wind from N.W.

Mr. Hill with threshing crew near Argonia, Kansas
Used with permission of Daniel Horn

1907

The World Series was only four years old in 1907. The Chicago Cubs won the World Series, beating Ty Cobb and his Detroit Tigers four games to none. 1907 is the busiest year ever seen at Ellis Island, with 1.1 million immigrants arriving there.

January 1, 1907: Rain prevented work today.

Jan. 2: Cut wreckage all day.

Jan. 3: Went to Alex. in a.m. and had two teeth filled as they had ached all day and night previous. Pd. $2.00 = teeth filling, 75-cents for mouth washes etc., 55-cents for clothing, 20-cents – dinner. Cut wood in late afternoon. Cold

Jan. 4: Helped butcher and cut wood

Jan 5: Gathered corn for Trammel at 3-cents per bu., Vaughan guaranteeing payment.

Jan. 6: Passed day reading etc.

Jan. 7: Gathered corn for Trammel at 83 bushels.

Jan. 8: Gathered 40 bushels – 60 lbs. corn in morning. Hauled cotton seed meal from Alex. in p.m. Rain in the evening

Jan. 9–18: Routine Cut wood. Repaired fences.

Jan. 19: Weather still strong today. Went to cyclone cellar last night but thankfully no cyclone came.

Jan. 20: At place all day. Weather warm

Jan. 21–23: Repairing fences

Jan. 24–31: Odd jobs, Hauled loads of feed, Cut wood

Feb. 1: Built fence. Went to town 25-cents = much needed haircut, 20-cents for lunch, 25-cents stamped envelopes.

Feb. 2–8: Cut wreckage, Completed wood cutting . Received $1 from Oscar Vaughan

Feb. 9: Repaired garden fence and plowed garden etc.

Feb. 10: Went to Alex and paid $2.50 for shoes. Warm sunny day.

Feb. 1–16: Worked in orchard clearing out stumps and old trees, clear and spring-like. Sent Cora $20.

Feb 17: Warm day, clear. Rounded up cattle all day

Feb. 18–21: Orchard work

Feb. 22: Prepared wood for use, wreckage and old posts, etc.

Feb. 23: Wreckage and orchard work—Measured wood I cut by cord. = 24 cords

Feb. 24: A "Norther" came last eve. And this day is cold and cloudy.

Feb. 25–27: Plowed

Feb. 28: Rainy did no work.

March 3: Went to Alex in morning. 60-cents = shirt, 25-cents cough syrup, 10-cents quinine. A little girl scared to death last night in Alex. by shooting in the streets. Rec'd $1.80 from Oscar V. in full of his account.

March 4–9: Did odd jobs about the place all week.

March 10: At place. Settled with Vaughan in eve, receiving check for $92.80 in full.

March 11: Walked to Chickasha in morning. Pd. 40-cents for grub, $3.00 =hat , purchased horse and bridle for $50.00, 25-cents for lodging, 25-cents Salvation Army, 25-cents = pocket book. Deposited $250.00 in Citizens National Bank and checked out $50 of same.

March 12: Pd. $14.00 = saddle, $2.50 for slicker, 25-cents grub, 50-cents horse care, 5-cents for rope. Left Chickasha at mid-day and rode 22 miles east to Dibble where I stopped all night. Warm travels until 4p, when a "Norther" came. The country is rolling and ½ with alfalfa.

March 13: Left Dibble and rode to Purcell by 1 p.m. and then onto Eason, 15 miles east where I put up at night. Country here very rough and timbered with oak. Land selling from $15 per acre up. Pd. $1.00 = Hotel bill, $1.00= overalls, 25-cents for horse feed, 15-cents spurs. Cold and cloudy

March 14: Left Eason and rode east and north to Romulus and then on to Maud. Spent night here. My pony stepped on broken plank in culvert bridge and threw both itself and me in the mud on bottom but luckily doing no more damage than skinning its leg. This occurred about 6 miles from Maud. Pd. $1.00 for Hotel, 50-cents feed. Maud is 3 year old town of 600-800 people – a saloon town and growing.

March 15: Left Maud and rode east by south to Holdenville, about 35 miles. Country here is mostly timber but some prairie near H. Land sells for $15-30 per acre though titles are risky. Pd. 40-cents for horse feed and care, 50-cents grub and lodging.

March 16: Left Holdenville at 7:30 a.m. and rode to Weleetka about 30 miles northeast timber country. Crossed north fork of Canadian River on ferry between Wetumka & Weleetka

March 17: Rode to Okmulgee timber country and rolling. Pd. 50-cents = horse care 50-cents lodging. Checked land sales here and they also are $15-30 per a acre. Bottomland is good but little of it. Warm.

March 18: Went to Okmulgee through Beggs to Sapulpha. Sapulpha is full of oil people and is growing considerably. Interesting lot.

March 19: Went to Tulsa by M. Tulsa is town of 13,000, is getting street cars. Remained in Tulsa day and night. Heard from home. Pd. 60-cents = grub, 75-cents horse care, 50-cents for lodging.

MARCH 20: Rode west to Prue about 35 miles over hills most of the way. Arkansas valley is very narrow all the way. This land is fair for cotton and grass.

MARCH 21: Went from Prue through Cleveland to 12 miles west of Cleveland. Expenses for self and horse = $1.25.

MARCH 22: Continued on my journey through Pawnee to within 10 miles of Red Rock. $1.25 expense for self and horse.

MARCH 23: To Ponca City $2.15 total expenses.

MARCH 24: Went to Newkirk, about 12 miles today. Country is prairie and good soil. Wheat looks healthy. Land sells at $8,000 -12,000 per quarter section. 65-cents expenses.

MARCH 25: Went north to Winfield, Kansas – some 30 mile ride. Land north of Newkirk is rocky stony land, thin soil. 60-cents for lodging and grub, 50-cents = horse Warm clear day.

MARCH 26: Winfield to Augusta – 32 miles north along valley of Walnut River valley is ½ - 2 miles wide. Alfalfa and wheat are leading crops. Good land in valley at $75 per acre. Prairie land is also thin and rocky. Pd. $1.50 = horse shoeing and feed. 65-cents for self = grub and lodging. Cloudy to very windy from S.

MARCH 27: Went northeast to Eldorado thence east to Reece, which is 40 miles from Augusta. Expense 55-cents

MARCH 28: Rain last night making ground a little muddy. Went northeast to Hamilton about 25 miles. Mostly upland. This is were feed crops are raised. Sells from $15 - $40 per acre. Continue to study crops and price of land. Expense = $1.20

March 29: From Hamilton to Emporia, another 30 plus miles. Emporia is town of 8,000 in valley county of Neocho and Cottonwood. Got much welcome shave, grub and lodging = 55-cents

March 30: Stopped at Miller in eve. Some rain turning colder. General character of ground is about same as south of here.

March 31: Rode to Seranton in the coal district. Land thinner and more clay. Pd. $1.20 for self and bronc.

April 1: Went northeast to Topeka. 75-cents for grub and lodging. 60-cents = self and horse. Country here more rolling hills. Dairying a leading industry in Topeka neighborhood. Cool southeast wind.

April 2: Rode to Valley Falls. Expense = $1.25 A very welcome letter from home was received.

April 3: Went to Denton This area's land is much richer and more rolling. Good wheat. Some rain in a.m. and late p.m.

April 4: Went east to St. Joseph, Mo. Very hilly – grass being leading crop. Pd. 65-cents for self and horse

April 5: Left St. Joe in cold light mist and went to Union Star – 25 miles northeast. Rough country, $1.40 total expense

April 6: Went to Stanberry = 20 miles Rain all day. Went through the cyclone strip today and yesterday, a path about 40 yds/ wide and 15 miles long in northeast direction. Nothing left in this area. Land fairly level to rough. Pd. $1.65 expense

April 7: Went to Grant City, riding 25 miles northeast. Changeable cool weather. Continues to be rough country Pd. $1.25 –self and horse

April 8: On to Mount Ayr, Iowa, Cold riding. Land very rolling and sells at $50 per acre. $1.15 total exp.

April 9: To Talmage, 30 miles north. Narrow strips of level country between broken ground. 50-cents = horse keep.

April 10: To Winterset. North country getting better more generally level. $1.55 exp.

April 11: To Waukee. Good country - low and black soil. Corn made 65 bushels last year. 95-cents = total exp.

April 12: Onward northeast to Madrid – 28 miles. Good country about all the way. Ground is more sandy. $1.75 = exp.

April 13: To Cambridge east. Looked for job today but landed none. Cold weather all week. N. E. wind prevailing – a few snow flurries! $1.80 exp.

April 14: To Nevada – town of 2000 plus $1.50 exp.

April. 15: To Radcliffe - North Scandinavian country slightly rolling. Pd. $1.25 expense

April 16–21: Worked part of time at livery barn. Recv'd $3.25 73-cents exp.

April 22–27: Went north 2 miles to A. L. Mossman's and worked remaining of week at $1 per day – 5 ½ days 75-cents exp. Continues cool days.

April 28: Cool cloudy – light rain

April 29–May 4: General farm work Wrecking house etc. 6 days of work.

May 5: At place

May 6–11: Plowing harrowing, disking etc. 75-cents for socks.

May 12–18: Steady weeks work at harrowing, work on house etc. Still very cool

May 19: Cora's 32nd birthday anniversary. Stayed at place today.

May 20–25: Routine farm work all wk. Heavy rain on 23rd and 24th. Pd. 80-cents = clothes and 10-cents= drugs

May 26: At place all day.

May 27–June 1: Steady work all week. Fencing, lathing, etc. Ma's 55th birthday anniversary on 30th.

June 2–8: Straight time, lathing etc. Cool

June 9: Day passed as usual. Read

June 10–15: Hauling material. Cultivating corn etc. Steady work

June 16: Hot clear day. Rode around country a few miles in p.m.

June 17–22: Cultivated corn and built fence. Weather warm.

June 23–29: Still cultivating corn etc. Pd 30-cents for envelopes. $9.50 for much needed clothes, Rec'd $10 from Mossman.

June 30: Rode horse north about 4 miles and played baseball!

July 1–3: Good corn growing weather. Cultivating corn.

July 4: Spent day in Radcliffe. 75-cents expenses. Ball games about all day. Warm Great day for baseball!

July 5–6: Worked in garden

July 7: At place all day. Hot and sultry.

July –13: Routine farm work. Settled with Mossman in eve of 13th, received check for $71.00 in full of a/ct. and saddle. Went to Radcliffe in eve and remained at Geo. Sheldon's. Pd. 10-cents shave

July 14: Remained at Sheldon's. HOT

July 15: Work for $1.00 day including board for a time. Repair work at barn.

July 16: Ditto yesterday.

July 17–Aug. 17: Work at Livery barn – driving etc.

Aug. 18–24: Routine work at barn. At various times since working here have received a total of $35 from Shelton. Have pd. $2.25- clothing, $1.25 washing, 90-cents. = shaving

Aug. 25–Sept. 3: Received $14 for work at livery barn.

Sept. 4–20: Regular work plus driving etc. Paid in full $14.00 Spent $1 = washing, 54-cents stamps and envelopes, 50-cents shirt, 60-cents for shaves.

Sept. 21: Heard from home today. Grandma is very low in health. Went to Iowa Falls and sent 1 doz. Carnations to her at Wolf Lake. Pd. $1.20 for flowers and express, $1.49 railroad fare and etc. Returned this eve. Corn along railroad is very poor.

Sept. 22–26: Same routine, received $6. Grandma is showing slight improvement.

Sept. 27–Oct. 2: Paid in full of a/c = $8 I left Radcliffe riding my horse south to Nevada. Considerable rain on the 1st. $1.25 expenses.

Oct. 3: Went from Nevada south to Elkhart. Cool

Oct. 4: Went to Colfax – a mineral water town. Expense = $1.15

Oct. 5: Rode on to Monroe. Rough country except for a strip between Skunk and Des Moines Rivers.

Oct. 6: Remain in Monroe thru Sunday. Very pleasant weather.

Oct. 7: Exp. $2.70 for self and horse. Rode around area until 1:30p. when I met up with a farmer and will work for him. Located northwest of Monroe.

Oct. 8–12: Worked on the farm and rec'd $5.25 on eve of 12th.

Oct. 13: Went to Mitchellville and remained over night. $1.60 expenses

Oct. 14: Rode north 3 miles to W. T. Haines where I went to work before noon at $1.00 per day, board and horse kept 'till corn shucking. Then 3 ½-cents per bu. for corn shucking.

Oct. 15–19: Farm work. To town on eve. Of 17th - $1.30 for mittens and soap etc.

Oct. 20: At place – reading, relaxing etc.

Oct. 21–23: Farm work

Oct. 24: Corn shucking by bushel began today. 28 bu. in a.m. and 26 in afternoon.

Oct. 25–26: Farm work. To town in eve of 26th. 90-cents for shave and purchased drawers.

Oct. 27: Cool N. W. wind. Stay at place all day. Lots of reading.

Oct. 28–31: Shucked corn on 28th Rain on 29th and 30th. Plowed on 31st. Only two half days of shucking corn. Pd. $6.00 for much needed overcoat, 63-cents for railroad fare, 15-cents = magazines. Shave 15-cents..

Nov. 1–3: To Mitchellville in evening on 2nd. Stayed at place.

Nov. 4–9: Shucked corn. A 12 acres field avg. 29 bus. per day, the remainder will make 40 bushels or more per acre. To Mitchellville in eve. 15-cents shave, 25-cents for liniment, 90-cents for mittens.

Nov. 10: Relaxed at place.

Nov. 11–16: Shucked corn.

Nov. 17–Dec. 5: Gathered corn most of the time. Finishing for Haines on 5th of December, having shucked 2400 bus at 3 ½- cents per bu. Settled with him in morning, receiving $97 for work. Got draft for $100.00. Paid $1.25 laundry and mending for 2 months, $1.60 overshoes, 65-cents for barbering. Attended farm implement and stock sale. Prices were not as high by 10% as last sales I attended.

Dec. 6: Left Haines at 9 a.m. and rode horse to a place 1 ½ miles south of Elkhart where I got job of corn gathering for a few days.

Dec. 7: Shucked corn. 35 & 43 bushels for day. Cloudy and some mist.

Dec. 8: Cloudy and rather a lonesome day. Miss family and friends.

Dec. 9: Stormy

Dec. 10: Finished corn gathering. 95 bushels.

Dec. 11: Rec'd $5.10. Went to Elkhart, thence toward Grimes. Put up at farmer Holts.

Dec. 12: Went west and south to Waukee and on to Boonville. 75-cents=expenses

Dec. 13: Boonville to Cummings.

Dec. 14–15: Cummings to Carlisle where I remained over until Sunday.

Dec. 16: Carlisle to Ford.

Dec. 17–24: Helped farmer McEntyre get up wood for saw, rec'd $6

Dec. 25: Rode to Pleasantville. Nothing resembles Christmas.

Dec. 26–31: Cut wood for T. Brown – pd. $3.50

1908

A BALL SIGNIFYING NEW YEAR'S DAY, drops in New York City's Times Square for the first time. On February 27th, a forty-sixth star is added to the United States flag, representing the State of Oklahoma. November of 1908, William Howard Taft defeats William Jennings Bryan, becoming the 27th President of the United States.

IN THE BACK OF THE JOURNAL there are entries showing he was employed in late 1907 by Mr. Mottem, W. T. Haines, A. L. Mossman, and B. J. Vaughan.

A notation states Mr. Mottem's agreement was Mr. Hill would be paid 75-cents per cord cut wood but he would be responsible in paying $3.00 per week for board.

Abruptly, this is where the formal entries end.

WBH's Great-Great Niece, Karen Hill Mail gave me WBH's hand-written account from 1960 about what he did in the years and months after his daybooks ended. It is as follows;

> Fall and Winter of 1906 and Spring of 1907 in Kansas and Indian Territory. I purchased and rode horse in March and April of 1907, from Indian Territory to Iowa—1,100 miles.
>
> On farm in Iowa and ditching from 1907-1910. Worked in Concrete Tile Plant until February 1913. After 3 months in

> Mississippi, back to Iowa. Excavating draining ditches for flood and water control in Iowa and Minnesota thru 1917.

He located in Charles City, Iowa in 1918, where he registered for the draft for WWI.

Papers state his occupation as a Grinder with employer, Hart-Parr.[40] In WWI he served at a camp in Iowa and worked in a machine shop. When called to action, he would be a foot soldier and sent to Virginia. He was ready to ship out but the War ended on November 11, 1918.

In 1920, he was living in Clear Lake, Iowa, as a Tiler. By May 1922, he moved to Detroit, Michigan where along with two other gentlemen, established an excavating business until December 30, 1924—To Louisville Kentucky for same firm until December 1927, returning to Detroit until September of 1932.

In 1933, upon the death of his mother, Sarah Agnes Shambaugh Hill he returned to the family home in Waterloo, Indiana. Mr. Hill now 57 years of age, remained there until his passing on June 15,1978.

Tintype of William Bert Hill, with permission of Karen Hill Mail

1893 Graduates of Waterloo High School, Waterloo, Indiana
Seated: Leora Yeagy, H. H. Keep, Supt., O. B. Arthur, Viola Powers, Principal
Standing: J. Lester Till, Dr. J. E. Graham, Fred Willis, W. Bert Hill

1890 Class, Right
Charles A. Hill

1890 graduation picture of brother, Charles A, Hill

Tintype of Cora Hill, used with permission of Karen Hill Mail

Photo button of Mary Jane North Shambaugh, Grandmother of WBH. He records numerous accounts in his journals about her. She lived in Wolf Lake, Kimmel, Indiana area.

WBH saved and wrote; "The 2 half-dollars are dated, 1876 = year I was born & 1893= the year I graduated from high school

Twenty-cent piece is one I had when I left home, Oct 1, 1895 and I carried for many, many years." W. Bert Hill

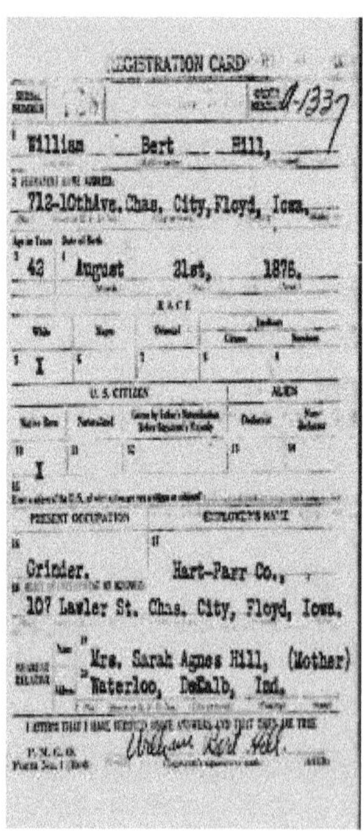

REGISTRATION CARD

1-1337

William Bert Hill,

712-10thAve. Chas. City, Floyd, Iowa.

43 August 21st, 1876.

RACE

I

U. S. CITIZEN | ALIEN

I

PRESENT OCCUPATION | EMPLOYER'S NAME

Grinder. Hart-Parr Co.,

107 Lawler St. Chas. City, Floyd, Iowa.

Mrs. Sarah Agnes Hill, (Mother)

Waterloo, DeKalb, Ind.

I AFFIRM THAT I HAVE VERIFIED ABOVE ANSWERS AND THAT THEY ARE TRUE

William Bert Hill

1918 Draft Registration Card from Charles City, Floyd County, Iowa. Employer: Hart-Parr Company, Occupation: Grinder. In WWI, he served at a camp in Iowa, the west side of the State and worked in the Machine Shop. When called to action he would be a foot soldier. Sent to Virginia and was ready to ship out but the War ended.

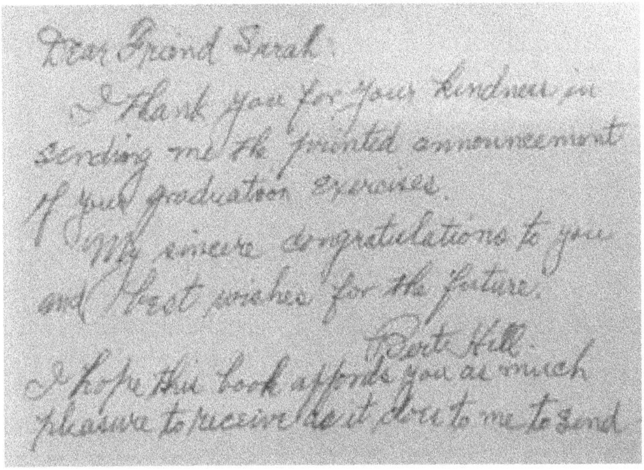

Dear Friend Sarah:
I thank you for your kindness in sending me the printed announcement of your graduation exercises.
My sincere congratulations to you and best wishes for the future.
Bertie Hill.
I hope this book affords you as much pleasure to receive as it does to me to send

WBH's graduation gift to me was The Oxford Book of American Verse, which included his 1893 graduation name card and my 1967graduation name card. The note was attached to the inside cover of the poetry book, "Congratulations and best wishes for the future. "

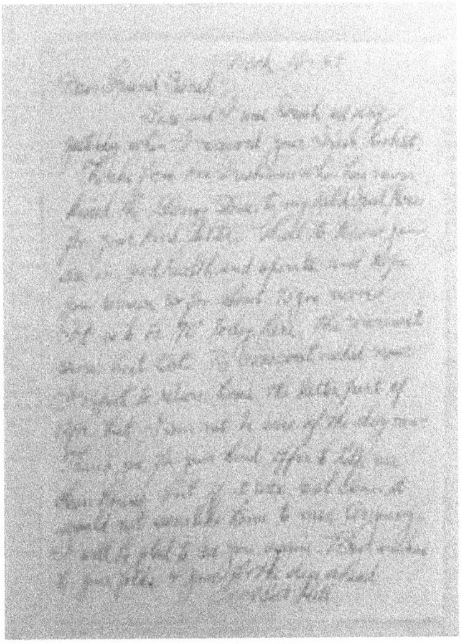

Letter dated, March 18, 1969. At 93 years young, WBH began spending the winters with niece, Laura Hill Smith in Michigan. His home was not winterized and the heat source consisted of a potbelly wood-fired stove.

Birthday boy

WBH's 99th birthday – 1975 – He is standing by the last remaining maple tree his father planted in the front yard. Notice a glimpse of his home in the background, which was demolished in the 1980's. The Evening Star newspaper, Auburn, Indiana

1975 WBH's 99th birthday. Pictured: WBH, Sarah and her daughter, Emily

Letter dated, February 4, 1976. WBH at almost 100 hundred years old, still maintained his legible handwriting and reminisced about our first introduction.

William Bert Hill's obituary, 1977. Picture was taken on his 100th birthday in 1976.

Bert Hill, 101, dies

WATERLOO — One of DeKalb County's oldest residents, Bert Hill, died at 8:45 a.m. today in Carlin Park Nursing Home at Angola. He was 101 years old.

Mr. Hill was born Aug. 21, 1876 in a home at [illegible] E. Douglas St., Waterloo. He returned in [illegible] and lived in the same home for about 44 years before going to Carlin Park.

His parents were Elijah and Sarah Agnes (Shambaugh) Hill. He graduated from Waterloo High School in [illegible] with a class of six. After that his travels took him throughout the west and midwest. At one time he was a partner in an excavating business.

His only survivors are one niece, Mrs. Edward Smith of Waterloo, and two nephews, William C. Hill of Belleville, Mich. and H.L. Hill of Cincinnati. A brother, Charles, preceded him in death in [illegible] and a sister, Cora Baumgartner, died in [illegible].

His funeral will be Saturday at 2 p.m. in [illegible] Funeral Home. Rev. Max Smith, pastor of Waterloo United Methodist Church, will officiate. Burial will be in Waterloo Cemetery.

Friends may call at the funeral home after 2 p.m. Friday.

Bert Hill
In 1976 photo

FAMILY TREE

Mr. Hill mentions many family members in his daybooks. Shortly after his death, his niece, Laura Hill Smith presented me with an envelope spilling over with handwritten notes that had been found in his desk. It contained random thoughts, baseball scores, recipes, addresses and notes about his relatives. I was able to compile, with additional assistant from his great-great niece, Karen Hill Mail, the following family information.

Dr. Elijah Hartshorn I	B.2/5/1754 Norwich, Conn. D.6/14/1839 Franklin, Conn. Father of Isaac Johnson Hartshorn
Jerusha Johnson Hartshorn	B.1/14/1760 Norwich, Conn. D.12/30/1807 Franklin, Conn. Mother of Isaac Johnson Hartshorn
Isaac Johnson Hartshorn	B.4/7/1795 D.8/26/1875 Father of Elijah Hartshorn Hill and twin Delia Hartshorn
Delia (Ellis) Hartshorn I	B. 1/29/1793 D. 6/11/1834 in childbirth (Delia and Elijah) Mother of Elijah Hartshorn Hill and twin Delia Hartshorn

Isaac and Delia's four (4) older sons:

Andrew	B.1822 D.1901 M. no children,
Asher	B. 3/15/1823 - New London, Conn. D. 6/3/1887 – Hamilton Co., Ohio Married Ann Mitchell B.1826 in Ireland D. 7/28/1900 Cincinnati, Ohio Daughter: Hattie Hartshorn
Isaac Franklin	B. 1824 D.1866 Unmarried
Samuel Ellis	B. 1827 Unmarried D. 4/1/1855 in GA.

Mr. Hill notes that Delia was born a few minutes before his father, Elijah. Soon after the birth of the twins, their Uncle David Hartshorn took Delia to raise.

A neighbor, **George W. Hill** and his wife **Terresie Louis (Porter) Hill** adopted Elijah Hartshorn Hill.

Delia (Hartshorn) Averill II	B. 6/11/1834 D. 8/31/1910 Soldiers Home, Vineland, N.J. Married Samuel Averill

Elijah Hartshorn Hill B. 6/11/1834 Corfu, West Batavia, N.Y. D. 7/17/1902 Buried in Waterloo, Indiana

Elijah served in the Civil War with Co. K. 18th Regiment Volunteer Michigan as a foot soldier. Marched through Ohio, Kentucky, Tennessee, Mississippi, Alabama to Georgia. Career: Millwright

Lucinda Young Hill (1st wife) B.4/26/1842 in Whiteford, MI. Married 1865 D. 3/6/1870

Daughter: **Delia (Hill) Wolcott** B.1869 D.1920 Married 1888 to Oliver Wolcott

Sarah Agnes Shambaugh Hill (2nd wife) B. 5/30/1852 Married 9/3/1871 D. 2/9/1933

Mother: Mary Jane North Shambaugh B. 02/25/1831 D. 11/15/1907

Father: William Shambaugh B. 07/05/1831 D. 06/27/1891

Sisters: Catherine Ellen "Ella" B. 09/28/1856 D. 11/23/1956

Alma Jane (M. 1886 J. A.Richmond)	B. 07/14/1861 D. 11/21/1922
Son: Carter Richmond	B: 1894
Brother: Henry Albert (M. 1887 Jennie Allen)	B. 09/07/1859 D. 09/03/1944
Son: Dr. Dewey Allen Shambaugh	B. 1889 D. 1977

Children of Elijah and Sarah Agnes (Shambaugh) Hill

1. Charles Austin Hill	B. 02/19/1873 D. 11/30/1959 Mina Evado (Hall) Hill (wife) B. 1874 D. 1943 Both are buried in Lakeside Cemetery, Port Huron, MI.

Charles and Mina's three (3) children:

William C. Hill	B. 04/15/1902 D. 1994 Married Ruth (Kennedy) Hill 1927
Daughter: Ann Hill	B.1931 Married William David Horn 1954

Ann and Wm. Horn's children:

Daniel Paul Horn	*B. 1956*
Thomas Edward Horn	B. 1958 D. 11/2022
Son: William Bert Hill	B. 5/7/1934 D. 4/15/2004 Married Louise (Hall) Hill 1957

William and Louise Hill's Daughter:

Karen Hill Mailer	*B. 12/18/1959*
Horace Leslie (Bud) Hill	B. 1905 D. 1991 Married Sally Wheeler abt. 1930 Daughters: Mary Catherine and Elizabeth Son: Richard Hill
Laura Agnes (Hill) Smith	B. 05/03/1907 D. 04/27/2006 Married: Heath Morris 1930

Two (2) Children: Charles and Nancy both died in infancy

Two (2) Adopted Children: Carol and Robert Morris

	Married: Edward Stapleton Smith 1977 B. 1896 D. 1993

2. William Bert Hill	B. 08/21/1876 D. 06/15/1978 Waterloo, Indiana Pearle Lamb (spouse) B. 06/21/1886 D. unknown M. 11/01/1926 Divorced 01/1928
3. Cora May Hill Baumgartner	B. 05/19/1875 D. 10/01/1920 Waterloo, Indiana Lorenzo Baumgartner (spouse) M. 10/1916

AMPLIFICATIONS

1897

1 The invention of the ***threshing machine*** occurred in the 1780's. Before the threshing machine, when grain was cut by hand, the method for separating the kernels from the straw was labor intensive. Grain was hauled to a barn where it was spread on a floor and was trampled by animals. The object was to knock the kernels free of the straw, which would be raked away. The remaining mixture was winnowed, by tossing it into the air where the wind was relied on to blow the chaff and lighter debris away from the heavier grain.

From 1897, the manuscript of W. H. Dill states "I recollect very distinctly an early threshing machine. It indeed was a beauty. It did not even separate the grain from the chaff and straw, but it drew crowds when set to work. Instead of being several weeks in flailing, tramping and winnowing out a hundred bushels of wheat, the farmer could thresh out that quantity in a day, and then take his time to run it through the fanning mill."

The threshing machine of yesteryear is the combine of modern times. Both machines remove the grain from the stalks. The main difference is that the combine is self-propelled and eliminates both the man-hours and the threshing crew that the old threshing machines used.

The operation of a ***corn sheller*** is similar to a threshing machine, but in order to deal with larger grain size and other differences of corn, the corn shellers were hand cranked. Whole corncobs were fed in and were pulled between two toothed wheels, usually made of metal. Each wheel spun the opposite direction of the other. The teeth pulled the kernels off the cob until there were no kernels left. The kernels fell out through a screen into a container (such as a bucket) placed underneath the machine. The cob was then ejected out, since it couldn't pass through the screen.

The main piece of equipment needed for ***husking/shucking*** *corn* was a hook. This steel peg or hook was strapped to the hand and was used to tear the shucks open on the corn. Many huskers wore gloves but some shucked barehanded. The most common method used in husking was to grip an ear with one hand, yank off the husk with the other hand, and twist the ear from the stalk.

A ***spring-tooth harrow***, sometimes called a drag harrow, is a specific type of tine harrow. It used many flexible iron teeth mounted in rows to loosen the soil before planting. It set in the ground and rose manually and could not back up. It was a good implement for rough work, and especially for stony ground. It was popular for orchard tillage, partly because the teeth would spring over the roots and with little damage to them. But on rough land the spring-tooth harrow was jerky and hard on the horses' shoulders. What made this harrow so popular was the durability and the ease with which obstructions were cleared.

There were approximately 294 brand/type of plows during the late 1800's and early 1900's. Most plows were variations on the time-tested, walk behind moldboard design with an iron plowshare attached to a wooden or iron beam. **Gopher plows** had a vertical disc that was used to cut through roots. Double, sulky and turn plows were more advanced implements. **Sulky plows** represented the most advanced models in the late nineteenth century, because the plowman actually rode the plow through the field.

2 ***The Waterloo Press,*** DeKalb County, Waterloo, Indiana's editor set his first type on February 4, 1859. THE PRESS would be an independent family newspaper, devoted to the news of the day. *Agricultural, Domestic Economy, Social Improvement, the Dissemination of General Intelligence, and the True Interests of DeKalb County, Indiana* "The policy of THE PRESS would be to attain an honorable position in its own way. It would be strictly "Independent in all Things and Neutral in Nothing" and will be governed only by the dictates of an honest judgment. The Civil War, fires and mishaps never stopped an issue from being printed. It was the oldest paper in DeKalb County, Indiana. It continued to be published until June 28, 1973. *Account taken from the 1902 DeKalb County Historical Book*

3 The principal role of ***corn*** planting during the 19th century was closely tied to the development of the Midwest. In the movement westward, corn found its major home in the woodland clearings and grasslands of Ohio, Indiana, Illinois and Iowa.

As an overview, in 1898, Mr. Hill writes that he is receiving 2½–cents per bushel for corn shucked. He could average 100 bushels per day and records that corn harvest is about 50 - 60 bushels per acre. Present corn yield per acre in Illinois averages 200 bushels. (2018). In 1903, he is paid by measuring bushels in a crib and also by weight. Daily bushels shucked averaged between 94 – 101 bushels at 2¾-cents per bushel. In 1904, Mr. Hill notes measuring cribs and also continues shucking by weight, (averaging 79.5 bushels, at a daily rate of 3-cents per bushel).

4 Since Mr. Hill's description of the ***Lincoln Monument*** in 1897, it has been altered numerous times. It is a fascinating read; the protecting of Lincoln and his family's remains, the numerous physical locations and the reconstructions that were needed to secure the monument. The Oak Ridge Cemetery was dedicated in 1860 and construction of the monument began in 1869. Their son, Eddie was buried in 1850 in the Hutchinson Cemetery in Springfield, Illinois. Tad Lincoln's remains were placed within the tomb following his death in July 1871, and in September, Lincoln's remains and the remains of his sons; Willie and Eddie were also moved to the unfinished structure.

By 1897 mounting maintenance costs and the prospect of a reconstruction of the obelisk made it inescapable that the State of Illinois would have to take over responsibility and oversee the sight. Upon an inspection they discovered the tomb would have to be rebuilt, because the original monument was built in clay, which rendered the entire monument unstable. It was at this time that the height of the obelisk was increased by an additional fifteen feet.

5 The sport of trotting has always been enjoyed and had a large following. Originally, trotting matches were raced from the saddle. But greater use of vehicles put the racing trotter between the shafts. Harness racing was born. The racing sulky underwent numerous changes. By 1897, a radical innovation was made in the sulky design, which created the ancestor of today's sulky by placing pneumatic-tired bicycle wheels on a high-wheeled sulky frame. This increased the potential speed of the trotter by lowering wind resistance and by increasing stability; therefore the "bike-sulky" was born.

Star Pointer and Joe Patchen were two of the most popular and successful harness race horses of this time. Many times open betting was a legal and a popular American pastime. They were all trotters but pacers soon gained acceptance with the first two-minute mile, recorded in 1897 by the pacer, Star Pointer. The horse that popularized pacing was Dan Patch, (son of Joe Patchen, foaled in 1897) one of the fastest (1:55 for the mile) and the most popular Standard breeds ever.

The Sacramento Daily Union dated October 2, 1897 headline read: "Star Pointer Still the King of Pacers." Defeats Joe Patchen on the track at Springfield, Illinois. When the two great pacers made their appearance they were greeted with cheers. Patchen won the first heat in a jog in 2:14, with Pointer about 300 feet behind. In the second heat the two horses started even, but Patchen soon broke and lost a dozen lengths. But down the stretch it was a fight between the two. Pointer gained the lead and passed under the wire half a length ahead. The third heat was a wildly exciting one and was a race for blood from the start with Pointer winning by five lengths!

1898

6 In 1872, ***Montgomery Ward*** opened and was the first mail-order house in existence, with a single page, sales sheet. By 1900, it boasted more than a 1,000 pages. In 1887 they moved to Michigan Avenue, into the Tower Building, which still stands today. (Aaron Montgomery Ward battled to create a lakefront park in Chicago and to preserve the land as open space. As a result Chicago possesses one of the most magnificent front yards in the world. What contributed to the success of the mail-order catalog sales was that the middle class income was on the rise and rural mail delivery, railroad transportation and factory production was increasing. The impact the mail order business had on rural America is a fascinating story and is a book in itself.

It is noted that Mr. Hill would purchase daily needs, salve, paper, postage stamps, candy, work mittens etc. from the local general store but he consistently ordered from Montgomery Ward.

The Waltham watch, which he purchased from Montgomery Ward, could be tracked since the serial number was recorded and he always kept meticulous records of this watch and its repairs. The grade name is Crescent Street, which refers to one of the manufacturer's many grade names of their watches. Waltham chose the names of board members, investors or prominent individuals, such as, Appleton Tracy & Co, William Ellery, Crescent Street, etc.

7 Mr. Hill felt *Mr. Hotsenpiller* was a good and decent man and felt sorrow at his passing. His obituary was found in his journal. It reads; A Ripe Age - Death of William Hotsenpiller of Ballard – ***William Hotsenpiller***

was born in Shenandoah County, Va., February 23, 1838 and died at his home in Chenoa Township Saturday, April 16, 1898, age 60. Dropsy was the cause of his death. April 4, 1861, he was married to Miss Frances Dunham. The household circle was completed by the birth of eight children. He was converted in early manhood and united with the Methodist Episcopal Church. The Oliviet Church was built in which he took undying interest and to the time of his death it was a cherished place. (Mr. Hill has numerous entries about attending Oliviet Church. where he made his first acquaintance with Mr. Hotsenpiller.) The funeral was held at the Olivet Church and a long procession followed his remains to the Lexington Cemetery.

8 The origins of the 1898 ***Spanish-American War*** began with the Wilson-Gorman Tariff of 1894. It put restrictions on sugar imports to the U. S. that severely hurt the economy of Cuba. In Cuba, then a Spanish colony, nationalists began a revolt against the ruling Spanish regime. Spain sent in General Weyler to stabilize the situation; many U.S. businessmen with investment interests in Cuba became concerned. The American public was stirred into an anti-Spain frenzy by the yellow journalism of men like Hearst and Pulitzer. By the time President McKinley came into office in 1897 the uproar over Cuba was continuing. The U.S. dispatched the *USS Maine* on a "friendly" mission to Cuba. On February 15, 1898 the *Maine* mysteriously blew up. The U.S. blamed a Spanish mine. McKinley declared war and by April, both U.S. and Spain had declared war. In order to ensure the world that it was fighting only for the good of Cuba, the U.S. passed the Teller Amendment, which promised to make Cuba independent after the war was over. Assistant Secretary of the Navy, Theodore Roosevelt ordered Commodore Dewey to attack Manila Harbor in the Philippines. On May 1st Dewey destroyed the Spanish fleet. The U.S. invaded the Philippines, Guam and Puerto Rico during the war. With heroics from the famous Rough Riders, the ground effort in Cuba was a success. On December 10, 1898, the Treaty of Paris was signed, ending the war. The U.S. liberated Cuba and got Puerto Rico, Guam and the Philippines as colonies for itself. After the war, the U.S. made improvements in the Cuban infrastructure and educational systems and prepared to leave. But in 1901, the U.S. forced the Cubans to insert the Platt Amendment into their constitution, which gave the U.S. a military base on the Island (Guantanamo).

9 ***Helena Amelia Rempis*** was a friend and schoolmate of Mr. Hill's. He always spoke of her kindness and sweet personality. The drowning accident had a large impact on the entire community. Six young folks in a small boat, on a deep lake; no thought that this combination would lead to such a tragedy. Ironically, Leonard Eugene Roby who knew how to swim also drown, after saving the others. *Waterloo Press, Waterloo, Indiana, August 18, 1898*

10 ***The Jucklins*** is an 1896 novel by Opie Read. It was a best selling book in the United States, with over one million copies sold, though it never appeared on the best-sellers list since its early and primary sales were of paperback copies sold on trains and newsstands. The story is set in the backwoods of North Carolina. Teacher, Bill Hawes lives with the Jucklins, a local farming family. Author reported that he sold the book for $700 to publisher, Laird and Lee. *Adaptations:* Adopted as a stage play and in 1921, a silent film version was released, which has been lost to time.

11 Many U. S. cities observed the end of the Spanish American War with celebrations. The ***National Peace Jubilee*** in Chicago, Illinois began on October 16 through October 22, 1898. President McKinley remained most of the week at the Jubilee making many speeches. The parade, on October 19th that Mr. Hill refers, by historical accounts was reported to be "one of the greatest parades that Chicago every witnessed. No one with eyes to see and a heart to feel could look upon that Great War and Peace Army without a thrill of deep patriotism. Most significant, was the formation of the hollow square, which enclosed the carriage of the President and served as his bodyguard. In front were naval reserves and to the rear, veterans of the land forces at Santiago. On the right flanked the Grand Army and Ex-Confederate veterans and more who made up the remarkable pageant." *Chicago Tribune*

1899

12 ***Dr. John E. Covey*** has numerous articles written about him in the Lexington and Chenoa newspapers. He attended Illinois Wesleyan University in Bloomington, Illinois, graduating in 1887. He immediately located in Lexington, Illinois. Townspeople spoke of his dedication to his patients. He was deeply involved and served in all local organizations. As a citizen he was enterprising and progressive, ready to assist in any enterprise of public benefit.

La Grippe is known today as influenza. In 1898 this highly contagious illness was of concern, and was known to be fatal. The following is a newspaper advertisement, typical at the time. The ads were placed strategically next to updates of local people's illnesses and their condition. "During the prevalence of the Grippe the past seasons, it was a noticeable fact that these who depended upon, "Dr. King's New Discovery", not only had a speedy recovery, but escaped all of the troublesome after-effects of the malady. This remedy seems to have a peculiar power in affecting rapid cures not only in cases of La Grippe, but in all diseases of the throat, chest and lungs and in most cases of asthma and hay fever of long standing. "Try it and be convinced. It won't disappoint." Free trial bottles at Kennedy Bros. and Co.'s Lexington and Schuirmann and Hops, Chenoa." *Taken from the Chenoa Clipper Newspaper, Chenoa, Illinois*

Frequently advertised and widely available, Dr. King's New Discovery products became well known enough to attract the attention of the medical profession, and were used as a symbol of the dangers of patent medicines.

13 ***Scours,*** common term is diarrhea. Even today, despite improvements in management practices and prevention and treatment strategies, diarrhea is still the most common and costly disease affecting young lambs.

14 "I must pay one day's work for ***poll tax,*** which I did on the 4th."

The very early poll taxes were general revenue measures, authorized as far back as the 1630's by the General Court in Massachusetts and Virginia colonial authorities. But the poll tax had fallen into disuse as a general revenue source by the Civil War. The more affluent white population had access to the polls, while the poorer white and black population would have trouble justifying trading rent, food and clothes for a vote at the ballot box. Voting was a wealthy man's game. The winning of elections was successful by approaching the few people who could afford to pay the poll tax, which effectively created a one-party state.

On January 23, 1964, the 24th Amendment to the Constitution was adopted. The heart of the amendment, Section 1 reads: The right of citizens of the United States to vote in any primary or other election for President or Vice President, for electors for President or Vice President, or for Senator or Representative in Congress, shall not be denied or abridged by the United States or any State by reason of failure to pay any poll tax or other tax. Illinois was the first state to pass the amendment.

Five states still imposed a poll tax as a condition for voting for state elections. Finally in 1966, the Supreme Court ruled that a poll tax was unconstitutional even in state elections. Stating; Voter qualifications have no relation to wealth nor to paying or not paying this or any other tax. So finally the end came to the poll tax.

15 The ***ABC Mining*** by Charles Bramble, published in 1898 can be read in its entirety on line. An example of information is as follows: Without the prospector there would be no mining and the world would yet be in the Stone Age. The author states, "One may not be very deeply learned in either geology or mineralogy, but he must have a keen eye and good natural powers of observation." The prospector keeps his eye open as he goes along and notes carefully the character of the fragments of rock he finds in the streams. Quartz, diorite, diabase and porphyry pebble are grounds for expecting a profitable result. Bramble warns a pick, shovel and pan must be handled skillfully, while the rife and shotgun must also be understood. The traveler must even rely upon the fish and game.

1900

16 There was a series of Pre-Columbian Native American *cliff dwellings* located in the Sierra Ancha ("broad range" in Spanish) Wilderness. The Salado people built them between 1280 and 1350. They used mud and rocks to construct multi-story dwellings or pueblos.

In 1900, Mr. Hill writes about his discovery of the ruins but mistakenly believes the Aztec Indians built them. Today the Salado communities of the river valley have been covered up by Theodore Roosevelt Lake but the elevated cliff dwellings remain. In 1907, Theodore Roosevelt set two relatively intact cliff dwellings aside as the Tonto National Monument.

17 ***Fort McDowell*** was established by the California Volunteers on the west bank of the Verde River in 1865. They were created to protect the area from Apache who roamed the Salt and Gila River Valleys. The camp was first called Camp Verde, but was later renamed to Camp McDowell after Major General Irwin McDowell. After numerous skirmishes, the victory of the Salt River Canyon Battle brought the campaign to a close. In 1890, it became known at the Fort McDowell Indian Reservation serving Mohave, Apache and Prima Indians.

18 In 1864, the town site of Prescott was surveyed and laid out along the Granite Creek, where gold had been panned. The town was designated the capital of the new territory of Arizona after it was separated from New Mexico. President Lincoln wanted the territorial capital in the northern part of the territory, far away from the Confederate sympathizing cities to the south. The City was named after the favorite author, at the time, William Hickling Prescott.

Headlines and article from the ***Arizona Miner***, Saturday, July 14, 1900, read "Prescott Swept By Fierce Flames", "A Sickening Scene of Disaster" The city was helpless without water to combat the fire. The fire started in a room over J. E. Burchard's bottling works on South Montezuma Street, where a man is said to have been lying in bed reading a paper. The flames made rapid progress and within minutes had burst through the roof and spread. Powder was sent for and a number of buildings were blow up in the hopes of saving the magnificent Scopel block, but all efforts proved unavailing. The flames lapped up the flattened buildings, sending their fiery forks high in the air, as if laughing at the futile efforts to stay their progress.. One after another succumbed to the flames, every building in the block to Granite Street being burned. While hundreds of men were engaged in fighting the flames and in removing goods to places of safety, the balance of the population, including women and children watched the appalling work of destruction. Around 3:30 a.m., the fire was under control but most of the downtown was gone. The scene during the fire was beyond all power of description. Wagons and buggies, men on horseback, men, women and children afoot were scurrying hither and thither, the human part of it being more or less excited. *(Mr. Hill's comments parallel this newspaper account.)*

19 A young engineer, George Washington Gale Ferris created the ***Ferris Wheel*** for the Chicago Exposition of 1893. Luther Rice was hired as the Construction Chief of the project. The cars were 24 feet wide and 10 feet high and weighed 26,000 pounds. Each car carried fancy twisted wire chairs for 38 of the 60 passengers. Conductors rode in each car to the height of 264 feet, to answer patron's questions or, if necessary calm their fears. The wheel weighed 2,382,244 pounds, including the 2,160 passengers. A trip consisted of one revolution, during which six stops were made for loading, followed by one nine-minute nonstop revolution. In July 1895, the Wheel was re-erected adjacent to Lincoln Park. Investors anticipated development of this area with restaurants, a band shell and a theater, which did not materialize. In 1900, when WBH rode on this Ferris Wheel it had been relocated to Lincoln Park but by 1903 the Ferris Wheel was dismantled and used at the 1904 St. Louis World's Fair. By May 11, 1906 a neglected Wheel came to its end and was demolished by dynamite, to become salvage.

20 ***J B. Clawson*** and his wife, Elizabeth Mason moved to Lexington, Illinois in 1880. Mr. Hill mentions numerous times "stopping at Clawson's, visiting with friends, staying at this boarding house until he would secure work". It is mentioned in J. B. Clawson's obituary about owning a restaurant but nothing that confirms a boarding house. But according to the census, he and his wife, Elizabeth did operate a boarding house in the early 1900's in Lexington, Illinois.

1901

21 ***Purdue University*** located in West Lafayette, Indiana had its origin in an Act of Congress, passed in 1862, which "Donated public lands to the several States and Territories, which may provide College for the benefit of Agriculture and the Mechanic Arts." In 1865, the State of Indiana accepted the grant and the sale of this land together with other gifts and established an endowment. A gift of $150,000 from John Purdue and other donations located the University on a beautiful site not far from the center of the City of Lafayette, Indiana. Dedicated in 1877, University Hall, originally called the Main Building is the oldest building still in existence in 2024.

In 1901 the Purdue Debris describes that the Winter Courses in Agriculture covers the two winter terms each extending from January to April. It states that, " The work differs from that of the regular courses, in that a minimum amount of text book study is required, and lecture and laboratory exercises constitute the most of the class work. This feature renders the work of much more value to the students, as they are taught to practice and apply the correct methods, rather than to evolve methods from underlying principles. Everything in the course is of direct practicability, and when the young man returns to the farm, the good results are immediate. The Winter Course does not take the place of the more thorough education, but in a measure forms a means whereby the farmer may become appreciative of the value of technical preparation in his life work."

22 In America, the history of the ***German Coach Horse*** is comparatively brief. It made its first appearance in the 1880's. Not much prior to 1890 did the breed receive recognition at American shows. *Crouch & Son*, of Indiana, were most actively and prominently identified with its promotion. Ento and Hannibal, owned by *Crouch & Son*, were distinguished in the show-ring. Winning against the severest competition for years in succession.

23 **The Cakewalk** was a pre-Civil War dance originally performed by slaves. It was first known as the "prize walk"; the prize was a cake. By the 1870's, a cakewalk was a popular feature of minstrel shows. The dance featuring fancy strutting and steps that was fluid and graceful. As the dance became more popular, they gave rise to their own form of music, an early predecessor of ragtime. The term "that takes the cake" was derived from this dance form.

24 On September 5, 1901, in Buffalo, New York while visiting the Temple of Music at the Pan-American Exposition, ***William McKinley***, President of the United States, was shot a few minutes after 4 o'clock in the afternoon. For a little over a week, he clung to life. During the days following an operation, it was hoped would save his life, confidence was high the President would recover. One bullet struck on the upper portion of the breastbone, glancing and not penetrating; the second bullet penetrated the abdomen. The abdomen was opened through the line of the bullet wound. It was found that the bullet had penetrated the stomach. The opening was closed after which a search was made for a hole in the back wall of the stomach. This was found and also closed. The further course of the bullet could not be found. That bullet, passing through vital organs caused an infection that resulted in his death. On September 14, 1901, he died from an infection. At the autopsy the surgeons probed for nearly an hour and a half trying to locate the bullet that had taken his life. It was never found. Unknown to medical professionals back then, it is believed he died of pancreatic necrosis.

The assassin, 28 year old, Leon Czolgosz, a blacksmith from Cleveland, Ohio confessed. He described with accuracy the preparations he had made to kill the President, how he had practiced in folding the handkerchief about his hand so as to conceal the revolver and described how he had shot President McKinley. He said he had been a student of Emma Goldberg, the Anarchist. She was arrested and held for two weeks then released when there was no proof she had any association with the assassin.

Emma Goldberg's story is worth researching. She created and edited, *Mother Earth* Magazine, an anarchist journal that described itself as "A

Monthly Magazine Devoted to Social Science and Literature" Alexander Berkman, another well-known anarchist, was the magazine's editor from 1907 to 1915. It published articles on a variety of anarchist topics including the labor movement, education, literature and the arts, state and government control, and women's emancipation, sexual freedom, and was an early supporter of birth control. Its subscribers and supporters formed a virtual "who's who" of the radical left in the United States in the years prior to 1920.

1902

25 ***Alexander Archibald Rice*** Obituary (Source: Saturday Press, Attica, Indiana 1/25/1902) A. A. Rice died at his home in Lafayette last Sunday morning from neuralgia of the heart. He was born near Waveland, Montgomery County, May 26, 1834 and was one of the best known men in this part of the state. He practiced law in Attica, three years prior to the war. When it broke out he was the first man to raise a company in Fountain County. He served as Captain of the Company, which was A of the 15th Indiana, afterwards serving with the 72nd and was later Assistant Adjutant General on the staff of General Joseph Reynolds. After the war he went into a partnership with Milford, his father-in-law at this place and in 1871 moved to Lafayette. Captain Rice was a man of many high qualities and was popular wherever he was known. Captain Rice frequently visited Attica and always had a pleasant greeting for each and all of his acquaintance. At the time of his death, he was teaching a Rural Law Class at Purdue University.

26 Feb 15, 1902 the Grand Opera House in Lafayette, Indiana introduces ***King Dodo**, a* light opera, and a musical comedy in three acts, music by Gustav Luders and lyrics by Henry Pixley. New York City was experiencing a theatrical bonanza in the late 1800's, which tempted the tycoons of Broadway to bring Gustav Luders to NYC to write the music for productions for Anna Held, Elsie Janix, Harry Bulger and Frank Moulan, the stars of NYC. Like Victor Herbert and many of the other composers who pioneered the field of American musical comedy, Gustav Luders was of foreign stock. He was born in Bremen, Germany in 1865. After serving for years in the Kaiser's army, he studied violin, piano and composition. In 1888 he came to America. The opera, *The Burgomaster* made Luder's an overnight success. His scores of *King Dodo, The Prince of Pilsen, The Sho-Gu* and *The Old Town* continued his popularity. In a brilliant but relatively short career that was marked by one success after another, Luder collaborated with two writers whose gift with words matched his ability with notes. Both came out of the editorial rooms of The Chicago-Times-Herald, one was Henry Pixley, the paper's editor-in-chief.

27 Orator and Author, ***Thomas Dixon, Jr.*** was born in 1864 in Shelby, North Carolina. He received a master's degree from Wake Forest, where he studied history and political science. Then attended Johns Hopkins University, where he became friends with Woodrow Wilson. He continued to find his way, leaving there and headed to NYC to study drama. Acting was not to be so he went home and received his law degree in 1885. He dabbled in local politics, became disillusioned, then went into private practice but would soon leave and become a minister. He was ordained a Baptist minister in 1886. By 1889 he left the ministry and began to lecture throughout the country. While on a lecture tour, Dixon began writing what would become his Ku Klux Klan trilogy. In, 1915, *The Birth of a Nation*—a silent film based on his Ku Klux Klan novels, *The Leopard's Spots* and *The Clansman.*

D. W. Griffin directed the landmark and notorious film, which is praised for its many cinematic innovations while rightly so was condemned for its overt racist agenda. Griffith's innovative techniques and storytelling power have made *The Birth of a Nation* one of the landmarks of film history. In 1992, the United States Library of Congress deemed the film "culturally, historically, or aesthetically significant" and selected it for preservation in the National Film Registry.

28 July 4th was celebrated in every city, town and village. ***Baseball*** was always being played in Bloomington, Lexington, Chenoa, Peoria and all surrounding towns. Lexington's baseball great, Ed Kinsella was a farm boy who made the professional baseball ranks in 1905, with the Pittsburgh Pirates. In Lexington baseball rivalries were played in Old Dawson Park, where Ed and others like Noah Henline, John and Bill Turnipseed, Melvin Barnard, Bert Franklin, Bert Stevens, Billy Bold, Charlie Hibbs and Billy Lawrence exercised their talents. *Daily Pantagraph*, Bloomington, Ill.

Where there was a park, there was a baseball game. In Lexington, Illinois, during the 1890's and early 1900's two parks were in use. One was just north of the T.P. & W. railroad track and west of Lexington Route 66, which was the scene of some hotly contested baseball games. The other ballpark was on the lots west of M.F. Quinn residence at 318 Owsley Street. Wild West shows and carnivals did business in these parks too.

One article from *The Chenoa Clipper* read; "GOOD BASEBALL GAMES**".** That is what may be expected when the home club enters the field. As the spring and summer season is almost here Chenoa will go to work to organize a baseball club, which has been talked about for several weeks past. It is very generally believed that a good club could be put in the field here and the exhilarating pastime derived from a good game of ball would tone up the system better than double doses of spring medicine. I have vivid memories of Mr. Hill welcoming me into his parlor to listen to baseball games, usually the Detroit Tigers on the radio. I would sit on his mother's settee and become mesmerized, as the announcer would announce the play-by- play. He loved talking about the games and would answer any of my questions. My loyalty to the Chicago Cubs and the game of baseball, I owe to my parents and Mr. Hill.

29 Front page of the *Waterloo Press,* dated; Thursday morning, July 24, 1902 carried the obituary of ***Elijah Hill.*** (Excerpt) WAS AN EXCELLENT SOLDIER and had many friends—his life's career has been an honorable one. The sudden death of Elijah Hill, which occurred last Thursday evening, was a shock to the community, as no one knew that his health was critical. He took his scythe to cut some grass and weeds for his chickens and suddenly collapsed with heart failure. The deceased had a good record as a soldier, was a number one mechanic, an expert millwright and a citizen who had few or no enemies. He was somewhat reserved in his habits, but was always genial and honest with those whom he became acquainted. He was an honorable citizen and his death takes from our midst one of the old time residents, who will be missed by all who knew him.

He was born in West Batavia, New York, June 11, 1834 and died at his home in Waterloo, July 17, 1902, aged 68 years, 1 month and 6 days. In 1840 he moved with his parents to Monroe County, Michigan where he lived until he enter the army. He enlisted in Co. K, 18th Regt., Michigan Vols. in July, 1862, and served until the close of the war. In 1865, he was married to Lucinda Young, at Whiteford, Michigan and in 1866 moved to Waterloo, where in the following spring he built the house in which he has since continuously resided. To them a daughter was born, Mrs. Della Wolcott, of Toledo, Ohio. In 1869 death entered his home and left him to mourn the loss of his companion. In the fall of 1871 he was married to Sarah Agnes Shambaugh, at Wolf Lake, Indiana. To them were born three children, Charles A. of Barberton, Ohio, Cora M. of Waterloo and Wm. Bert of Lexington, Illinois who with their mother mourn a good husband and father.

30 The ***Corn Carnival*** was a late summer attraction in Peoria, Illinois from 1898 to approximately 1905, located at the corner of Globe and Hamilton streets. The octagonal building, which seated 7,000, was first built as the Tabernacle Theater for religious meetings. As the Corn Palace, the entire theme of decoration was Corn, both inside and out. Typically, a week long carnival provided music, bands, and street shows. A Governor's Day celebrated with a parade, bicycle races, and husking matches.

1903

31 ***Flinch*** was introduced and invented in 1901 by A. J. Patterson. He grew up on a farm in Eaton County, Michigan and graduated from high school at the age of sixteen. He worked as a bookkeeper at a stationary store, Beecher & Kymer in Kalamazoo, Michigan. He was playing cards and came up with the idea for Flinch. He decided to create the game and the deck. Later, he ran the Flinch Card Company out of the stationery store that was renamed Beecher, Kymer and Patterson. It is the seemingly simple but surprisingly difficult card game in which players attempt to discard from their stockpiles of 10 cards, by playing them in numerical sequence. Flinch is still being sold and played, after more than a century since its creation.

1904

32 ***The Golden Age of Quackery***

About 1890, Dr. Samuel Hartman moved to Columbus, Ohio and created several remedies and ***Peruna*** for catarrh was born. His genius was defining catarrh as the root cause of virtually all known diseases. His advertising for the cure for pneumonia, which was catarrh of the lungs and so, was tuberculosis, appendicitis, chronic indigestion, mumps and many more ailments. Hartman claimed Peruna would cure them. Frederick Schumacher became the super salesman of the company and succeeded in making Peruna the largest selling proprietary medicine in the United States. A bottle contained ½ pint of 90% proof spirits, 1.5 pints of water, a flavor cube and a little burned sugar for color; cost 18-cents to produce and he charged $1.00. (Catarrh, today is defined as bronchitis)

Quinine tablets – Advertised to be used for a cold in the head. Bromo Quinine is listed also as a laxative and cure for headaches and La grippe. The inventor was E. W. Grove.

The ***Malena*** Company manufactured the basic compound. Malena was meant to be used either as an ointment or salve, and later added Malena Liver Pills, Worm and Blood Tablets, as well as Gu-Ma-Gum- "the best chew for a cent". The pitch for the Liver Pills, a laxative, was straightforward: "Constipation leads to death. Use Malena Liver Pills and don't die." Chauncey York founded the Malena Company. He was born in New York City in 1850. He was a graduated of Penn State University. Married and had a son, Harry, who carried on the business through the 1920's.

Perry Davis Pain Killer was patented in 1845. It is the first nationally advertised remedy specifically for pain. Of all the patent medicines manufactured, none possessed a more worldwide reputation than this. Christian missionaries around the world distributed it. In its heyday, Perry Davis' "vegetable elixir" was widely regarded as a wonder drug. Its ingredients mainly opiates and ethyl alcohol, were entirely natural. Since it was a registered trade brand name, there was no legal requirement to make its ingredients public on the bottle. It was advertised that it could be taken internal and used externally.

33 In 1903, St. Louis hosted The ***Louisiana Purchase Exposition*** to celebrate the centennial of the 1803 Louisiana Purchase. It was built on over 1,200 acres in the heart of St. Louis and was the largest fair ever held. There were over 1,500 distinctive buildings surrounded by broad boulevards, water vistas, fountains, trees and lush lawns. For seven months, the city became the "World's University". There were 12 major classifications, such as Transportation, Art, and Education that were housed in Palaces. The Palaces were ornate, detailed showplaces, with massive columns and spired towers. Electric lights, a recent innovation for the turn of the century was used lavishly both for illumination and decoration. The Palaces comprised five million feet of exhibit space. The Agriculture Palace alone covered 23 acres. Just one of the medium sized Palaces required 95,000 sq. feet of glass, windows and doors, 450 tons of steel and 7,000,000 feet of lumber. Since these were temporary construction, their outsides were covered with 800,000 square feet of a mixture of plaster of paris and hemp fiber.

The Festival Hall, crowned by a gold leafed dome was larger than the dome of St. Peter's Basilica in Rome; it housed an auditorium that seated 3,500 people. It also housed the world's largest organ, with 10,159 pipes. After the fair, the organ was dismantled and eventually by 1911 it was loaded onto 13 railroad cars for shipment to its new home in Philadelphia. It was reassembled at Wanamaker's Department Store in Philadelphia, which is now Macy's.

St. Louis paid special attention to planning multiple music genres daily throughout the fair. There were daily organ concerts in Festival Hall. In October, the French organist ***Alexandre Guilmant*** played a series of 40 recitals on this magnificent organ made by the Los Angeles Art Organ Company.

The fair was the birthplace of several American culinary institutions: hot dogs, ice cream cones, and ice tea. It also popularized a health drink known as Dr. Pepper and a health food called peanut butter. Fairgoers were also introduced to a new confection called "fairy floss", now known as cotton candy.

1905

34 In 1874 the Chautauqua movement was started as a summer camp for Sunday school teachers on Chautauqua Lake in New York State. Gradually the movement spread, especially throughout the Midwest. It broadened into a great educational and moral forum. The Chautauqua was well received in the Midwest because of the isolation of the population and the lack of opportunity for entertainment. It was a place for impersonations, vocal and instrumental music, dramas and operas. Typically they would erect a large tent, in a wooded or lakeside area. The event would last for a week with a schedule including one or two well-known speakers.

The Chautauqua Institute is still going strong at Chautauqua Lake in the State of New York.

35 Obituary of ***Nellie Adreon*** read, "Crossed the River". Mr. and Mrs. Ed Adreon mourn the loss of their daughter Nellie, who died Wednesday night of typhoid fever. She was an attractive girl, 15 years of age. The funeral will be held Friday afternoon from the Roman Catholic Church in Chenoa. The afflicted family have the sincere sympathy of this wide circle of acquaintances in this their hour of sorrow and bereavement. *Chenoa Clipper*

36 As Governor of Wisconsin, 1901-1906, La Follette championed numerous progressive reforms, including the first workers' compensation system, railroad rate reform, the minimum wage, non-partisan elections, the open primary system, direct election of U.S. Senators, women's suffrage, and progressive taxation. His goals included the recall, referendum, direct primary, and initiative. All of these were aimed at giving citizens a more direct role in government.

The Wisconsin's 1905 legislature was to elect a U. S. Senator. La Follette nominated himself and was confirmed, but he kept serving as

Governor and left Wisconsin's U.S. Senate seat unfilled until January 1, 1906, when he finally resigned and went to Washington. La Follette won instant fame as a Senator not controlled by special interests. He was a man with conviction and was proud of his principles. When Mr. Hill heard him speak in October of 1905, La Follette was still serving as Governor. He ran an unsuccessful bid for President in 1912 against Teddy Roosevelt but continued as Senator until his death in 1925.

37 The headline from the *Chenoa Clipper* dated November 9, 1905: SIGN OF TERROR IN OUR CITY LAST WEEK - Takes Refuge In Vault And Defies The Whole Town – **William LeDuc,** farmer, gets enraged over business matters, turns Desperado, kills his brother-in-law, shoots a prominent retired farmer and does the wild west act to perfection.

Recently with the help of his brother-in-law, Charles Nickel's, President of the State Bank of Chenoa, had secured a loan to settle his pending divorce from his wife in the amount of $2,850. Despondent over his personal life and financial woes, he loaded his 38-revolver and took his recent purchase of 5 boxes of cartridges and went to the bank. Without warning Mr. Nickel's was shot and killed. Then the demon turned his gun on everybody else in sight. Victor Nickel escaped and gave the alarm that the bank was being robbed and his father had been shot. Nickel called people from every direction, who ran with guns thinking there was a raid on the bank. An immense crowd surrounded the bank with nearly two hundred guns. The cry was started that the bank was being robbed and everyone was shocked to learn that William LeDuc, the genial, joking inoffensive farmer was "out for blood" and doing all the shooting without any attempt to take any money.

The City Marshal, A. J. Statler was near by when the shooting began and ran into the bank, just as LeDuc shot Jones. LeDuc's adopted son, Ralph Christie was at this time pulling at his coat and crying and begging him to quit and asking him what he was doing. From the position the boy was in the Marshall was afraid to shoot, from fear of hitting the child so he called: "Look out! I am going to shoot" At this LeDuc dodged behind a big desk and yelled at the boy to get out of danger. A dual of revolvers commenced. LeDuc took refuge in the vault for hours and continued to shoot randomly. LeDuc said he would surrender but began shooting. The local doctor injected a large quantity of ether into the vault but LeDuc closed the second door and lay down and covered his face so as not to be overcome. Next David Whiteside brought a couple of bee smokers and used sulfur and cayenne pepper and a rubber tube inserted into the vault. Again LeDuc closed the second door, which helped him only get slightly sickened by the fumes. They promised not to hurt him, assured he would be protected and would receive a fair trial, but when the door was open a little way again, he began to shoot. He had gained his point, a little more fresh air before he shut the vault door. Finally, after much conversation he surrendered. LeDuc was hurriedly taken out the back way and placed in a carriage with two deputies and driven to Lexington, where they boarded the midnight train and the prisoner was safely landed in the county jail at Bloomington.

1906

38 ***Charles F. McColm*** Obituary read, "Lexington Man Answers to the Call of the Savior"

He was born in Adams Co. Ohio, March 14, 1857 and was brought by his parents to McLean Co. Illinois as a child. He was never married, and practically speaking his home was always with his parents. He assisted his father in carrying on the farm, except when teaching. He was a lover of books and study. By diligent study at home he qualified himself for teaching, and pursued this important calling with marked success for ten years. He was finally compelled to relinquish this work on account of failing health. He had been in feeble health for a number of years and the past winter was particularly hard on him, but with his accustomed courage and energy he held to his daily duties when many times he ought to have been at home in bed. Saturday he was taken suddenly and seriously ill and died at 12 o'clock. Mr. McColm was a modest unassuming gentleman and was highly esteemed by all who knew him. He was a pleasant man to meet and will be greatly missed in Lexington. The funeral was held from the M. E. church at 2 p.m. the Rev. William Woolley officiating. Besides his aging parents there are two sister and three brothers that he leaves behind. (A side note states he was 49 years old and died of spotted fever. Medical professionals of the 21st century believed that this spotted fever was what we now call typhus, which is spread by ticks, lice and fleas.)

39 "Big Pasture" 1906 marked the last great opening of Oklahoma lands to settlement. The land did not go to the man first on the ground or to the one who was lucky in drawing a certain number, but to the one who had the most money to offer. The "Big Pasture" was an area of about 450,000 acres, in the southern portion of Comanche Country.

Entry on October 8 and 9th, Mr. Hill states, "I spent time in Indian Pasture". His entries in the back of this daybook states, *Field Notes*: Land may be examined at Fredrick, T. 2, 3,4, and 5 S.R. 14, 15, 16 W.rem. of Big Pastures at Lawton. Accompany blank forms for bids; affidavits and a $200 check on the National Bank for 1/5 audit amount was obtained from Land Office at Lawton. He was interested in bidding. He diligently entered 35 plus descriptions, by section of acreage. Over a six-day period in December, the Lawton land office of the Department of the Interior received 7,621 sealed bids totaling $2,286,300.

40 Hart-Parr's Charles City factory was built in 1901 and was the birth of the farm tractor industry. The first production run of 13 tractors was in 1902-3. They were rated at 17-30 horsepower. One of these tractors is in the Smithsonian collection. Hart-Parr is recognized as the first commercially successful farm tractor and Charles City, Iowa as the birthplace.

ACKNOWLEDGMENTS

I WISH TO ACKNOWLEDGE the libraries in several Arizona communities, especially Gila County Historical Society in Globe Arizona, and the library and archives in Prescott, Arizona, for providing helpful knowledge of their historic state. Much appreciation is given to the Bloomington, Illinois, Historical Society. This organization and their volunteers provide a priceless commodity to their community! A very special shout-out goes to Dorothy Myers and Jackie Rever at "The Fort" in Lexington, Illinois, for their enthusiasm and assistance. They house a treasure trove of data. The Ford County Historical Society in Paxton, Illinois, and Jean and Cynthia Swanson were very helpful through emails in helping me decipher depots, railroads, and churches in their area.

A special thank you to Mr. Hill's great-great niece, Karen Hill Mail. In 2020, I discovered Karen Hill Mail's family tree and reached out to her. She responded and we immediately became friends! She has been so helpful by providing me with family pictures and stories. Karen's father was named after his Great-Uncle Bert!

Also, a sincere thank you to Mr. Hill's great-great nephew, Daniel Paul Horn, who very generously provided me with family pictures.

I wish to thank, Emily Hitchcock, who many years ago encouraged me to believe in this project. I am grateful to Clair Fink, who advised me throughout this process.

There are no words adequate enough to thank my daughter, Rachel for her consistent and caring support.

Scan here to hear an audio interview conducted by the Eckhart Public Library in Auburn, Indiana, around the time of W. Bert Hill's 100th birthday. A rare glimpse into the life and memories of a man who witnessed a century of history. Take a listen and step back in time as W. Bert Hill shares his experiences, bringing the past to life in his own words.

ABOUT THE AUTHOR

Sarah Dunn was raised in Indiana and lived there for fifty years. She and her husband are retired and now live in Columbus, Ohio, with her dog, Bess.

www.ingramcontent.com/pod-product-compliance
Lightning Source LLC
Chambersburg PA
CBHW030816090426
42737CB00010B/1299

9781633378766